Debbie Hell
from Shayla.
Christmas 2018

W9-AWI-079

Making It

Making It

RADICAL HOME EC
for a
POST-CONSUMER WORLD

Kelly Coyne & Erik Knutzen

RODALE

Mention of specific companies, organizations, or authorities in this book does not imply endorsement by the author or publisher, nor does mention of specific companies, organizations, or authorities imply that they endorse this book, its author, or the publisher.

Internet addresses and telephone numbers given in this book were accurate at the time it went to press.

© 2010 by Kelly Coyne and Erik Knutzen

All rights reserved. No part of this publication may be reproduced or transmitted in any form or by any means, electronic or mechanical, including photocopying, recording, or any other information storage and retrieval system, without the written permission of the publisher.

Rodale books may be purchased for business or promotional use or for special sales. For information, please write to: Special Markets Department, Rodale Inc., 733 Third Avenue, New York, NY 10017.

Printed in the United States of America

Rodale Inc. makes every effort to use acid-free ∞, recycled paper ♻.

Book design by Roman Jaster

Illustrations by Teira Johnson

Library of Congress Cataloging-in-Publication Data

Coyne, Kelly.
    Making it : radical home ec for a post-consumer world / Kelly Coyne and Erik Knutzen.
        p.   cm.
    Includes bibliographical references and index.
    ISBN-13   978-1-60529-462-9 paperback
    ISBN-10   1-60529-462-4 paperback
  1. Home economics.   2. Sustainable living.   3. Simplicity.
4. Consumer education.   I. Title.
    TX158.C7589 2010
    640.73—dc22   2010023680

Distributed to the trade by Macmillan

    6   8   10   9   7   paperback

We inspire and enable people to improve their lives and the world around them.
www.rodalebooks.com

*To anyone who is in their kitchen,
garden, or garage right now, making it.*

Contents

Introduction   *1*

The Five Principles of Making It   *5*

SECTION ONE: DAY TO DAY   **7**

01>   Olive Oil Lamps   *8*

02>   Thinking around the Toothbrush   *11*

03>   Homemade Tooth Powder   *14*

04>   A Minimalist Mouthwash   *15*

05>   Giving Up the Bottle: Four Natural Shampoo Alternatives   *16*

06>   Hair Rinses   *21*

07>   Deep Conditioning   *23*

08>   Styling Gel   *24*

09>   A Quick Facial   *25*

10>   A Close Shave   *26*

11>   A Roman Bath   *27*

12>   Body Polish/Hand Scrub   *29*

13>   Homegrown Medicine   *30*

14>   Herb and Fruit Infusions   *36*

SECTION TWO: WEEK TO WEEK   **41**

Weekly Cooking   *42*

15>   Vegetable Stock   *44*

16>   Whole Chicken Stock   *46*

17>   How to Cook Beans   *48*

18>   Cooking Whole Grains   *50*

19>   One-Bowl Meals   *52*

20>   The Dog's Pot   *55*

21>   Serious Bread   *58*

22>   Homemade Condiments   *61*

23>   Old-Fashioned Vinegar-Based Drinks   *65*

Cleaning, Washing, and Mending   *68*

24>   Making Your Own Cleaning Products   *69*

25>   Laundry Day   *75*

26>   Basic Mending   *84*

SECTION THREE: MONTH TO MONTH   89

The Transformational Power of Salt   90

27 > Sauerkraut   91

28 > Kimchi   94

29 > Gravlax   96

30 > Nukazuke   97

Indoor Gardening   100

31 > Microgreens   101

32 > Sweet Potato Farm   104

Herbal Medicine and Beauty   108

33 > Medicinal Honey   109

34 > Foraging Feral Greens   111

35 > Drying, Infusing, and Tincturing Herbs   115

36 > Making Salves   120

37 > Moisturizing Cream   127

38 > Deodorants   131

39 > Keeping the Bugs Away   133

40 > Curiously Homemade Peppermints   134

41 > Cloth Pads   137

SECTION FOUR: SEASON TO SEASON   147

42 > Making Soap the Easy Way   148

43 > Making Soap the Hard Way   157

44 > Cabbage Patch pH Indicator   163

45 > How to Slaughter a Chicken   165

Projects for the Garden   174

46 > Starting Seeds and Planting Your Garden   175

47 > How to Prepare a Bed for Planting   181

48 > Grow Lights on the Cheap   182

49 > Free Fertilizer from Weeds   187

50 > Saving Seed   189

51 > How to Espalier   192

The Magic of Fermentation **198**

52> Making Vinegar *199*

53> Making Mead *203*

54> Making Home Brew *207*

SECTION FIVE: INFRASTRUCTURE *217*

55> Drip Irrigation for Vegetables *218*

56> Seedling Flats *223*

How to Compost **226**

57> A Compost Bin Made of Shipping Pallets *230*

58> Slow Compost *232*

59> Fast Compost *234*

60> Building a Dry Toilet *237*

61> Worm Farming *242*

62> A Mash Tun *248*

63> A Wort Chiller *253*

64> A Solar Cooker *255*

65> Build a Chicken Coop *261*

Backward Beekeeping **270**

66> Getting Started with Beekeeping *271*

67> Bee Acquisition Method 1: Swarm Capture *277*

68> Bee Acquisition Method 2: Cutout *281*

69> Build a Honey Extractor and Collect Some Honey *288*

70> Make a Native Pollinator Habitat *291*

Resources *296*

Acknowledgments *301*

Index *302*

Introduction

Last June, we got a call we'd been expecting for weeks. It was from our beekeeping mentor, Kirk Anderson. He said, "I've got a shop vacuum full of 4,000 bugs here for you. Are you ready?" We were ready. We wanted to be beekeepers. To do so, we'd have to pass through a rite of initiation: transferring the contents of a feral beehive built in a derelict shop vacuum into our waiting hive boxes. It wouldn't be a pretty process—bees rarely take well to having their hives chopped to pieces—but this procedure, called a cutout, would not only save the bees from the exterminator's wand but also give us a backyard source of raw, organic honey and beeswax. It would be worth a few stings.

Soon after that call, we found ourselves standing in our backyard in sparkling white bee suits, surrounded by an enormous cloud of unhappy bees. Thankfully, Kirk was there with us, wielding a butcher knife like a surgeon, his practiced calm the only thing standing between us and chaos. Both of us were thinking that of all the crazy things we've done, this had to rank right up there among the craziest. And yet we'd never felt so alive. Staring into the golden heart of that cracked-open hive was like staring into the fierce, intelligent eye of Nature herself.

The Acquisition of the Bees was one of a string of ongoing adventures that have gradually reshaped and reformed our lives and our home over the past decade. For the most part, our adventures play out in the domestic sphere, in our kitchen and yard. We find fascination in these most ordinary spaces. In the compost heap, our garbage transforms magically into soil. In the garden, seeds sprout and flourish and turn back to seeds. In the kitchen, flour, water, and bacteria mix to make bread. And in the dark recesses of our cabinets, apple juice becomes vinegar and honey becomes wine. Each of these processes raises challenges and questions that lead to more exploration and further adventures.

We didn't start all of this with a particular agenda. The way we live now is the result of a series of actions rising out of seemingly random decisions that, in retrospect, followed a logical path. And that path was dictated by the things we were learning. To turn Zen for a moment, you could say we didn't shape the bread loaf, the bread loaf shaped us. As did the chickens and the bees, the vegetable bed and the worm bin, the laundry line and the homemade soap. Once we discovered the pleasure of making things by hand and the enchantment of living close to the natural world (even though we lived in the heart of Los Angeles), there was no going back to our old ways.

It all started reasonably enough. Twelve years ago, when we lived in an apartment, we decided to grow tomatoes in pots one summer because we were starved for a decent tomato. We didn't know much about tomatoes, but somehow we managed to grow a few. After that first bite of a succulent homegrown tomato, still warm from the sun, our fate was sealed. We'd never buy tomatoes from the store again.

Next we learned to bake bread, and we started to keep herbs in pots. Bit by bit, we began to replace the prepared foods that we'd eaten all of our lives with homemade meals. The microwave gathered dust. The impetus behind this slow change was pleasure—and a dose of common sense. We figured out that what we could grow or make was inevitably better and usually less expensive than what we could buy. This gave us ample incentive to expand our knowledge base. We moved into a house and planted a vegetable garden. Once we had a little space, things started to snowball.

For the longest time, we didn't understand that our various activities— baking, gardening, brewing, etc.—were parts of a whole. They were just things we liked to do. Only after we began to blog about our experiments did we form a unified theory of housekeeping. We realized we were practicing old-fashioned home economics—not the sort of home economics that made for an easy elective in high school, but its original, noble form, in which the household is a self-sustaining engine of production. Instead of buying our necessities prepackaged, we produced them. We disconnected as much as we practicably could from a system of production we didn't agree with and didn't want to support. Our guiding principle is the adage that *all change begins at home.* The larger forces of politics and industry may be beyond our control, but the cumulative effects of our everyday choices have the power to transform the world.

In time, our blogging led to a book offer. While researching our book, we met people who were remaking their lives in accordance with their ideals. They inspired us and galvanized our resolve. We realized we were part of a wave rising through the culture, a network of backyard revolutionaries who weren't content to buy into a "green lifestyle" based on a slightly tweaked version of consumerism but instead were challenging the foundations of 21st-century consumer culture itself.

We did our best to put what we'd learned, and what we believed, on paper. *The Urban Homestead* was published by the always prescient Process Media in 2008. While *The Urban Homestead* contained projects, at heart it was a book of ideas. When it came time to write *Making It,* we knew it had to be a project book, a practical toolbox for transforming ideas into action. We also wanted to show how many of these projects are interdependent and interrelated, how tools and skills from one project apply to and are expanded upon in another, because that is the nature of the home arts. One project calls up the next.

For instance, if you're growing your own vegetables, you'll end up with a lot of vegetable scraps and trimmings, which should be composted, because you'll need compost to grow more vegetables. Compost becomes vegetables and vegetables become compost. If you want to make your own medicines, you plant herbs. The flowers on the herbs feed honeybees, who make the wax and honey used in homemade medicine—wax and honey you can access if you keep a beehive. Interdependent systems are the hallmark of a homegrown household. The economy and elegance in these interconnecting relationships are poetic and, for us, reassuring. The compost heap and the beehive remind us of our place in the world. We're not free agents, floating above it all, but integral parts of the system—us and the chickens and the worms and the nettles and the sunshine.

HOW TO USE THIS BOOK

One of the questions we're asked most frequently is: "How do you have time to do all this stuff?" The flip answer is that we got rid of our TV. The real answer is much more complicated. But the heart of the question is not how *we* have time to do this stuff, but how *you're* going to find time to do this stuff.

The answer is that you do what you can, as you can. When you are passionate about something, the time you need will appear. Beyond that, everything becomes faster and easier with practice. The trick is to learn how to schedule it in and plan ahead. This is a key difference between our accustomed lifestyle of convenience and the home arts. The Quickie Liquor Mart is always open. The home brew needs a month to ferment. The home brew is worth the wait.

To help you plan ahead, we've arranged this book by time, both the time spent on a project and how frequently that particular project is done over the course of the year. It begins with the easy projects, most of which take only a few minutes to put together, little things you can start doing right away. From there it moves to weekly, monthly, and seasonal projects, and it ends with big infrastructure projects that are undoubtedly challenging but that you only have to tackle once. We don't intend for you to read the book in order. Just dive in.

Throughout the book, we use the same basic tools and ingredients as much as possible, not only to save you money and trips to the store but also to show how the basics can be stretched in many different directions. We're telling you this now, lest you think we're secretly sponsored by the United Consortium of Olive Oil Manufacturers. You'll see what we mean.

The old home arts revolve around process, locality, specificity, improvisation, and intuition. The great challenge in writing this book was reducing projects full of complex variables into step-by-steps. We've done our best to adapt them to this format, but we expect that you will sometimes have to ignore what we say and go ahead and do what you think is best. Much of our learning has been through trial and error and happy accidents, so we'd encourage you to embrace the accidents and begin improvising. These projects are for you. Make them your own.

The Five Principles of Making It

START BY TRYING ONE PROJECT IN THIS BOOK AND BUILD FROM THERE, SLOWLY. You can't transform your lifestyle overnight. Only engage with projects that engage you. Follow your passion, and see where it leads.

LAUGH AT YOUR MISTAKES. The mark of a true DIYer is a high tolerance for failure. In fact, if you're not failing, you're not learning. Disaster is inevitable and usually pretty funny when you look back at it. Both of us can still be reduced to helpless giggles when describing Kelly's first attempt to sew. To give you a visual, just imagine what would happen if Frankenstein's monster made himself a dress out of stretchy, moose-print fabric.

FOLLOW YOUR INTUITION. Learn to balance the left brain and right brain. The left brain helps you systematize and repeat successes, but it's your right brain that gives you those all-important gestalt moments. Intuition tells you that your dough looks right, that your body is craving the nutrients in a particular plant, that your compost needs more water, or that the sauerkraut is ready. Always trust your gut.

TRUST NATURE. Many of these projects involve natural processes. Oftentimes, you will be in the role of an observer or a shepherd more than a creator. Watch, listen, and learn. Admire. And intervene as little as possible.

KEEP LEARNING. You never really master the home arts, you grow into them. They are a school that will engage your energy and imagination for the rest of your life.

Day to Day

In this section we focus on the daily needs, like tooth brushing and face washing, and also little emergencies that might pop up at any time, like a scraped knee or sore throat. Unlike the big projects that come along later in this book, these projects are perishables and consumables, things you whip up as you need them, using ingredients found in your pantry or backyard. Warning: These are gateway projects that may addict you to a more homegrown lifestyle.

01 › *Olive Oil Lamps*

PREPARATION: 5 min

Since this book is all about rethinking your relationship to the common products and systems in your home, we thought it would be appropriate to start off with a project that brings new light to the household.

Oil lamps are one of the most elemental forms of lighting. The Romans used clay lamps filled with olive oil. The Inuit used soapstone dishes of seal oil. Scottish fishermen used little tin lamps filled with fish oil. Lamps fueled with ghee are still used to light temples in India. Oil lamps are inexpensive, nontoxic alternatives to paraffin candles and petroleum-fueled lamps. But the true beauty of these lamps is their flexibility and simplicity. They can be improvised in a few seconds with items found around the house (which is handy in a power outage) but can also be made into beautiful objects to grace your dinner table.

Oil lamps work best when the wick is submerged in oil, there's lots of airflow, and—this is most important—the flame sits just above the oil pool. If the flame is too far away from the fuel, it won't burn long. If you look at ancient lamps in museums, you'll see that they share a common design that facilitates

these principles. They are usually palm size and always shallow. In most, the flame is not placed centrally but instead burns at the rim of the container, where the wick rests on an sloped edge, against a lip, or in a spout of some sort.

YOU'LL NEED

A SHALLOW VESSEL. The first lamps were probably made of large scallop, clam, or oyster shells, and these still make pretty lamps. A little china saucer works well. So does a jar lid, but you'll want to pull out a little V-shape lip in the edge of the lid with pliers so the wick has a place to rest. We'll also show you a lidded variation made out of a round mint tin that burns from the center. It works because it has big holes punched in the lid for airflow.

A WICK. This can be made of a bit of kitchen twine, a shoelace, a string tie from an old blouse, or a thin strip of T-shirt. Just make sure it's 100 percent natural fiber. In olden times, they used the piths of reeds or twisted moss. The broader the wick, the bigger and brighter the flame. The wick doesn't have to be long because it doesn't burn down much.

THE FUEL. We recommend olive oil, though you're welcome to experiment with other fats. Olive oil of any grade burns slowly, without smoke or odor. If you have a bottle of olive oil that has gone rancid, this is a great use for it.

PUTTING IT TOGETHER

A LAMP MADE OF A DISH OR A SHELL

Fill your shell or dish with oil and lay the wick across the bottom, arranging the end of the wick so it pokes off the side about ½ inch out of the oil. For more light, use two wicks. Give the oil a couple of minutes to fully saturate the wick, then light the lamp. Tilt the vessel, if necessary, to make sure the oil is pooling at the base of the flame. Nesting one saucer or shell inside another facilitates this sort of tilting and can help to stabilize a tippy shell. Refill whenever you notice the distance growing between the oil and the flame. Time between refills varies by shell depth and whether you have multiple wicks, but a teaspoon of oil burns for about an hour. A good-size shell should see you through a dinner party.

SAFETY

Of course you'd never leave a flame unattended, but what if your lamp gets knocked over? Olive oil is not very volatile, so the spilled oil will not ignite into a blazing inferno. However, the wick may continue to burn if it isn't doused in the accident.

A LAMP MADE OUT OF A CANDY TIN

The shallow shape of a candy or mint tin is ideal for making an oil lamp. The lid is a nice addition, because it makes spills less likely. Punch a hole in the center of the tin's lid for the wick. Make the first puncture with the tip of a knife blade, then widen the hole using a screwdriver. Work from the top of the lid so that the ragged edge is hidden. The hole should be broad enough that the wick is not pinched or constricted. To allow sufficient oxygen flow, you will need to punch a second, smaller hole off to one side to help draw air. Use a broad, stiff wick for this sort of lamp. A shoelace or string tie would be ideal. Poke one end through the central hole and coil the rest in the bottom of the tin. Fill the tin with oil and allow the wick to saturate a few minutes before lighting.

02 ›

Thinking around the Toothbrush

PREPARATION: 5 min

A plastic brush with nylon bristles is considered an indispensable part of dental hygiene, but what did people use before its invention? What is used today in parts of the world where the toothbrush hasn't been adopted?

Modern toothbrushes date their popularity to 1938, when quick-drying nylon bristles were invented. Prior to that, brushes were made with animal bristles, which tended to shed and mold, and which probably didn't taste great, either. The combination of nylon bristles and plastic handles made for a hygienic, practical brush—but at a cost. Those brushes have immortal life spans in landfills, and while eco-friendly recycled handles and replaceable heads are available, they don't challenge the dominant paradigm that the toothbrush is a plastic, disposable item.

Alternatives exist. You might adopt them because you're trying to reduce the plastic waste in your household, or you might just keep them in mind in case a zombie apocalypse cuts you off from your usual toothbrush supply. If nothing else, they're convenient for camping trips. Try one or two of these techniques in conjunction with ordinary brushing. Your brushes will last longer, and over time you might find you don't miss your brush.

TOOTH CLOTHS

A tooth cloth cleans the teeth, and your finger massages the gums nicely along the way, which is something dentists are always trying to get us to do better.

Take a 5-inch square of slightly textured fabric, like linen or oxford cloth. (You can make a mountain of these squares with a yard of inexpensive fabric or old, clean shirts. Use pinking shears to cut them out and you can get away with not hemming them.)

Wrap a square around your forefinger and use it to rub your teeth clean. You can use a dentifrice, if you wish, by dampening the cloth first and then adding toothpaste or tooth powder. The cloth doesn't clean between the teeth, true; but that's why we floss. Wash and reuse the cloths.

SAGE

This strongly aromatic and antiseptic herb will leave your mouth fresh, and the texture of the leaves cleans teeth well. If you grow sage, it's worth keeping a few fresh sprigs in a vase in the bathroom. When it's time to brush, just rub a leaf over your teeth and gums, using as many leaves as it takes—two to four in most cases.

How to Choose a Twig

How do you find a good chew-stick tree in your neighborhood or yard? In every region, certain trees have been identified through traditional use as being valuable for this purpose. These trees will contain antibacterial or otherwise mouth-friendly agents, making them ideal for dental use. Question local wild food experts and search history texts for leads on interesting plants in your area. Don't use just any twig. The majority of them will be inert—meaning not particularly useful—while other trees are poisonous, such as olean-der, yew, holly, and (of course) poison oak and poison sumac. You'd be in for a world of hurt if you chewed on their branches. *Always be certain of your plant identifications.*

Harvest twigs respectfully, taking only a bit at a time from any one tree and using pruning shears or a sharp knife to make a clean cut rath-er than breaking branches off with your hands. Here are a few common North American trees you might start with:

FLOWERING DOGWOOD (*Cornus florida*), found mostly east of the Mississippi. Its spectacular floral displays make this a popular ornamental tree, easy to find in both city and suburb. *Gunn's Domestic Medicine: or Poor Man's Friend, in the Hours of Affliction, Pain, and Sickness*, by John C. Gunn (1835), says the twigs of young dogwood are "tooth-brushes of nature's presenting, in-finitely better than those made of hog's bris-tles." The dogwood was used as a "chaw stick" throughout the Ozarks, where the European set-tlers probably learned of its efficacy from the local indigenous people.

BIRCH, especially *Betula lenta*, known as black birch, cherry birch, and sweet birch. It gives off a distinct wintergreen aroma when you scratch the bark, so you'll know you've found the right tree. This twig makes a pleasant, minty-tasting toothbrush. Note that *Betula lenta* has smooth, gray bark instead of the white bark we typically associate with trees in the birch family.

OAK (*Quercus*, any type). This is one tree that most of us can identify with ease, if only by the acorns lying on the ground beneath it. Oaks are especially rich in tannic acid, which has power-ful astringent and antibacterial properties. Oak preparations have long been associated with the treatment of bleeding gums and ulcers of the mouth.

SWEET GUM (*Liquidambar styraciflua*). Another popular ornamental tree, sweet gum is easily identified by its brilliant fall colors and star-like fruit—not an edible fruit, but a gumball-size seedpod covered in sharp spikes, making it the bane of many a lawn owner. Sweet gum twigs are slightly astringent/tannic but basi-cally flavorless.

OTHER TREES that have been used for chew sticks include spicebush (*Lindera benzoin*) and sassafras (*Sassafras albidum*). Root-beer-flavored sassafras has a bad rap for being poisonous, but that toxicity occurs in the context of ingesting high doses of commercial extracts. An occasional nibble at a sassafras twig won't hurt you.

LICORICE STICKS, the dried roots of the lico-rice plant (*Glycyrrhiza glabra*), are a mail-order alternative for those of you who don't want to go around surreptitiously pruning your neigh-bors' trees. Licorice roots are sweet and taste intensely of licorice—as you might expect. They draw out a lot of saliva, especially when you first start chewing, and so aren't good for brushing while reading. On the upside, that juice freshens the breath; helps digestion; and eases canker sores, coughs, and sore throats. Excessive lico-rice intake *might* cause hypertension in some individuals, so if you already have high blood pressure, proceed with caution. Licorice sticks are sold processed and flavored, which makes them more expensive than twigs from nearby trees, but you can purchase unprocessed sticks from a bulk herb supplier on the cheap.

TWIGS OR CHEW STICKS

Toothbrush twigs or chew sticks were used in the West well into the 20th century and are used to this day for teeth cleaning in many parts of the world.

Chew sticks are slender, fresh twigs, measuring approximately ¼ to ⅓ inch in diameter and 6 inches in length. Choose them from an appropriate tree; see "How to Choose a Twig" on the opposite page. If twigs are too dry to chew into a brush form, soak them overnight. Otherwise, you don't have to prewash or prepare the twigs in any way before use.

Peel back the bark on one end by about ¼ inch, using your fingernail or a paring knife. Chomp the peeled part between your molars to break up the fibers, which creates a soft, blunt little brush. While the cleaning action of an ordinary toothbrush is a generalized sweep from side to side, the movement of the twig is more specific and refined, the action a gentle up and down. It makes you aware of the shape and edges of each tooth. The more slender the twig, the tighter the control.

Chew sticks are not usually used with dentifrice (though you could if you want). There are other ways to freshen breath, as explored in Project 4. Not using toothpaste means you are not tied to the sink while brushing—you can brush while reading or watching TV. This leads to more thorough brushing. The same twig can be trimmed and reused. On top of that, they are free, locally sourced, and perfectly biodegradable. What's not to love?

03 ›

PREPARATION: 2 min

Homemade Tooth Powder

Powders of chalk, charcoal, salt, and various ground medicinal barks and herbs are the oldest dentifrices. More recently, baking soda has become a sort of "people's toothpaste." Many of our grandparents used it during the Great Depression, and its simplicity and low cost make it a fantastic alternative to artificially sweet, chemical-loaded commercial toothpastes.

Baking soda is primarily a deodorizer and a mild abrasive. It is less abrasive than salt and certainly less abrasive than the silica (sand) found in many whitening brands of toothpaste. Moreover, baking soda's abrasive qualities break down quickly when it comes in contact with water or saliva. The taste is undeniably salty, but it leaves your mouth clean and fresh, with no lingering aftertaste. Just be sure to rinse well after use.

YOU'LL NEED

* Small jar with lid (A baby food jar works well.)
* Baking soda (sodium bicarbonate), approximately ¼ cup
* Peppermint essential oil (or anise essential oil)

PUTTING IT TOGETHER

Fill the jar with baking soda. Flavor it by adding a few drops of essential oil, then shake to distribute the oil. Let your nose be your guide as to exactly how much oil to use, but start off by trying 10 drops per ¼ cup of soda.

To use, wet your toothbrush (or other brushing implement) and dip it in the jar. If you are especially concerned about your breath, add 1 single drop of peppermint essential oil to the bristles of your brush before you begin. Brush as usual, and rinse well.

Note: A small jar is ideal because the essential oils fade over time, so it's best to mix the powder in small batches. It's also more hygienic, since you'll be dipping your brush in the jar. It's doubtful that nasty bugs can live in that saline environment, but you should clean the jar before refilling it.

VARIATION: Instead of using essential oil for flavor, mix 1 part baking soda with 1 part dried and powdered sage leaves. Sage is especially good for troubled gums.

04 › *A Minimalist Mouthwash*

PREPARATION: 5 min

Here's a simple mouthwash, a liquid variant on the tooth powder. It freshens the mouth any time of the day without dosing you with alcohol, harsh antiseptics, and artificial flavors. It's particularly useful in conjunction with toothbrush twigs, since they're used without a dentifrice.

YOU'LL NEED

* Glass jar or bottle with a lid and at least a 1-cup capacity (A jelly jar works well enough for this purpose, but an attractive bottle would be more fun.)
* 1 cup water
* 1 teaspoon baking soda (sodium bicarbonate)
* Peppermint essential oil
* Tea tree oil (optional)

PUTTING IT TOGETHER

Fill the jar or bottle with the water and 1 teaspoon baking soda. Add 4 drops of the peppermint essential oil and 1 or 2 drops of the tea tree oil, if using. The optional tea tree oil makes the mouthwash more antiseptic. Shake well before each use.

Simple Ideas for Fresh Breath

Drink a glass of water. Stale breath is often the result of dehydration. Drink a big glass of water when you wake up, and alternate water with coffee and tea during the day.

Take a tip from India: Keep a bowl of fennel seeds around the house and carry a small vial of them in your bag. Fennel seeds not only freshen the breath after a meal, but they also promote digestion. You can buy the festive sugared kind at Indian markets or harvest fennel seeds in the wild. Other breath-freshening seeds include anise, dill, and cardamom.

Chew on a sprig of fresh Italian parsley or a few mint leaves. If you're packing a lunch, remember to put a few sprigs from your garden in your lunch box. Nibbling on organic citrus rinds is also a good trick.

Enjoy one of the Curiously Homemade Peppermints (Project 40).

05›

Giving Up the Bottle: Four Natural Shampoo Alternatives

Commercial hair care products treat hair as a blank canvas. Shampoos strip it of its natural oils. Conditioners replace those oils with synthetic equivalents. Styling products shape chemically subdued hair into many forms, usually in conjunction with heat. Those styling products leave a heavy residue on the hair that must be stripped daily with shampoo, then reapplied.

DRY SHAMPOO

On days you oversleep, or when you wish to stretch intervals between washings, spot-treat greasy hair with dry shampoo. Cornstarch absorbs oil very well but can give a grayish cast to dark hair. Brunettes might prefer to use unsweetened cocoa powder. Put a towel over your shoulders to protect your clothes. Rub a small amount (½ teaspoon or less) of either cornstarch or cocoa powder between your fingers and work it into the hairline, wherever hair is the most oily. Don't spread it farther than that area, and use as little powder as possible. Leave it in a minute to absorb oil, then brush out the powder.

The combined effects of daily applications of detergents, heat, and drying chemicals make the hair lifeless and dull, completely dependent on styling products to give it the body and shine it should have naturally.

Hair cleaned by natural, gentle methods is strong and shiny and resilient. It doesn't need conditioner, because it retains its natural oils. It doesn't require styling products, because it retains its natural weight and texture. All it needs is a little brushing to bring out its shine or a touch of oil to tame its curl.

The transition from a heavily processed hair care regime to a simple one takes a bit of adjustment. First and foremost, you must give up the notion that shampooed hair must be so clean that it squeaks. Squeaky hair is overwashed hair. All of our shampoo alternatives will clean your hair, but your hair won't squeak between your fingers in the shower. It will have more texture when wet than you're accustomed to. This is the feel of its natural oils—not dirt. Those natural oils will give hair weight, body, and shine. At the start of this transition, your hair may seem more greasy than usual. This is because your scalp, accustomed to harsh daily cleansing, is overproducing oil. After a few weeks of gentle washing, your scalp will adjust to the new routine and stop producing so much oil. As a result, you may ultimately find that you can go longer and longer between washings.

Alternative 1: Homemade Shampoo Bars

By ditching the bottle for the bar, you save money, packaging, and space in the shower. If you've ever tried to wash your hair with a bar of commercial body soap, you'll know it leaves the hair gunky and coarse. Homemade soap is a different beast. It is much gentler than its commercial counterparts because it is made with high-grade oils, and because it retains all its natural glycerin. Glycerin, a moisturizer, is a byproduct of the saponification process. Because glycerin adds value to more expensive products like face cream and lipstick, it is usually extracted from mass-produced soap in the factory and sold off for those uses. If you make your own soap, you get to keep all the glycerin—and feel the difference. Homemade soap formulated for the hair gently cleans hair and scalp without overstripping natural oils. As a result, no conditioner is necessary.

YOU'LL NEED

* Our Peppermint-Rosemary Shampoo Bar or our Genuine Castile Soap (see Project 42). You can also buy shampoo bars at health food stores and through online retailers.
* Bottle of vinegar rinse, as described in Project 6 (optional)

PUTTING IT TOGETHER

To use a shampoo bar, just rub it with water between your hands to build up lather, then work that lather into the scalp, just as you would normal shampoo. Follow with a vinegar rinse (Project 6) to rinse away any lingering traces of soap (this is important if you have hard water) and to restore the pH balance of your hair, leaving it shiny and manageable.

By the way, shampoo bars work well on the body, too, streamlining your shower routine and minimizing clutter in the bath.

PREPARATION: 2 min

Alternative 2: Baking Soda Shampoo

Diluted baking soda makes an excellent clarifying shampoo. It's the strongest alternative shampoo, too strong for daily use, but it excels at removing product buildup and is good to employ when your hair needs a deep cleaning.

YOU'LL NEED

* 1 tablespoon baking soda (sodium bicarbonate)
* 1 cup water
* Spray bottle (optional)
* Vinegar rinse (Project 6)

PUTTING IT TOGETHER

Dissolve the baking soda in the water. (Never exceed this ratio of 1 tablespoon soda to 1 cup water. In fact, the less baking soda you can contrive to use, the better.) Pour the mixture over your hair or apply it with a spray bottle, then work it through. Always follow a baking soda shampoo with a vinegar rinse.

PREPARATION: 45 min

Alternative 3: Garden-Grown Shampoo

Intrepid DIYers might ask how they'd manage to wash their hair if they didn't have access to baking soda or the materials for soap making. The answer is that you could grow shampoo in the garden. Soapwort (*Saponaria officinalis*), also known as bouncing bet, fuller's herb, or sweet Betty, is a pretty, sweet-smelling, flowering perennial herb that contains saponins, which are natural surfactants, in its roots and foliage. Europeans brought this plant to the New World specifically for washing, and in many places it has naturalized and grows wild. Soapwort is easy to grow from seed—it grows all over the United States—and will cheerfully take over your yard if given half a chance. It's considered an invasive plant in some places, which to our way of thinking is a virtue. This means it's hardy and fast growing, a plus for a plant that you intend to harvest in quantity.

Use the flowers, leaves, stems, and roots to make a liquid cleanser for hair or body. Harvest the roots in the autumn and dry them for winter use, but don't dry the green parts—the foliage is best used when fresh. Dried soapwort root is sold by bulk herbal suppliers.

YOU'LL NEED

* 1 ounce dried or fresh soapwort root, crushed; or 10 fresh stems, approximately 6 to 8 inches long, roughly chopped
* 3 cups water (Distilled water or rainwater is best.)
* 2 tablespoons dried herb of your choice, or 2 handfuls of fresh herbs (optional; see the list of hair-enhancing herbs on page 20.)
* 10 drops of any essential oil, for scent (optional)
* Plastic squeeze bottle or spray bottle

PUTTING IT TOGETHER

In a stainless steel or enamel saucepan, combine the soapwort and water. Bring to a boil and simmer gently, covered, for 15 minutes. Turn off the heat and stir in the additional herbs, if using. They are not necessary but can be added for scent or hair care properties. Cover the pot again and let everything steep off the heat for at least 30 minutes. Strain out the solids, add essential oils for extra scent, if you like, and bottle the liquid.

Soapwort liquid is thin, and its cleaning properties are mild. You have to use more of it to wash your hair than regular shampoo—about 1 cup, depending

Soapwort plant

on the length of your hair. Spray or pour the mixture over dry hair and work it through until your hair is saturated. It will not lather. Leave it on for a few minutes (the length of your shower, for instance), then rinse well. Avoid getting it in your eyes, because it will sting.

Soapwort shampoo will spoil quickly, so store it in the refrigerator and use it in 3 to 5 days.

PREPARATION: 30 min

Alternative 4: Soap Nut Shampoo

Soap nuts are the fruit of the soap nut tree, *Sapindus mukorossi*. They are sold as a natural laundry soap alternative, but they can also be used to make shampoo. The saponins in soap nuts are more concentrated than those in soapwort, so they make a stronger shampoo. See page 82 for more information about using and buying soap nuts.

YOU'LL NEED

* 10 soap nuts
* 1 quart water
* 10–15 drops of essential oil in your choice of scent (optional)
* Spray bottle or squeeze bottle

PUTTING IT TOGETHER

Combine the soap nuts and water in a stainless steel or enamel saucepan. Simmer at low heat for 20 minutes. Remove from the heat, strain out the nuts, and cool. When the mixture is cool, stir in the essential oils, if using, and then bottle the mixture.

The liquid is thin, so it may be easier to apply with a spray bottle. Work the mixture into the scalp and through the hair, but don't expect it to foam. In fact, it won't feel like it's doing much at all, but it *is* cleaning. You just have to learn to trust it.

Soap nut tea doesn't spoil fast, like soapwort shampoo, but it is still a natural product. Store most of it in the fridge to keep it fresh, and transfer a cup or so at a time to a smaller bottle for the bath. It's fine to leave out for a couple of days at a time.

Hair-Enhancing Herbs

CALENDULA, or pot marigold, petals are soothing and conditioning, good for an irritated scalp. Over time they may also brighten blond and red hair. Use the petals only, dried or fresh.

CHAMOMILE leaves hair soft and smelling wonderful. If used as a leave-in rinse, it brightens blond hair over time. Use the flowers only, dried or fresh.

LAVENDER is very cleansing and stimulates hair growth. Use the flowers only, dried or fresh.

PEPPERMINT adds a nice scent and a bit of a tingle to any hair product. Use the leaves, dried or fresh.

ROSEMARY has long been considered one of the premier hair herbs. It stimulates the scalp and leaves hair shiny. If used as a leave-in rinse, it may darken hair slightly over time. Use only the needles stripped from the branches, not the woody parts. Fresh rosemary works best.

SAGE, like rosemary, is a cleansing scalp tonic that may darken hair over time. Use the leaves, dried or fresh.

STINGING NETTLE has no scent, but it is one of the best all-around herbs for hair. It is conditioning and nourishing and is particularly recommended for controlling dandruff. Use the leaves, dried or fresh. If they're fresh, handle with gloves until you get the leaves into boiling water. Both drying and brief boiling or steaming will de-sting the nettles.

06›

Hair Rinses

Here are two quick and easy recipes for hair rinses that will bring shine and manageability to your hair, cost almost nothing, and are purely natural, which is good for both you and the environment.

Vinegar Rinse

Vinegar is a mild acid that helps balance the base nature of soaps and detergents to restore the natural pH balance of your hair. A diluted solution of vinegar smooths the cuticles on the hair shaft, leaving your hair easy to comb out and shiny and manageable when it dries, eliminating the need for store-bought conditioners.

YOU'LL NEED

* ✱ 2 tablespoons apple cider vinegar
* ✱ 2 cups water or 2 cups herbal infusion (page 116)
* ✱ Squeeze bottle or spray bottle

PUTTING IT TOGETHER

Pour the vinegar and water or herbal infusion in the bottle you plan to use in the shower. Shake to combine. No heating is necessary. Make more or less of this mixture if you like, but always use the ratio of 1 tablespoon vinegar to 1 cup water, because too much vinegar will dry the hair. In fact, you may prefer a more dilute version: 1 tablespoon vinegar to 2 cups water.

After shampooing, work the rinse through your hair, saturating it from roots to ends. Let it sit a minute, then rinse thoroughly. The odor will vanish when your hair dries.

When the vinegar rinse is made with water, it should last indefinitely, because neither water nor vinegar is prone to spoil. If it's made with an herbal infusion, it will be more likely to spoil. You don't have to refrigerate it, but use it within 2 weeks.

Leave-In Herbal Rinses

Herbs do the most good for your hair when they're left on instead of rinsed away. Herbal rinses can add scent and shine, improve the condition of the scalp, and even subtly influence hair color. See "Hair-Enhancing Herbs" on the opposite page for examples of herbs you might like to try in your rinses.

YOU'LL NEED

* 1 ounce dried herbs, or enough fresh herbs to loosely fill a quart jar
* 2 cups boiling water
* Quart canning jar

PUTTING IT TOGETHER

Use fresh herbs whole—you don't have to chop them. Pour enough boiling water over the herbs to fill the jar completely. Cap it, and leave the herbs to infuse for as long as you can, anywhere from 20 minutes to overnight. Strain out the herbs.

After your shower, towel-dry your hair and comb the rinse through your wet hair, using enough to coat hair from roots to ends. Leave it in. Be aware that some herbs might leave yellow stains on light fabrics, so be careful if you get dressed while your hair is still wet.

Use the entire quart over the course of a week, or store it in the refrigerator for up to 2 weeks.

07 ›

Deep Conditioning

PREPARATION: 1 min

Hair oiling is an ancient—and still widely practiced— technique for taming long hair. It might sound like a recipe for a greasy head, but if done with a light hand, oiling is a simple, natural way to gloss those dry, frizzy ends and make your hair shine with good health.

YOU'LL NEED

* **Extra-virgin olive oil, organic virgin coconut oil, or any other high- quality oil you prefer (Olive oil is a light conditioner. Coconut oil is better for dry or damaged hair.)**

PUTTING IT TOGETHER

Start with dry hair. Rub a small amount of oil between your hands, just enough to make your palms shine. Working in sections, coat your hair from roots to ends with the oil, replenishing the oil when your hands no longer shine. If your scalp is dry, oil your scalp as well. If your hair is oily at the roots, coat only the ends of your hair. How much oil you apply in total will depend on your hair length and texture; the goal is not to end up heavily greased but, instead, slightly glossed. To improve the penetration of the oil, wrap your head in a towel for about 20 minutes. A warm towel feels particularly nice. After that 20 minutes, rinse out with warm water and follow with a wash—or leave the oil in, if it doesn't look greasy.

08 ›

PREPARATION: 15 min

Styling Gel

When flaxseeds are soaked in water, they release a thick, mucilaginous gel that works very well as a styling product. We've heard that the flappers used this formula to keep their spit curls in place. We don't know if that's true or not, but we do know that this gel provides clean, light hold for only pennies a batch. Better yet, it contains no alcohol or perfume or chemical ingredients with names too long to pronounce.

YOU'LL NEED

* 1 tablespoon whole flaxseed
* 1 cup water

PUTTING IT TOGETHER

Simmer the flaxseed in the water until the water is reduced by half. Using a fine-mesh strainer, strain out the seeds immediately, while the water is piping hot. When the liquid cools, it will thicken to goop.

For general hair management, apply a small amount of the gel to damp hair; brush it out when dry. Use larger amounts on wet hair as a setting gel.

Keep the gel in a covered container in the fridge.

09 ›

PREPARATION: 1 min

A Quick Facial

Exfoliation lifts away dead skin cells, revealing fresh skin and allowing moisturizers to penetrate better. So if your skin is looking dull or if your hands are rough and dry, grab a box of baking soda. Baking soda is a gentle abrasive, mild enough to exfoliate delicate facial skin without irritating it. A quick baking soda facial will leave your face clean and glowing and costs pennies. There's simply no need to use anything else.

YOU'LL NEED

* Baking soda (sodium bicarbonate)
* Water

PUTTING IT TOGETHER

FACE

Pour a nickel-size pile of baking soda in your palm and add enough water to make a paste. Using your fingertips only (not your palms), work the soda in circles over your face and neck. Don't scrub vigorously; let the baking soda do the work on its own. Rinse with cool water, pat dry, and apply a moisturizer.

HANDS

Rub a little baking soda between your wet hands, paying attention to the backs of the hands and knuckles. Rinse and moisturize.

FEET, ELBOWS, ETC.

Keep a jar of baking soda by your bathtub. After a long soak, use baking soda by the handful to scrub away dry skin.

10 ›

⏲
PREPARATION: 1 min

A Close Shave

When gentlemen go before the mirror to shave, they have the choice of using aerosol foams comprised of who-knows-what, or soap and a shaving brush. The shaving brush ritual is nice but soap can dry the skin, leaving it tight and uncoforable. Shaving with oil is less common, but one that is worth exploring.

There are shaving oils on the market, but despite their high prices, they are basically scented vegetable oil. Instead, try shaving with olive oil. Plain olive oil gives a smooth, close shave; cleans the skin as it works; and moisturizes it, too. How's that for a one-step product? Erik converted to oil after his first try. And of course shaving oil works well on legs—or whatever else you feel inclined to shave.

If you are prone to razor bumps on your face or legs, a light scrub with baking soda and warm water prior to shaving, as described in Project 9, sweeps away dead skin and softens the hair, which help prevent infection. Constant scrubbing might be harsh on your skin, so if you shave daily, you might find it works best to use baking soda only once or twice a week. Be sure to rinse well before you start to shave, because you wouldn't want salty baking soda residue in a shaving cut.

YOU'LL NEED

* Olive oil. If you find you don't like the feel or smell of olive oil, try other rich, quality oils like sweet almond, sesame, or grapeseed oil—but don't use cheap cooking oils, like corn or peanut oil.
* Bottle, such as a repurposed hand soap dispenser
* Essential oil (optional). Citrus, sandalwood, rosemary, and lavender, or some mix thereof, are classic scents for both men's and women's shaving products.

PUTTING IT TOGETHER

If you want to add scent, transfer the oil from its original container to a smaller bottle, then add a few drops of any essential oil you like and give it a shake to mix. Remember, essential oils are quite strong. Preferences vary, but you probably won't need to use more than 5 to 10 drops of essential oil per cup of olive oil.

Massage a small amount of the oil into warm, wet skin. There's no need to slather it on. It may be strange at first to shave with oil alone if you're accustomed to foams and creams. You might even miss the entertainment of cutting neat paths through foam, but think about how much easier cleanup will be! Just shave, rinse with water, and pat dry. Don't wash afterward. Leave what little oil remains on your skin as a moisturizer. In fact, if you're shaving your face, go ahead and massage the oil over your whole face before you shave, not just the beard area, so you don't end up with a baby-soft jaw and a craggy, dry brow.

11 › *A Roman Bath*

PREPARATION: 1 min

This project was inspired by ancient history. The Greeks and Romans knew about soap, but they didn't use it to bathe. They cleaned themselves with olive oil, massaging it over their bodies and then scraping off the oil, dirt, and dead skin with a curved device called a strigil.

Next time you are in a museum with collections from ancient Greece and Rome, look in the display cases for these little bronze or bone squeegees as well as the bottles that held their perfumed oils. You will also see them being used in art of the period depicting bathing scenes.

Soap isn't necessary for daily cleansing. In fact, it dries the skin with overuse, leading to all sorts of problems, from uncomfortable dryness to breakouts. It is perfectly possible to clean both your face and your body with oil alone. Oil dissolves impurities and feeds the skin.

YOU'LL NEED

A GOOD OIL FOR WASHING. We use olive oil because it is widely available and relatively inexpensive and because it's always around the house. Olive oil will not block your pores or cause breakouts. Castor oil is a powerful cleansing oil and is often combined with olive oil for this purpose, especially for oily skin. Or try sweet almond oil, grapeseed oil, or avocado oil—each has its own unique characteristics but are more expensive than olive oil. Some oils are best left for cooking: Coconut oil is rather drying and heavy on the skin, so it's not ideal for cleansing. Cheap oils (like corn, peanut, or canola oil) will not benefit skin at all.

ESSENTIAL OIL to scent your cleansing oil (optional). Be aware that some essential oils, like peppermint, might irritate your skin. A few drops of lavender essential oil is a safe bet.

PUTTING IT TOGETHER

FACE WASHING

Under normal cleansing regimes, delicate facial skin is first stripped of all its natural oils with soap, then shocked back into pH balance with acidic toners, then rehydrated with moisturizers. Cleansing your face with oil reduces the number of steps in your routine, saves money, and yields healthy, glowing skin. Oil washing is particularly useful during the winter, when the skin is under constant assault from cold, dry air.

Pour a coin-size dollop of oil in your palm. Warm it by rubbing your hands together, then gently massage it into your face, using your fingertips only.

This light massage is beneficial for your skin and a necessary part of the process. Enjoy it. You are both encouraging your skin to renew itself and dissolving impurities. Remove the oil with a warm, wet washcloth. It should be a smooth cloth—you don't want to scrub your face. Oil is an exfoliating agent in itself, so you don't need to be rough. If you use a white cloth, you'll see all the dirt and oil that you're lifting off. If your skin feels tight afterward, follow up the cleansing by massaging in a little more oil or applying a moisturizer.

BODY WASHING

We wish we could do this after a long soak in a decadent Roman bath. Instead, we have to settle for the end of a shower, when a little time in warm water has opened pores and softened the skin. Turn off the water and, while still in the shower, smooth a generous amount of oil over your body. Then use a loofah sponge or a washcloth to lift dirt and body oils, pausing once in while to rinse out the sponge or cloth. This scrubbing invigorates the skin and awakens the body. The best way to massage the skin is in long strokes leading from the extremities toward the heart. When you're done, take a quick rinse. After you dry off, you can apply yet more oil or another moisturizer, if you feel you need it.

12 › *Body Polish/Hand Scrub*

Fancy jars of salt scrubs are staples of gifty boutiques, but it's easy to make your own. As we saw in the last project, oil is a great cleanser. Combined with salt, oil becomes a substance that works two ways: first, as a fancy, spa-quality body polish; and second, as a down-and-dirty hand cleaner that strips away sticky chain grease and engine grime.

There's no need to use harsh solvents for a hand cleaner—oil dissolves oil very nicely. Erik barely knows what the word *exfoliate* means, but he has a jar of scrub that he uses after he works on his bike. The difference between a body polish and a hand cleaner is nothing but marketing.

You can whip up a jar of scrub in 5 minutes, either for yourself or as a gift.

YOU'LL NEED

* Clean, widemouthed container with a lid
* Fine-grain sea salt (Coarse salt is too hard on skin.)
* Oil. You can use olive oil or, if the mood strikes you, more expensive, quality skin oils like sweet almond or avocado or grapeseed. Cheap oils like corn oil or canola oil work well enough in a hand cleaner but won't do much for the skin. Use oil that you've infused with herbs (see Project 35) to harness their delicate scents, colors, and healing properties.
* Essential oil (optional)

PUTTING IT TOGETHER

Fill the container about three-quarters full of the sea salt, then stir in the oil bit by bit until you have a slurry, something that feels good to your fingers—neither too dry and grainy nor too runny.

If you wish, scent the scrub with a few drops of essential oil. Be careful with camphoraceous oils like peppermint and eucalyptus, because they might feel a little intense on freshly scrubbed skin.

13 ›

Homegrown Medicine

Cuts and bites, coughs and colds, upset stomachs, and aches and pains. These are the little emergencies that send us running to our medicine cabinet. It turns out that a lot of these common ailments can be treated with plants from your garden, plants that can be easily foraged, or ingredients you'll find in your pantry.

Directions for how to make the medicinal honeys and herbal salves, tinctures, and infusions mentioned here appear in Projects 35 and 36. You will find descriptions of useful weeds in Project 34.

BEE, WASP, AND HORNET STINGS

First, for bee stings, remove the stinger immediately with your fingers. Contrary to popular belief, you don't have to scrape it out with a credit card. Wasps and hornets don't leave a stinger behind, but the rest of the treatment is the same. Chilling the sting site is the best way to minimize your body's response to the venom. Wash the bite with soap and water if it's available, then apply ice or a cold compress. If no ice is available, submerge the bite in cold water. Taking an antihistamine will also help minimize itching and swelling. It may not be homemade, but it is sensible. Plantain will help too. See "Bug Bites and Local Irritations," below.

BLEEDING, SUCH AS FROM SHAVING CUTS OR KITCHEN ACCIDENTS

Apply a yarrow leaf (*Achillea millefolium*) directly to the wound. Bruise the leaf a little first to bring out the oils. Yarrow not only inhibits bleeding, it is antiseptic as well. Try it—you'll be amazed at how fast it works. To stop a nosebleed, bruise a yarrow leaf, roll it up, and put it up the nose. Yarrow is easy to grow in the garden, but it grows wild, too. Make a yarrow salve to use on cuts when the plant is unavailable.

BUG BITES AND LOCAL IRRITATIONS

Common plantain (*Plantago major*) is an ubiquitous and useful weed found in lawns and sidewalk cracks just about everywhere in the city or countryside of North America. (See Project 34, Foraging Feral Greens, to learn how to identify this plant.) Chew fresh leaves and smear the pulp juice directly on the bite. You'll find the taste bitter, but it's not poisonous. In fact, we add young plantain leaves to salads sometimes. In the winter, soak dried leaves in hot water to rehydrate them and then apply to the irritation. For more serious situations, apply wet, pulverized leaves as a poultice; put a whole leaf over the poultice to hold it in place; and put a bandage over that. Plantain salve is good for all sorts of skin eruptions and irritations.

BURNS

The juice from a fresh-cut *Aloe vera* leaf works well, as does honey. Aloe has cooling properties that feel good immediately after a burn, while raw honey can help prevent infection and scarring. You can combine the two of them to make a burn gel. To treat sunburn, try soaking washcloths in cold, strong black tea and laying them over the burnt skin. When the cloths get warm, refresh them with more cold tea.

COLDS

At the first suspicion that she may be getting a cold, Kelly starts eating raw garlic, at which time Erik reminds her that there's no scientific basis for any sort of cold cure, to which Kelly replies that since she started eating garlic, her colds are never as bad as his and they last half as long. If you'd like to give her method a try, eat a clove of raw garlic the first moment you suspect you have a cold. The most palatable way to do this is to butter a cracker or slice of bread and spread crushed garlic over the butter. Butter cuts some of the sting. Sprinkle some salt over it all, and it almost tastes good. Eat at least two cloves a day, one in the morning and one at night, and keep doing this for 3 to 5 days, until you're well out of danger. Don't use roasted or canned garlic, because heat kills garlic's natural antibiotic qualities.

COUGHS

A spoonful of honey will go a long way toward quieting any cough. For dry, tickling coughs, drink tea made of fresh or dried mullein leaf (*Verbascum thapsus*), but be sure to strain the tea after brewing to remove the tiny hairs on the leaves. Several other herbs that may be growing in your yard are good for coughs. The following herbs have expectorant qualities: common plantain (*Plantago major*), red clover flowers (*Trifolium pratense*), and fresh thyme (*Thymus vulgaris*). Licorice (*Glycyrrhiza glabra*) is probably not growing in your yard, but if you have licorice root on hand (perhaps because you use the roots for toothbrushing), it makes a tea with wonderful soothing qualities and good flavor. It could be combined with any other of the herbs already mentioned. To make a tea, use 1 teaspoon crushed licorice root to 1 cup water, and simmer for 10 minutes.

CUTS AND SCRAPES

Honey is a potent antibacterial ointment. The best sort to use is raw, because pasteurization (heating) degrades the healing properties, but any honey will do in a pinch. We always keep a small jar of raw honey in the medicine cabinet. It might crystallize after a long time, but it never goes bad. Smear honey on the wound just as you would apply a topical antibiotic, then put a bandage over the cut. It may sting slightly, but that twinge doesn't last more than a moment. *Aloe vera* is good for cuts, too.

DEHYDRATION

In cases of chronic vomiting and/or diarrhea, dehydration is a serious concern, especially for children. After a serious loss of fluid, rehydration with plain water is impossible because the body's supply of minerals has been depleted. Dissolve ½ teaspoon table salt (sodium chloride), ½ teaspoon salt substitute (potassium chloride, which is found near the salts and seasonings in the grocery store), ½ teaspoon baking soda (sodium bicarbonate), and 6 teaspoons sugar in 1 quart water. If you don't have access to salt substitute, make a solution of 1 teaspoon salt and 6 teaspoons sugar. This second mix lacks potassium, so as soon as possible, introduce potassium-rich foods like banana, avocado, papaya, spinach, sweet potato, or wild nettle greens. Whichever hydrating solution you use, feed it spoon by spoon, if necessary, until the patient tolerates it, then give as much as the person can drink. Even if the patient is vomiting what you give, some of the liquid will stay down, so keep spooning.

DIARRHEA

Make extrastrong tea out of fresh or dried blackberry leaves (*Rubus fruiticosus*) or red raspberry leaves (*Rubus idaeus*)—about 2 tablespoons of leaf per cup of water—and drink it on the hour as needed. Harvest these leaves in the spring when they're most potent, then dry them for convenient use. Be sure not to mistake poison ivy for these plants. When not in fruit, they look somewhat similar and grow in the same places. Just remember that poison ivy plants have no prickles. If you want to buy the leaves, raspberry leaf tea is easy to find in the tea section of health food stores, but blackberry leaves must be ordered from herbal supply companies.

HEADACHES

Headaches arise from so many causes that it is difficult to describe a universal treatment. Many headaches are caused by stresses to the neck muscles arising from the head-forward position of driving, biking, and using a computer. When a headache strikes, it's a good idea to stop whatever you're doing and change position. Do some gentle neck stretches, or lie down and try to relax your whole body. Rub your temples and nape with lavender, peppermint, or rosemary essential oil. Carry a blend of these oils, either diluted in a little bottle of neutral oil or in the form of a salve. If your hands and feet get cold when you have a headache, soak them in very warm water. It helps the head, believe it or not. Even better, take a warm bath with the above essential oils sprinkled in the water—only be sparing with the mint, because it can make your skin tingle long after you've left the bath. Try putting gentle pressure on your closed eyes with the heels of your hands, or use a flaxseed-filled eye pillow. And yes, take a pain reliever. See the entry on pain.

ITCHY, RED, IRRITATED SKIN

Take a bath and add a cup of baking soda to the water—this is our house cure-all for mild conditions. More ambitious but highly effective for serious itching, such as that caused by chicken pox, is an oatmeal bath. Grind regular oatmeal into a fine powder and add a couple of cups of the powder to bathwater. Keep the water temperature comfortably tepid, since hot water will only worsen angry skin. Common chickweed (*Stellaria media*), a ubiquitous weed, is soothing and cooling. Make a strong tea with fresh or dried chickweed; when the tea is cool, use it as a skin wash or add it to bathwater. It's well worth having a chickweed salve around for general use, but if you're out and about you can just pulverize or masticate chickweed and apply it straight to the skin.

MUSCLE ACHES AND STRAINS

Nothing feels better on overworked muscles than a warm bath with Epsom salts. It's a classic treatment, and it really works. Also excellent for all bruises, strains, pulls, and other muscle and joint injuries is comfrey oil or comfrey salve (*Symphytum officinale*).

NASAL CONGESTION

If your nose is miserably plugged up and runny, irrigate your nasal passages with lukewarm saltwater to flush out excess mucus and soothe inflamed tissues. Mix up a solution of ¼ teaspoon sea salt (not iodized salt) in 1 cup lukewarm water and load it into a bulb syringe. Standing over a sink, ease a bulb syringe just a little way up one nostril, aiming it at the top your same-side ear. Squeeze gently until you empty the syringe. You should feel water passing to the back of your throat, your mouth, or even your opposite nostril. Flush each nostril twice. If you don't have a bulb syringe, lean over a bowl of saltwater, block one nostril and snort the water up the other. It's a mess, but you'll feel so much better afterward.

SAFETY

If you're allergic to aspirin, don't drink willow bark tea. All medical precautions regarding aspirin should be applied to willow bark tea.

PAIN

Salicin, the active ingredient in a traditional pain remedy, willow bark, was identified in the 19th century and refined into acetylsalicylic acid, aka aspirin. While willow bark and aspirin are not the same thing, they behave similarly in the human body. Willow bark tea is a mild but effective treatment for pain, especially low, throbbing pain such as that from headache, backache, and arthritis. Simmer 1 or 2 teaspoons crushed dried willow bark in 1 cup water for 15 minutes, then let it steep covered for another half hour. Drink up to 3 or 4 cups a day, as needed. You can also use a tincture of willow bark for convenience and portability. Take 1 teaspoon of tincture at a time, mixing it in a little liquid before swallowing, up to three or four times a day. See Project 35 to learn how to make tinctures.

Willow bark tea is usually made from the fresh young bark of one of these four trees: white willow (*Salix alba*), black crack willow (*Salix fragilis*), purple willow (*Salix purpurea*), and black willow (*Salix nigra*), though other willows have similar properties. You can buy willow bark at health food stores and through herbal suppliers, or you can gather it in the wild. Harvest the bark from young willow branches in the spring, when the bark is easy to peel. Neatly prune a small branch so that you don't scar the tree. Peel off the bark, cut it into thin strips, and dry it for storage—or use it fresh.

PIMPLES

Not an emergency, but mortifying enough. Dab raw honey on pimples before you go to bed. Honey keeps the pimples from becoming infected and cools and moisturizes angry skin.

SORE THROAT

Gargle frequently with 1 tablespoon apple cider vinegar (preferably raw) diluted in a glass of water or with 1 teaspoon sea salt in a glass of warm water. With luck, you'll stop the infection it its tracks. Also, sip warm water mixed with lemon and honey—use infused, medicinal honey for extra punch. For a throat that has already been ripped raw, make a soothing demulcent tea out of flaxseed. Just simmer 2 teaspoons flaxseed in 2 cups water until the volume is reduced by half, leaving 1 cup of liquid. Strain the seeds out and drink it hot, because when it cools it will thicken to the consistency of egg whites.

STUFFY HEAD/IRRITATED SINUSES

Make a steam tent by pouring boiling water into a bowl on your kitchen table and adding aromatic herbs like mint, rosemary, eucalyptus, and lavender or grated fresh ginger. If you have fresh herbs, add them by the fistful. Dried herbs work, too—even mint tea bags will work. You can also sprinkle essential oils of the same herbs in the hot water. Lean over the bowl, drape a towel over yourself and the bowl, and breathe the steam until the water cools.

Chew whole Fennel

UPSET STOMACH

If the symptoms come from simple overindulgence, peppermint is your best bet, because it relaxes the stomach and promotes digestion. Make a cup of strong peppermint tea or eat several strong peppermint candies, such as our Curiously Homemade Peppermints (Project 40). If the queasiness is not from an overfull belly but from motion, nerves, illness, or morning sickness, then turn to ginger to warm and soothe a sick stomach. Grate an inch or so of fresh gingerroot and simmer it for 5 minutes in 1 cup water. Flavor with lemon or honey, if you like. Or, if you're on the move, nibble on candied ginger. Half a teaspoon of baking soda mixed in a small glass of water effectively neutralizes acid indigestion, but it should never be used if your belly is already uncomfortably full, because baking soda releases carbon dioxide in the stomach, making the discomfort worse and potentially leading to dangerous straining of the stomach muscles.

SLEEPLESSNESS, ANXIETY

Try sipping chamomile (*Matricaria recutita)*, vervain (*Verbena officinalis*), valerian (*Valeriana officinalis*), catnip (*Nepeta cataria*), or linden flower (*Tilia* spp.) tea. The first four plants are easy to grow in the garden, or their teas can be found in health stores. Linden flowers must be harvested from the linden tree, also called a lime tree, but not to be confused with the citrus tree. If none grow in your area, you can find linden tea in health food stores and stores that sell European foods, because it's popular in Europe. Chamomile and linden taste best of all these remedies and are both traditionally considered safe sedatives for children.

Wild lettuce (*Lactuca virosa, L. serriola*) and the flowers of hops (*Humulus lupulus*) are both excellent sedatives but very bitter, so they are best taken in the form of a tincture: 1 teaspoon in liquid before bed. Wild lettuce is a common weed that is practically guaranteed to be found in your nearest vacant lot—it's also the ancestor of salad lettuce. The milky sap in its stems and leaves is such a powerful sedative that it was long used as an opium substitute or to adulterate opium. Hops vines are fragrant, beautiful plants and a must for your garden if you make your own beer. Hops works well in combination with other sedative plants—hops and valerian are a classic combination, for instance.

YEAST INFECTIONS

Garlic kills yeast. For women, insert one peeled clove of garlic just as you would a tampon before going to bed at the first signs of a yeast infection. Don't worry, you'll be able to fish it out in the morning. It sounds strange, but it works. Repeat every night for 3 to 5 nights. Use plain, live-cultured yogurt for external itching. Acidophilus capsules, which are sold in the refrigerator section of health food stores, can also be used as suppositories to restore healthy bacteria levels in the wake of a yeast infection. Insert one or two capsules a day for a few days.

14 › Herb and Fruit Infusions

Day to day around this homestead, our liquid intake consists of coffee, tea, beer, wine, and water, water, and more water. This is all well and good, but when we're looking for a change, we drink one of these.

PREPARATION: 5 min
WAITING: 4–10 hours

Green Elixir

Herbal tea—a teaspoon of herb steeped in a cup of water for a few minutes—is pleasant, but it doesn't capture much of the nutritional potential of herbs. To take full advantage of the rich vitamin and mineral content of plants, you need to soak a good quantity of herb in water for hours. This process is called infusion, and infusions are nature's power drinks.

We first learned of strong herbal infusions through the writings of an herbalist named Susun Weed, and ever since we've been quaffing infusions around the house as part of our regular routine. The flavors are strong, but they grow on you, and the infusions have powerful positive effects. Homemade herbal infusions are like energy drinks and vitamin pills rolled into one. They're also inexpensive, and the ingredients might even be growing in your backyard. Once you get used to the process, it's no more difficult than keeping a supply of iced tea in the fridge.

Our favorite infusion, good for men and women and people of all ages, with no medicinal cautions that we know of, is made of stinging nettle (*Urtica dioica*). Nettles can be foraged in most parts of the country and are in no danger of being overharvested. They are nutrient powerhouses: loaded with vitamins A, C, and D; iron; potassium; manganese; and calcium. This beautiful emerald green infusion is both energizing and deeply nourishing—a tonic, in other words. When you drink it, you know you are doing your body good. The flavor is best described as a cross between green tea and vegetable broth. See Project 34, Foraging Feral Greens, to learn how to identify and harvest stinging nettle.

YOU'LL NEED

* 1 ounce dried or fresh nettles or herbs (One ounce of dried, chopped nettles measures about 1 cup; 1 ounce of fresh leaves stripped from their stalks would fill half a quart jar.)
* Quart jar
* 4 cups boiling water

PUTTING IT TOGETHER

Add the fresh or dried leaves to the quart jar. Pour the boiling water over the nettles or herbs to fill the jar. Cap it and walk away for at least 4 hours. After a maximum of 10 hours, strain out the herbs, squeezing the plant matter to get all the good juice out. Drink the resulting concoction over the next 36 hours or so—either chilled, at room temperature, or gently reheated. It will start to lose nutrients after that and eventually spoil.

PREPARATION: 10 min

Aguas Frescas

If nettle infusions seem a little stern to you, but you want something special to drink, try *aguas frescas. Vitroleros,* huge beehive-shaped jars filled with colorful *aguas frescas* (fresh waters), are a fixture of our landscape here in Los Angeles. They sit at market stands and on restaurant counters and show up at backyard parties and picnics. Fresh and fruity and lightly sweet, a big glass of *agua fresca* is the ideal antidote for sultry summer weather and the natural complement to a plate full of savory little tacos or a *pupusa* swimming in cheese and hot sauce.

Aguas frescas are made of many things, but we're going to focus on those made of ripe fruit blended with water. Sometimes they are flavored with herbs or spices, sometimes they are sweetened with sugar. There are endless flavor possibilities for a budding mixologist to explore—cucumber and lime with salt and chile, anyone? Or what about a watermelon and basil combo? You can get as fancy as you like, yet a single-ingredient *agua fresca* can be mind-blowingly delicious if the fruit is ripe and in season. Here's a basic *fresca* formula.

YOU'LL NEED

* **3 cups peeled and chopped fruit. Classic choices are watermelon, cantaloupe, strawberries, pineapple, guava, cactus fruit, cucumber, and citrus. But more "northerly" fruits would work well, too—peaches and blueberries and raspberries come to mind. The riper and sweeter the fruit, the better. This is an ideal use for slightly overripe fruit. Remember, if your fruit is flavorless, your drink will be, too. Sugar and lime juice will help not-so-great fruit, but they can only do so much.**

* **Juice of 1 lime (optional) (Lime makes everything better.)**

* **Sugar, if necessary, to taste. Simple syrup works best, because dry sugar will not want to dissolve in cold water. Agave nectar works well, too, but add it sparingly because it's quite sweet.**

* **Extras: Handful of chopped mint, pinch of sea salt (really brings out melon flavors), pinch of powdered chile**

* **6–8 cups water**

PUTTING IT TOGETHER

Put your fruit and any sugar, herbs, and spices in a blender along with 2 cups of the water. (Don't use all 6 to 8 cups of water at once or the result will be a foamy mess. Use just enough water to puree the fruit.) Blend the fruit until smooth. If you don't have a blender, use a fork or potato masher or similar tool to pulp the fruit as best as you can.

For a clear beverage, strain the pulp through a fine-mesh colander or cheese-cloth, pressing to release all the juice. Otherwise, just toss the pulp into your serving pitcher and add the rest of the water. (The slightly chewy quality of an *agua fresca* is part of the experience.) Chill well and serve with or without ice.

Makes 4 servings

Section Two

Week to Week

The following projects are about ongoing cycles of maintenance and renewal. Weekly cooking, housekeeping, and laundry are the indispensable (some would say inescapable) rituals that make a house a home. Adopt a DIY stance toward these necessities, and you'll not only eat better, but you'll make your home a welcoming, comfortable, and nontoxic oasis.

Weekly Cooking

We cook the majority of our meals at home and buy very little prepared food. We do this for a bunch of reasons. It saves money (lots and lots of money), it minimizes the amount of packaging waste that moves through our kitchen, and it keeps our diet simple and healthy.

Like any other aspect of a DIY lifestyle, the transition from prepared foods to home cooking is best done gradually, through passion rather than duty. That is to say, the last reason you want to cook at home is because "It's good for you." Or, even worse, "Because it's good for the environment." These are abstractions, and abstractions don't motivate you when you come home from work hungry. An improved diet and a reduced carbon footprint are side benefits of cooking from scratch. The driving force behind all real change is pleasure.

We splurge on certain indispensable foods, like cheese, chocolate, and wine. Meanwhile, most of our meals are constructed out of fresh produce from our garden and inexpensive staples: flour, sugar, dried beans and whole grains, dried fruit, seeds, and nuts. Staples are cheap, even in the grocery store, but especially when bought from bulk bins or through a food co-op. Staples keep well and pack a lot of calories into a relatively small space. A well-stocked pantry is not only the basis of home cooking but also the backbone of emergency preparedness. At any given time, we probably have about 2 weeks' worth of food in our pantry, enough to weather a garden-variety disaster, but perhaps not enough for the whole Mayan calendar thing.

We weren't born eating this way, and we still buy prepared foods once in a while. This has been a long transition. What set us on the Way of the Bulk Bin was a love of bread. The drive to make interesting bread sent us searching for all sorts of flours and whole grains, many of which we could only find in bulk bins. Soon, the breads we were making were better than those we could buy. For the same reason, we grow our own vegetables because they taste so much better than store-bought. Once you realize that what you make tastes better than what you buy in the store, it's hard to go back to eating out of boxes.

As we began to learn our way around exotic flours, we also began to expand into other bulk items and found that basic, elemental foods satisfy like nothing else. Canned beans are salty and slimy. Dried beans cooked with love are a whole different order of experience. Whole grains brought new flavors and textures into our lives. Bit by bit, our diet started to change.

STOCKING UP

Of course, cooking from scratch takes time, and all of us are pressed for time. The secret is advance preparation: doing the bulk of your cooking on one weekend afternoon and stocking your refrigerator with basics that can be transformed into quick meals during the week. The building blocks of quick meals are stock, precooked grains, and beans and bread. All of these can be made ahead of time and transformed into different meals throughout the week. We've also included some recipes for condiments and some old-fashioned drink concentrates. Spend one afternoon a week stocking up on these basics and reap the benefits all week long.

STORING BULK FOODS

Insect contamination is the biggest danger with bulk foods. When you come home with bulk items, transfer them to jars or plastic containers with tight lids. Leaving food in plastic bags is the surest way to invite infestation, and if something comes home already infested (this is a possibility), keeping the food in jars contains the damage. We use a lot of quart and half-gallon canning jars in our pantry. The glass doesn't absorb odors, is easy to clean, and lets us see what we have, and the lids are sturdy enough to keep insects out. If you suspect that a package of grain or flour might have been exposed to infestation, popping it into the freezer for 4 days will kill any hidden creepy crawlies.

Where Do I Put All This Stuff?

Storing bulk foods can be a challenge if you have a small kitchen. When we started down this road, our few cabinets soon began to overflow with jars. We fantasized about a new house with a walk-in pantry, but we came up with a solution that works for us and might work for you.

Make a pantry by lining any open section of wall with narrow shelves. Our pantry is in a hallway off the kitchen and is made up of eight long shelves cut from 1 x 5-inch lumber. Five inches of depth is all you need to stow away jars, cans, and boxes. Narrow shelves don't take up much floor space, and they're easy to inventory and manage. Everything is right in front of you, nothing is hidden. Mount the boards on simple shelf brackets, and space them at varying heights, like bookshelves, so the bottom shelves are taller and the upper ones have just enough headroom to store pint jars and cans. In one afternoon spent with a saw and a drill, you can add mountains of storage space to your kitchen.

15 ›

PREPARATION: 40 min

Vegetable Stock

Stock makes everything taste better. It makes good use of singleton vegetables and scraps that might go to waste otherwise and, in the case of meat, allows you to extract every bit of nutrition from leftovers and bones. If you have stock on hand, you can make good soup fast. Stock also lends flavor and nutrients to beans and grains and sautés. A warm cup of stock on its own is an excellent pick-me-up. So the first task in weekly cooking is to make sure you're stocked up on stock.

Gather sound vegetable trimmings during the week and keep them in the fridge or freezer for cooking day. Don't save anything bruised or rotten, but vegetable tops and trimmings, peels of scrubbed vegetables, leftover onion halves, and the like can all be set aside for a new life. You can include almost any vegetable in your stock, including potatoes, mushrooms, and tomatoes. The only questionable vegetables are members of the Brassica family—strong-flavored vegetables like cabbage and mustard greens that can dominate the flavor of your stock. Use them sparingly.

Stock is an improvisational process, but a classic vegetable stock is composed of onion, carrots, celery, garlic, and fresh herbs. To this base, add anything else you have lying around.

YOU'LL NEED

- * 1 onion
- * 2 stalks celery
- * 2 carrots
- * 1 clove garlic
- * Olive oil
- * 1 bay leaf
- * Other vegetable scraps or singletons you have on hand and fresh herbs like parsley and thyme (optional)
- * Sea salt and black pepper

PUTTING IT TOGETHER

Coarsely chop the onion, celery, carrots, and garlic. In the bottom of a stockpot, heat a little olive oil. Add the vegetables and the bay leaf and cook over medium heat for about 10 minutes, until softened. At this point, throw in any additional vegetables or herbs, also coarsely chopped, and cover with a generous amount of water. Bring it to a simmer and cook for 30 minutes total. Add salt and freshly ground pepper to taste as it cooks. After a half hour, the vegetables will have given over most of their goodness and flavor to the broth. Strain the stock into a storage container and keep it in the fridge, or use it immediately for other cooking projects.

Stock keeps for a week in the refrigerator. You can also freeze it for later use.

ROASTED VEGETABLE VARIATION

If you want a vegetable stock with more depth of flavor, preroast your vegetables. Preheat the oven to 400°F. Toss coarsely chopped vegetables in olive oil, salt, and pepper. Lots of roasted garlic is the key to the rich flavor, so include an entire unpeeled head of garlic. Cut off the top, so that the end of each clove is open. Put the head of garlic and all of the vegetables in a roasting pan and roast for about an hour, or until tender. Give them a couple of stirs as they roast so they brown evenly. When the vegetables are tender, transfer them to a stockpot, reserving the head of garlic. Squeeze each clove of garlic over the stockpot to release all the yummy roasted paste inside. Fill the pot with water, add fresh herbs like thyme and parsley, bring to a simmer, and cook for another half hour, stirring occasionally. Strain out the solids.

16 ›

PREPARATION: 4 hours

Whole Chicken Stock

If you're a meat eater, nothing beats chicken stock. It lends savor to everything it's cooked with and forms the basis of comforting chicken soups, sauces, and gravies. Nowadays, when most of our meat comes precut and wrapped in plastic, we've forgotten about bones—not to mention knuckles and whole heads—but these parts are the basis of good stock, both in terms of flavor and nutrient value.

Gelatin-rich stock was once considered a healing food, and it still should be. A bone-based broth is rich in calcium, magnesium, phosphorus, protein, and all that good stuff that helps sick people get better and healthy people stay well. Meat stock also allows us to put every part of an animal to good use, which is not only practical but a mark of respect for the animal that gave its life to feed us.

The following recipe is a good use for a chicken deemed too old and tough for roasting. This is a very basic stock. Feel free to add more seasoning, but remember the stock can be seasoned later, in its final applications. This recipe will produce a rich, gelatinous stock and a supply of stew meat for other dishes.

YOU'LL NEED

* 1 large onion
* 2 stalks celery
* 2 carrots
* 2–3 peeled cloves garlic (optional)
* 1 whole free-range chicken (3–4 pounds)
* 2 tablespoons vinegar, any sort
* 1 teaspoon sea salt
* A few grinds of black pepper
* Sprig of thyme
* 1 cup chopped parsley

PUTTING IT TOGETHER

Chop the onion, celery, and carrots into 1-inch chunks. The garlic cloves can be left whole.

Rinse the chicken inside and out. Cut off the wings and legs and divide the legs into drumsticks and thighs. You don't have to be tidy. The neck is fair game for stock, as are the gizzards and even the feet, if you have them and wish to use them. Use the skin, too.

In a stainless steel pot with a 6- to 8-quart capacity, add the chicken pieces, chopped vegetables, garlic, vinegar, salt, pepper, and thyme. Cover with cold water, about 4 quarts, and bring to a boil. Skim off all scum that rises to the top. Put a lid on the pot, turn down the heat, and simmer for 4 hours. Yes, 4 whole hours! After 2 hours, check the condition of the meat. If it's falling off the bone, fish the carcass out of the pot and pick it clean. The meat can be set aside for soups, tacos, salads, etc. You do this halfway through, rather than at the end, to prevent the meat from overcooking. If the chicken was a tough old bird, it might need the full 4 hours of cooking. Once the meat is picked off, return the bones and skin to the simmering stock.

Add the parsley in the last 15 minutes of cooking.

Strain the stock while it is still hot by passing it through a colander to catch the bones and spent vegetables. The finer the strainer, the cleaner the stock. Add more salt and pepper to taste, if necessary.

Put the hot stock in the fridge to cool. As it cools, most of the fat will rise to the top in a solid, white layer. Remove that layer with a spoon and transfer it to a lidded container and store in the fridge or freezer. This can be used as a flavorful cooking fat, so shouldn't be wasted. It shouldn't be left in the stock, either, because it will give it a greasy mouth-feel. When cool, the stock will turn gelatinous. This is exactly how it should be. That gelatin is the nutritious legacy of the bones and the hallmark of real meat stock. Transfer the stock to smaller containers to freeze for later use.

17›

PREPARATION: 15–60+ min

How to Cook Beans

If the only beans you're acquainted with come from a can, you're in for a treat. Home-cooked beans are not only creamy and savory, they're also a cheap, versatile superfood. Beans are high in fiber and low in sugar and have the caloric density of meat. This magic combination of low sugar, high fiber, and high calories means that a meal of beans keeps you satisfied and on an even keel for a long time.

Even better, they're full of healthy antioxidants. Cook up a pot of beans on the weekend and use them all week long. One day they might be in a salad, the next day they're tossed with pasta, a third day they're in soup or pureed into a dip or rolled up in burritos. Beans are nothing if not versatile.

YOU'LL NEED

* ✱ Dried beans, such as black beans, kidney beans, lentils, and split peas (When deciding how many beans to use, keep in mind that beans triple in volume when they're soaked and cooked.)
* ✱ Water
* ✱ Sea salt and black pepper

PUTTING IT TOGETHER

Beans have a bad rap as being hard to cook. That's not true. They're just misunderstood.

TO SOAK OR NOT TO SOAK

Dried beans don't have to be soaked before cooking, although presoaking makes the cooking time a little shorter. The downside to soaking is that oversoaked beans turn mushy in cooking. Never soak beans for more than 12 hours. Eight is ideal. So if you want beans for dinner, set them out to soak before you go to work in the morning, not the night before. Small beans, like lentils or split peas, don't need to be soaked.

To soak beans, pour some beans into a bowl. Run your fingers through the beans and make sure you don't see any tiny pebbles or other foreign matter. Give the beans a quick rinse and then fill the bowl with three times more water than beans. Soak for 8 hours.

COOKING

Drain the presoaked beans. If the beans haven't been presoaked, sort through and rinse before cooking. Put either type into a big, heavy-bottom pot. Cover unsoaked beans with 3 inches of cold water; cover presoaked beans with 2 inches of water. Bring the pot to a boil, then reduce the heat and simmer, partially covered, for as long as it takes.

The older the beans, the longer they need to cook. It's hard to tell how old beans are just by looking at them. You might be able to see beans chipping or crumbling: These are hints that they're old. This doesn't mean they're *bad*—dried beans have an almost indefinite shelf life—it just means they'll take longer to cook. Generally speaking, unsoaked beans take anywhere between half an hour and 2 hours to cook. The shorter cooking time is for small beans like lentils. Larger dried beans, like black beans or kidney beans, cook in about an hour if they're fresh but could take 2 hours if they're old. Presoaked beans generally take about 45 minutes to an hour. It's hard to generalize, because freshness varies so much.

All this means you have to resign yourself to a variable cooking time. For this reason, it's good to prepare beans on your cooking day, when you'll be in the kitchen anyway and can keep your eye on them. Let your beans simmer, and check them every 15 minutes. All you have to do is make sure the water doesn't boil off. As long as you keep them covered in water and the heat steady, they'll get done. Taste for tenderness. When you think they're getting close—when they're soft enough to bite but still a bit crunchy—add salt and pepper to the water. Salting too soon makes the skins tough, so it's best to add salt in the last 15 minutes or so. When they're tender, drain off the excess water.

Refrigerate cooked beans in a covered container for up to a week.

18 › *Cooking Whole Grains*

🕐
PREPARATION: 20–60 min

We know we're supposed to eat more whole grains, but we don't always know how to go about it. We eat "whole grain" crackers and buy cereal "with whole grains." All the while, we're missing the deliciousness of REAL *whole grains.*

Whole grains range from the familiar, like brown rice and oatmeal, to the more exotic, like quinoa and spelt. Find a place for them in your daily meals. Buy a grain that you don't know anything about and experiment with it. They're each a little different, but they all have a place at the table.

Think about rice. We know what to do with rice: Pile stuff on top of it, roll it in burritos, make it into a pilaf. Well, *any* whole grain can be used the same way. Grains also can take the place of pasta in hearty salads and soups.

Like dried beans, whole grains have an undeserved reputation as being hard to cook. They're not. You don't even need a recipe.

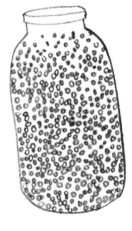

YOU'LL NEED

* **Any type of whole grain, such as brown rice, oatmeal, quinoa, spelt, millet, barley, and wheat berries**
* **Salted water or stock**

PUTTING IT TOGETHER

Put the whole grain into a pot. Cover with 1 inch of salted water or, better yet, stock. (Cooking in stock makes whole grains taste heavenly and increases their nutritional value.) Bring the liquid to a boil, turn down the heat, and simmer uncovered, stirring occasionally, until the grain is tender. All you have to do is keep the grain from drying out and burning. It's okay if you add too much liquid, because you can drain off any excess at the end. The grains are done when they taste done to you. The fastest-cooking grains are millet and quinoa, which cook in about 15 minutes. Most grains (including brown rice, barley, wheat berries, and spelt) take about 45 minutes. Wheat berries and spelt tend to stay a little chewy no matter how long they're cooked—that's just their nature.

If you put a lid on your grains when you turn off the heat and let them steam for a few minutes while you do other things, they'll absorb the last of their water and finish off nicely. This works particularly well with rice.

Put the cooked grains in a covered container and keep them in the fridge for up to a week. (The exception to this is rice, which doesn't reheat well, except as fried rice.) If you toss cooked grains with a little oil while they're still warm, they won't stick together. For a quick snack or light meal, reheat whole grain in a skillet with a little butter and oil and season with salt and pepper.

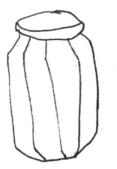

One-Bowl Meals

One of the keys to regular home cooking is leaving recipe books behind. They're a great source of ideas, but day to day you need to be able to improvise with what you have on hand. And if you cook like we do, you'll be working with fresh vegetables, precooked beans and grains, stock, and perhaps a little meat, cheese, and eggs. The trick is to learn to combine them into endlessly variable one-bowl meals.

Liberate yourself from the idea that dinner has to consist of several dishes. Sure, sometimes you might want to pull out the stops and do some fancy cooking, but it helps if you have a repertoire of simple meals that can be pulled together fast.

The following recipes are examples of this kind of cooking.

PREPARATION: 30 min

Italian Fried Rice

Fried rice is a comfort food, and making it is a great way to use up leftovers. Fried rice is best when cooked with day-old rice instead of fresh rice, which will tend to clump in the pan. Traditional fried rice is made with Asian-style vegetables, like bok choy or snow peas. We don't grow these things in our garden—they're great, but the climate in Los Angeles is similar to the climate in Italy, so we've been successful growing more heat-tolerant Italian vegetables. In this recipe, we combine fried-rice technique with Italian-style ingredients and seasonings. Adapt this recipe to whatever vegetables and grains you happen to have on hand. You can't go wrong.

YOU'LL NEED

* 1 bunch of sturdy greens, like bitter Italian dandelion, kale, or Swiss chard
* 1 tablespoon olive oil
* ½ onion, chopped
* 2 cloves garlic, chopped
* Big pinch of red pepper flakes
* 3 cups precooked spelt (or any other sturdy whole grain)
* ¼ cup stock (optional)
* Splash of dry white wine (optional)
* Handful of chopped pancetta or fried bacon bits (optional)

* 1 egg, beaten
* Sea salt and black pepper
* Parmesan cheese, grated

PUTTING IT TOGETHER

Wash and trim the greens, chop them into ribbons, and put them in a steaming basket. Steam until bright green and wilted.

In a large skillet, heat the olive oil. Add the onion and cook until transparent, then add the garlic and pepper flakes and cook another minute. Add the steamed greens and cook them for a minute or so in the hot oil so they pick up flavor. Add the spelt or other grains to the skillet 1 cup at a time, tossing them with the greens and cooked onions. If you have stock on hand, add about ¼ cup to help hydrate the grains and add flavor. This is also a good time to slosh in a little bit of white wine.

If you're using pancetta or bacon bits, add them now. Then clear a hole in the center of the pan and pour in the egg. Let it cook undisturbed for a minute or so, until opaque. Then toss it with the greens and grains until bits of scrambled egg are distributed throughout the dish.

Take the pan off the heat. Season with salt and pepper. Put the dish into bowls and top with the Parmesan cheese.

Makes 2 servings

PREPARATION: 30 min

Quick Soup

If you have stock, beans, and grains in the fridge, soup is only minutes away. Let minestrone be your inspiration. This classic vegetable and bean soup originated as a way to use up kitchen leftovers. Its flavors would vary from kitchen to kitchen and season to season. A spring minestrone might feature baby peas and carrots and be light and fresh. A summer minestrone would be big and bold, full of chunks of eggplant and zucchini and tomatoes.

Use the following recipe as a loose guideline for constructing your own soups on the fly. Don't let the lack of a particular ingredient stop you from making soup. Honor both the season and the contents of your pantry. It's all good.

YOU'LL NEED

* 3 tablespoons extra-virgin olive oil
* 1 medium onion, chopped
* 1–2 cloves garlic, peeled (optional)
* 1 cup mixed vegetables, like carrots, celery, potatoes, and hard squash, chopped into spoon-size pieces
* 6 cups stock

* 1 cup tomatoes, canned or fresh, diced
* 1 cup leafy greens, cut into thin ribbons
* 1 cup precooked beans, such as white beans, kidney beans, cranberry beans, or garbanzos
* 1 cup precooked grain, any sort
* Handful of chopped fresh herbs, like parsley or basil
* Sea salt and black pepper

PUTTING IT TOGETHER

In the bottom of a soup pot, heat the olive oil and cook the onion for about 5 minutes, until it softens. Add the garlic, if using, and any firm vegetables and cook for a couple of minutes. Add all the stock, throw in the tomatoes, and bring to a simmer. Simmer for about 15 minutes, until the hardest vegetables soften. (If you're not using vegetables that require long cooking, proceed to the next step as soon as the stock is simmering.)

Add the leafy greens, beans, and grains. If the soup seems a little thick, add boiling water by the cupful to thin it to the consistency you prefer. Simmer about 10 minutes more, just until the greens are tender and the beans and grains are hot. Ideally, at this point the tomatoes should be broken up, the firm veggies like potatoes spoon-ready, and the greens and other tender vegetables still bright. Finish by adding the fresh herbs to the pot; salt and pepper to taste.

Serve drizzled with olive oil.

Makes 4 servings

20 ›

PREPARATION: 30 min

The Dog's Pot

Our dog is undeniably spoiled, so part of our weekly cooking time is devoted to him. He eats premium-brand kibble, but supplementing that with matching canned food is more than we can afford. In a period of madness, we tried cooking all of his food, but he's so large it was like cooking for another person—another person who required a special diet. The logistics were too complicated. (If he were a Chihuahua, the story might be different.) Yet a diet of 100 percent dry kibble seems equivalent to living on nothing but energy bars and soda crackers. We found a compromise solution in soup.

Every week we make a batch of soup and feed it to the dog as a kibble topping. He loves his soup, and it gives him access to the vitamins found in fresh vegetables and a protein boost from meat scraps, as well as adding more moisture into what would otherwise be a dry, kidney-straining sort of diet.

A friend told us that his Egyptian grandmother always had two pots stewing on the back of the stove. One was a stockpot for people, and the other a pot for the dogs. This recipe honors that waste-not, want-not sensibility.

The great thing about cooking for dogs is that they'll love whatever you give them. There's no need to worry about seasoning the dog's pot or getting the ingredients right. It might look disgusting, but that will only make it more appealing to dog sensibilities. Moreover, because this is a supplement to kibble, not the whole diet, you don't have to worry about trying to balance the nutrients in a scientific manner. The soup will change from week to week, depending on the scraps you have available, and that's okay.

While it's fine for a bit of cooked food to find its way into the soup, plate scrapings aren't good for dogs. It's far better to use unprocessed foods, like trimmings.

YOU'LL NEED

FRESH VEGETABLES, SCRAPS, AND PEELINGS. Save them up all week in a bag in the fridge or freezer. Dogs are omnivorous scavengers, not carnivores, and they really do like vegetables. If you've ever found your dog nibbling grass, you know they crave the vitamins in greens. They don't digest raw vegetables well, so precooking vegetables helps dogs get the most out of their food. Dogs love sweet veggies like carrots and squash but also seem to appreciate green stuff like spinach and broccoli. Potatoes, sweet and regular, are good for this, too, and our dog adores

tomatoes. The only vegetables you should withhold are onions and onion family members, like leeks and garlic. These are toxic for dogs in quantity.

PROTEINS AND FATS. Dogs need more protein than we do. High-quality protein helps them recover from injuries, surgeries, and chronic illnesses. So you should save your meat trimmings, scraps, and bones for the dog's pot. Animal fat is also an excellent—and much appreciated—soup addition, in small quantities. Unless your vet directs otherwise, you don't have to withhold animal fat from dogs for the sake of their health—their weight, yes, their health, no. In other words, the calories in fat won't help an obese dog slim down, but it won't make your dog keel over from a heart attack, either. They crave fat, and fat is good for their skin and coats. Far better they get the fat in their soup, in a relatively unprocessed form, than in junk food treats. If you strip skin from chicken, save a piece of the skin for the soup. If you keep bacon grease in a can, add a spoonful to the pot. If you don't eat meat, or you eat so little you never have scraps, you might consider buying a little meat for the dog. A couple of chicken thighs go a long way in a soup.

WHOLE GRAINS. Dog kibble is grain heavy, so the soup doesn't need to include grains. However, a bit of grain makes the soup thicker and easier to serve. If you have leftover cooked grains, like rice, toss them in. Some dogs are allergic to wheat and corn, but they'll likely do well with any other type of grain.

PUTTING IT TOGETHER

Throw everything you have in a soup pot, fill the pot with water, and bring to a boil. Don't add any salt or seasoning. And don't worry about quantities. It might end up a thin soup or a thick stew. Anything you cook up will result in a broth that dogs will like and will do them some good. Simmer until the vegetables are soft and the meat cooked through. When it's all done, fish out any bones. Cooked bones are dangerous because they splinter and can perforate a dog's throat or intestines.

If you wish, you can blend the soup with a stick blender or in a countertop blender to make the soup more homogenous and easier to digest, but this isn't strictly necessary. Transfer the soup to a covered container, refrigerate, and dole it out by the scoopful over kibble. It only keeps about a week, so adjust the quantity you make to the size of your dog.

21 ›

PREPARATION: 1¾ hours
WAITING: 16 hours

Serious Bread

VOLLKORNBROT, *"whole kernel bread" in German, is a dense, whole grain bread popular in northern Europe but difficult to find elsewhere. It's so dense, in fact, that it's the black hole of breads, able to suck SUVs into its gravitational pull. VOLLKORNBROT is made with whole kernels of wheat and rye, flaxseed, and sunflower seed. A loaf weighs more than 2 pounds when it comes out of the oven. One slice is a meal.*

Vollkornbrot has such a high moisture content that you can make it on the weekend and nibble at it for the rest of the week. It never seems to dry out. Also in its favor is that it's a no-knead bread, and it requires no shaping. Making this bread is a 2-day process, but most of that time involves letting the dough sit.

You can find wheat and rye berries (i.e., whole kernels of wheat and rye) in your typical health food store bulk bin. Rye flour is often sold in bins, too, or in bags alongside regular flour. Crack the wheat and rye berries by throwing them in a blender or a food processor for a few seconds, or grind them in a grain mill. Process the berries in batches so they don't overwhelm the appliance. You're done when there are no more whole kernels and all kernels are chopped in half at minimum—finer is better.

YOU'LL NEED

* 4 ½ ounces wheat berries, cracked
* 4 ½ ounces rye berries, cracked
* 4 ½ ounces whole wheat flour
* 4 ½ ounces rye flour
* 1 ½ teaspoons sea salt
* 2 cups water
* 3 tablespoons sourdough starter (whole wheat, rye, or white) or ½ teaspoon active dry yeast
* 2 ½ ounces whole wheat berries
* ½ cup flaxseed
* ½ cup sunflower seeds (optional)
* 1 ½ tablespoons barley malt syrup (optional)
* Handful of rolled oats

KELLY: Erik, I notice the *Vollkornbrot* recipe is made with sourdough starter, not yeast.

ERIK: It's better that way.

KELLY: But how many people keep a sourdough starter? Can't it be made with packaged yeast?

ERIK: They should make their own sourdough starter. All it takes is flour and water. Sourdough bread tastes better, stays fresh longer, and is more nutritious. Think of all that beautiful wild yeast out there, waiting to be harnessed.

KELLY: But realistically…

ERIK: Really, it's not that hard. It's how this bread is made. The sourness of the starter melds with grains and makes the flavors deeper, richer. And once people have a starter, they can make other loaves, sourdough pancakes, all kinds of things. Nothing can really replace the flavors wild yeasts bring to the table. Store-bought yeast is for chumps.

KELLY (GETTING STERN): Chumps like us. We use it in focaccia. There has to be an alternative, or people won't bake this bread. It's hardly raised at all, so it can't matter that much.

ERIK (ROLLING HIS EYES): Okay, okay. I'll work up an alternative. But seriously, they should try it with the starter.

PUTTING IT TOGETHER

DAY 1

STARTING THE SPONGE

Just before you go to bed, combine the cracked wheat berries, cracked rye berries, whole wheat flour, rye flour, salt, water, and sourdough starter in a large bowl. If you're using yeast instead of starter, dissolve the yeast in the water before adding it to the other ingredients.

At the same time, place the whole wheat berries in a separate bowl and add enough water to cover. Let both the sponge and the wheat berries sit, covered, overnight.

DAY 2

INCORPORATION

The next morning, drain the water off the soaked wheat berries and stir them into the sponge. Add the flaxseed and the sunflower seeds and malt syrup, if using.

Note: This will be a very moist and sticky bread dough.

PROOFING

After incorporating the seeds and soaked berries, allow the dough to sit in the mixing bowl for 3 to 8 hours. This is all proofing means—letting the dough rest undisturbed so that its flavor and texture improves. This flexibility of schedule means you can bake this bread whenever it's most convenient for you. Cover the proofing bowl with a plate, or a larger upturned bowl, to keep the dough from drying out. The bread will proof best at regular room temperature. If your house is cold, find a warm place for the bowl to sit.

The dough will not rise much. This proofing period is more about developing flavor than gaining loft. Just trust that it will be done enough after 3 hours. If you poke at it after 3 hours or so, you'll notice that it has changed a little. The dough will have some air in it, even if it looks sort of inert on the outside.

BAKING

Grease a 5 x 9-inch loaf pan *very well* with butter, being sure to grease the corners of the pan, and sprinkle a single layer of rolled oats across the bottom to prevent sticking. Turn the dough out of the bowl and into the loaf pan. You'll probably have to use a big wooden spoon to transfer it glob by glob. Smooth the top with the back of the spoon.

Don't preheat the oven. Just stick the loaf pan on the center rack of the oven and set the temperature to 425°F.

Bake for 40 minutes, then pull the pan from the oven and loosely cover it with a piece of aluminum foil to keep the top of the loaf from browning too much. Bake for another 40 to 45 minutes, then pull it out to take a look. When done, the top will be golden brown and the sides of the loaf will pull away slightly from the sides of the pan. What little you can see of the sides should be golden brown. Test the loaf with a knife to determine whether it is finished. Insert the knife in the center; the blade should come out clean (or cleanish—it might have slight traces of dough on it). Even when finished, this bread is damp and dense.

Remove the finished bread from the pan straight away. Run a butter knife around the edges of the loaf pan to loosen the loaf. Using oven mitts, knock the pan on the countertop, invert it, and give it a shake. The loaf should slide free. Leave it to cool, if you can restrain yourself. This is one bread that is not necessarily better hot out of the oven. It improves somewhat if left alone to cool undisturbed.

How to Make and Maintain Sourdough Starter

To create a sourdough starter, mix 1 cup white flour with 1 cup water. Put this in a lidded glass jar—a quart or pint canning jar works fine—and keep it on the kitchen counter. Each day, pour off half the contents and add ½ cup flour and ½ cup water to replace what you poured off. This is called "feeding the starter"—you are literally giving fresh food to the yeast culture. Without regular feeding, the culture weakens and then spoils.

Pour off and feed every day for a week. You'll begin to see some changes in the odor and consistency of the starter as wild yeasts begin to colonize it. Air bubbles are a good thing. If liquid forms at the top, just stir it back in. The only bad sign would be truly nasty smells or outright

mold, and this would happen only if you'd neglected your starter. After a week, you'll have a viable white flour starter that you can use for baking. The starter will become stronger and more flavorful over time.

To make a whole wheat or rye starter, simply start feeding this white starter with whole wheat or rye flour instead of white flour. Remember to feed your starter every day, especially wheat and rye starters, which can go rancid fast without regular attention. If you go on vacation or know you won't be baking for a while, put the starter in the fridge. It can nap in there for a couple of weeks, but not forever. It might take a few days of feeding after it comes out of refrigeration to get back to full strength.

22› *Homemade Condiments*

The nice thing about making your own condiments is that you can customize them any way you wish. That and the fact they are delicious. Experiment with these basics. Once you see how easy it is to make your own, you'll be converted.

PREPARATION: 5 min

Mayonnaise

Come on, live a little! Don't deny yourself homemade mayonnaise. The secret to making mayonnaise is to be sure that the eggs and oil are both at room temperature before you begin and to combine them very, very slowly. It's an emulsion. Make it with a whisk. The egg and oil don't want to combine—you have to coax them together. If you add the oil too quickly, you'll end up with a thin, greasy liquid instead of mayonnaise.

YOU'LL NEED

* 2 egg yolks, at room temperature
* 1 tablespoon lemon juice or vinegar
* Sea salt and black pepper to taste
* ¼ teaspoon dried mustard or paprika (optional)
* 1 cup sunflower oil (or a similar mild oil), at room temperature

PUTTING IT TOGETHER

TO MAKE MAYONNAISE BY HAND:
of room to whisk. Whisk for a minute or so until the yolks turn thick. Add the lemon juice or vinegar, and a pinch of salt and pepper and the paprika or mustard, if using, and whisk another half minute to incorporate. Then start adding the oil, drop by drop. The first addition of oil is the most critical—this is when the emulsion happens. Add a few drops of oil, beat until creamy, add a little more. It should start thickening by the time you've added the first ⅓ cup of oil. After that point, you can add the oil a little faster.

TO MAKE MAYONNAISE WITH A BLENDER, A FOOD PROCESSOR, OR A STAND MIXER:
Follow the same protocols as hand mixing. Blend together the eggs, lemon juice, and seasoning first, until well incorporated. Then start adding the oil in a slow, steady drizzle, bit by bit, while the blender or processor is running. The mayo may thicken before you're done adding the oil, which might cause a countertop blender to choke. Just scrape down the sides and carry on. The result will be a very creamy, thick mayonnaise. Alternatively, you could make the recipe with 1 whole egg

and 1 egg yolk instead of 2 egg yolks, which will make the mix a teeny bit less thick and easier on your blender.

For both methods, taste and add more salt or pepper or lemon juice if needed. If the mayonnaise sets up too thick, add a spoonful of hot water.

VARIATIONS

Add minced garlic or juice from a garlic press to make aioli. Stir in chopped herbs. Crumble in blue cheese. Add cream and a spoonful of curry powder. Add a spoonful of wasabi.

What do you do with homemade mayonnaise? Of course, it's a great dip for almost anything, a nice side for meat and fish, and indispensable for egg and tuna salad, but we like it best with vegetables. There's a type of salad called Russian Salad, made with chilled diced potatoes, mixed vegetables, and cubes of meat tossed in a generous quantity of mayo. We do variations on that dish using boiled potatoes as a base and adding whatever we've got coming out of our garden, as well as pickles, olives, chunks of cheese, or hard-cooked egg. All of that is tossed with shameless quantities of mayo and some extra lemon juice and salt and pepper to brighten it up. It's one-bowl eating at its best, perfect for summer cooking. Sometimes the mix is as simple as potatoes and bitter greens; other times we've put everything in there but the kitchen sink. No matter what you use, the mayo binds it into eating perfection.

Keep the mayonnaise in the fridge and eat it all within a few days.

Makes 1 cup

PREPARATION: 5 min
WAITING: 1 day

Mustard

Mustard is so simple to make, and so easily adapted to your own preferences, you'll wonder why you ever bought it in a jar.

YOU'LL NEED

* 6 tablespoons whole mustard seeds (All yellow works, or use half brown seeds and half yellow seeds for a more pungent mustard. Buy mustard seeds in bulk for the best prices.)

* ⅓ cup dry white wine

* 2 tablespoons white wine or apple cider vinegar

* ½ teaspoon salt

* Pinch of ground allspice

* Couple of grinds of black pepper

PUTTING IT TOGETHER

In a glass bowl or jar, combine all the ingredients and refrigerate overnight. In the morning, you'll find that the seeds have soaked up most if not all of the liquid.

Transfer the mix to a food processor or blender or use a mortar and pestle. Add 3 to 4 tablespoons of water and grind the mustard to the consistency you like.

The flavor improves after a couple of days in the fridge, although you could use the mustard right away if you must. Taking this basic recipe as a starting point, customize your mustard any way you like: Add herbs and spices before the overnight soak, or add honey when you pulverize it to make a sweet mustard, or add a little horseradish if you like your mustard hot. To make bright yellow mustard, stir in a small spoonful of turmeric.

Transfer the final product to a glass jar. It will keep in the fridge for weeks.

Makes 1 cup

Harissa

PREPARATION: 3 min
WAITING: 10–40 min

In our house, *harissa* is the hot sauce we reach for the most. It goes on eggs, into stews, over tacos, even on chips. *Harissa* is a hot pepper condiment native to North Africa and most often associated with Moroccan cuisine. The recipe varies from region to region and from house to house.

We asked a Moroccan friend how to make *harissa,* and he shrugged and said, "You just grind peppers with garlic and oil and add a little salt." It's that simple. You can find *harissa* recipes that are much more elaborate, but elaborate doesn't mean better.

Each time we make *harissa,* it comes out a little different, but it's always good, because peppers, garlic, and salt are natural mates. In combination, they make the tongue happy. The big variable is the peppers. We hesitate to recommend any particular type of pepper because we want you to make it with whatever peppers are local and convenient to you.

You can use fresh peppers or dried peppers. Fresh-pepper *harissa* is bright red-orange and can be blazingly hot. It looks like the *harissa* that you buy in cans or tubes in import stores. *Harissa* made with dried peppers is a deep, sultry brown. Its flavor is richer and more mellow than the fresh version. It reminds us of the Mexican sauce called *mole.* In the summer, we make fresh-pepper *harissa* from hot Italian long peppers that we grow in our own garden. For the rest of the year, we make it with dried chiles sold in our local Latin market, like chiles negros, ancho chiles, and New Mexico chiles. Use whatever peppers you prefer. If you don't like much heat, use roasted red peppers to dilute the heat of fresh peppers.

The following hypothetical harissa recipe is just to start you off. Once you have the basics down, improvise and find a balance that works for you.

YOU'LL NEED

* 4 ounces dried peppers or 8 ounces fresh peppers
* 3 cloves garlic, peeled
* 1½ teaspoons salt

* 3 tablespoons olive oil
* Optional seasonings: 1 teaspoon ground cumin, 1 teaspoon ground coriander, 1 teaspoon ground caraway (any one or all three), 1 tablespoon chopped fresh mint leaves, lemon juice to taste

PUTTING IT TOGETHER

Pull the stems from the peppers, open them up, and remove the seeds. If you are using dried peppers, pour boiling water over them and let them soak for a half hour first. Be careful not to touch your face while stemming and seeding, and wash your hands well after handling peppers. Otherwise you might suffer the same fate as Erik, who visited the restroom after seeding fresh hot peppers…. Well, the less said of the incident, the better.

Transfer the peppers to the bowl of a food processor or a mortar and pestle. Add the garlic and salt. Begin to process or grind. Drizzle in the olive oil as you go. Don't add much oil now, just enough to make a smooth paste. If you wish, add the additional spices, mint leaves, and lemon juice, according to taste.

Store the *harissa* in a jar. Smooth the surface down and cover the surface with a layer of olive oil to help keep it fresh. Restore this layer after each use. It will keep for a few weeks.

Makes about 1½ cups

23 ›

Old-Fashioned Vinegar-Based Drinks

If you're trying to avoid high-fructose corn syrup, you'll know how hard it is to find a sweet beverage in the store that doesn't contain it. Those you can find tend to be pricy. Home-made drinks make it easy to reduce your sugar consumption. They return sweet drinks from the realm of the mundane to their rightful place as special treat. You might drink a whole can of soda without even noticing, just because it's in your hand, but you'll drink a small glass of club soda and flavored syrup with more conscious pleasure.

Oxymel, *sekanjabin*, and switchel are three sweet vinegar-based drinks of ancient lineage. We don't consume nearly as much vinegar as our ancestors did—particularly if our ancestors came from northern climes where citrus does not grow. Once upon a time, only rich folk could afford citrus, which meant that for most people vinegar was one of the only means of making food taste tangy and bright.

Vinegar also was widely used in pickling and often mixed with water to purify it. It makes sense that people would make sweet beverages with it as well. Keep in mind that they were using unpasteurized vinegar, such as you might buy in the health food store or make yourself (see Project 52). Raw vinegar not only has richer, more subtle flavors than distilled vinegar, but it is also a healthful, fermented food.

If your palate leans toward the adventurous, make up a few of the following recipes and keep them on hand for visitors or sudden soda cravings. They might taste odd at first, but they are genuinely addicting.

PREPARATION: 5 min

Oxymel

Oxymel means "acid-honey." It's a blend of honey and vinegar. The ancient Greeks and Romans used this widely as a beverage and as a vehicle for medicine—they'd infuse the oxymel with different herbal concoctions. Its use carried forward well into medieval Europe and beyond. As a simple drink, it has long been considered a refreshing and restorative beverage.

YOU'LL NEED

* ½ cup honey
* ½ cup mild, tasty vinegar, like apple cider, white wine, or fruit vinegar

PUTTING IT TOGETHER

The classic proportions are 1 part honey to 1 part vinegar, but you can adjust this to taste. In a saucepan, warm the honey gently, then stir in the vinegar (they won't mix cold). Pour the syrup into a clean bottle. It will keep indefinitely.

A spoonful of straight oxymel is good for a sore throat. Stir a couple of spoonfuls into hot water or tea for a soothing, expectorant drink. Or stir it into cold water to make a refreshing, lemonade-like beverage.

Makes 1 cup

PREPARATION: 15 min

Sekanjabin

This traditional Iranian vinegar beverage was once used as medicine—just like oxymel—but it is still drunk for pleasure to this day. You can find premade *sekanjabin* syrup for sale in Middle Eastern markets. *Sekanjabin* is an Arabic transcription of a Farsi term, *sirka-anjubin,* which means "honeyed vinegar." Despite this, all the recipes we've found are made with sugar, though we're sure it could also be made with honey. In general, *sekanjabin* is a type of beverage more than a specific recipe, so be inventive and alter it as you like. Here's a basic *sekanjabin*.

YOU'LL NEED

* 4 cups sugar
* 2 cups water
* 1 cup apple cider vinegar or white wine vinegar (Fruit vinegar would be good, too.)
* 1 cup fresh mint leaves

PUTTING IT TOGETHER

Combine the sugar and water in a saucepan and heat gently for about 5 minutes, until the sugar is dissolved. Bring to a simmer, add the vinegar, and continue to simmer, until the mixture thickens a little. Test it by raising your spoon and watching how fast the liquid runs off it. When it slows, the syrup is ready. Add the mint and infuse for 5 minutes. Keep the heat low so your syrup doesn't caramelize. After 5 minutes, take it off the heat and let it cool.

Strain off the mint leaves and pour the syrup into a very clean bottle. Like the oxymel, this keeps indefinitely.

Mix with sparkling or still water at the ratio of 1 part syrup to about 4 to 8 parts water, depending on how strong you like it. On special occasions, serve *sekanjabin* with a little shaved cucumber on top.

DOCTORING YOUR *SEKANJABIN*: Try adding about ½ cup fresh lemon juice when you add the vinegar. Or, add 1 to 3 ounces of grated ginger and/or the peel of a lemon when you add the mint and let it infuse for about 20 minutes. Or, add crushed fresh fruit to the blend and let sit overnight, then strain off the fruit.

Switchel

Switchel, or haymaker's punch, is *sekanjabin* by way of the prairie. This sweet water was served during the summer to hot and tired field workers as the prairie equivalent of a sports drink. Laura Ingalls Wilder mentions it in *The Long Winter:*

> *Ma had sent them ginger-water. She had sweetened the cool well-water with sugar, flavored it with vinegar, and put in plenty of ginger to warm their stomachs so they could drink til they were not thirsty. Ginger-water would not make them sick, as plain cold water would when they were so hot.*

Like *sekanjabin*, this drink is more like a concept than a specific recipe. Every farmwife made her own version. Play with the types of sugar and the amount of vinegar until you come up with something you like.

YOU'LL NEED

* 1 cup apple cider vinegar
* 1 cup molasses (If you don't like molasses, substitute white sugar, brown sugar, or honey, or do a half-and-half blend. Also, you can up the quantity of sugar to tone down the vinegar bite.)
* 1 ounce grated or sliced ginger, to taste, or 1 teaspoon ground ginger

PUTTING IT TOGETHER

In a saucepan, heat the vinegar and molasses or sugar until they're well blended. Add the fresh ginger and simmer a couple of minutes more to warm it, then take the pan off the heat and let the ginger infuse for about 15 minutes. Skip this step if you're using powdered ginger—just stir it in and you're done.

Strain off the ginger. The flavors mellow the longer they are left to sit, so making the syrup the day before you need it is a good thing, but not imperative. It will keep well.

When you're ready to serve, add all of the syrup to about 1 quart of cold water and stir well, or portion it out glass by glass.

If you want to be authentic, add about ¼ to ½ cup ground oatmeal to the diluted switchel before serving. Most of the oatmeal will settle to the bottom of the pitcher, and this is fine. The idea is that the oats add body and smoothness to the switchel. Make ground oatmeal by chopping rolled oats in a blender.

Cleaning, Washing, and Mending

Doing the laundry and cleaning the house are weekly rituals of renewal. Preparing your own cleaning products and laundry soap makes the ritual more personal and intellectually engaging. It's hard to imagine housecleaning as empowering, but the power is there when you decide which substances you and your family breathe, touch, and ingest on a daily basis. Commercial cleaning products and laundry detergents are some of the most toxic substances in the home. Take a look at the warnings on the back of their packaging. Ask yourself if you really want to wipe your counters, mop your floors, and coat your clothing with such aggressive chemicals. Rather than worry about potential chemical exposure, it's easier to disengage and make your own cleaning products. Once you switch to homemade, you'll walk down the cleaning aisle of the supermarket and marvel at all the brightly colored, highly specialized bottles of cleaners that you don't need and don't miss.

24 ›

Making Your Own Cleaning Products

Recipes for cleaning products are everywhere, and you should certainly experiment to find mixes that work well for you. Our philosophy is "Simple is better," so most of our recipes and recommendations are based on a single ingredient used correctly, and we use the same ingredients for many different purposes.

As you convert to this way of cleaning, the space beneath your sink will become blissfully uncluttered. All you need are a couple of spray bottles, some rags, and a few key ingredients. It feels good to get rid of all those bottles of who-knows-what chemicals and lurking toxins. As you transition to nontoxic cleaning, you can use up what is already in your cupboards or take your half-empty bottles to a hazardous waste drop site. This is a safer way to dispose of chemicals than sending them to the landfill.

Get ready to go sleek and minimal. The following is all you need to clean your entire house and do the laundry:

FOR BASIC CLEANING:

* 1 gallon distilled white vinegar
* 1 large box or bag baking soda (sodium bicarbonate)
* 1 quart liquid castile soap, like Dr. Bronner's

We used to look askance at borax and washing soda, believing them to be unnecessarily harsh for day-to-day cleaning. Recently, we've started using them in homemade laundry powder and experimenting with them in housecleaning. While they need to be used with more caution than baking soda, soap, and vinegar and kept out of reach of children and pets—they've earned their place in our home as less-toxic cleaning alternatives for really tough jobs.

FOR ADVANCED CLEANING AND LAUNDRY:

* 1 box laundry borax (sodium borate, also called sodium tetraborate)
* 1 box washing soda (sodium carbonate)

A few other items get called into play now and then, like lemons, cornstarch, and olive oil, but they're things you're likely to have in the kitchen. You'll also want to gather up some rags and spray bottles. We're big on cleaning with rags, which we make out of old kitchen towels and T-shirts. They're sturdier than paper towels and more hygienic than sponges. Use a fresh rag for every job, gather them up into a "rag load," and launder in hot water.

Any of the recipes that follow can be scented with essential oils to make cleaning more fun, but that step is entirely optional.

ALMOST UNIVERSAL SPRAY

Combine 1 part vinegar with 1 part water in a spray bottle.

This 50/50 blend of vinegar and water is the homemade mix you'll reach for most often. Use it to wipe down counters, tile, tables, appliances, bathroom sinks, toilet seats, and mirrors and windows. It requires no rinsing. However, it doesn't work well on heavy grease—it's best for shining and gentle cleaning, disinfecting, and deodorizing. Yes, deodorizing! The smell of vinegar vanishes when it dries, taking other odors with it. The scent of vinegar might seem strange at first, but soon you'll associate it with cleanliness and realize it's a more wholesome scent than chemical fumes and artificial perfumes. Vinegar disinfects because it is a mild acid. Up the disinfectant strength by adding a few drops of tea tree oil to the spray bottle and shaking well before each use.

Here's a tip for windows and mirrors: The secret to a streak-free shine is polishing until dry with an old, lint-free T-shirt or even newspaper. You don't need much vinegar to clean windows—your bottle of 50/50 blend will be convenient for quick touch-ups, but if you're doing a lot of windows, use about ¼ to ½ cup vinegar in a bucket of hot water. Wipe with a wet rag and polish dry. If you get bad streaking, you're probably seeing remnants of wax leftover from commercial window cleaner. A squirt of dish soap in the vinegar mix will take care of that.

> **WARNING**
> Don't use vinegar spray on marble or granite countertops. It might damage the stone.

SPRAY FOR GREASY SURFACES

Pour 1 to 2 tablespoons of liquid castile soap in a quart spray bottle and top off with water.

It's a dilute mix because it doesn't take much soap to do a lot of cleaning. Use soapy water on sticky refrigerator doors, grimy appliances, and stovetops. While this could be used as a general-purpose cleaner, like the vinegar spray above, we've found that surfaces wiped with the vinegar spray stay cleaner longer. Our theory about this is that traces of soap left behind attract dirt. So to work less, use soap only when it's really needed, and use the vinegar spray the rest of the time.

Want to use your own homemade bar soap in your spray? You can improvise a watery liquid soap which is good for cleaning by pouring 1½ cups of boiling water over ½ cup of grated Coconut Laundry Soap (Project 42) and stirring until it dissolves. If you experiment with other types of bar soap, be aware that bar soaps dissolve in unpredictable ways, depending on their composition. A simple alternative is to let the soap dissolve gradually. Place a few pieces of soap, roughly 1 or 2 tablespoons, in the bottom of a spray bottle full of water. It won't be particularly pretty, but the soap will dissolve over time and create soapy water strong enough for this purpose.

If you want to boost the cleaning power of this soap spray for extratough jobs, add a tablespoon of borax.

SUPER-NATURAL DISINFECTANT

Many common herbs are full of disinfectant powers and pleasant scents. Instead of reaching for disinfectant sprays, use a strong infusion of herbs in water to wipe down cooking surfaces, the inside of the refrigerator, cutting boards, doorknobs, and the like.

Pour 1 cup boiling water over 1 heaping tablespoon of dry herbs or over a handful of fresh herbs. Let it sit for 20 minutes, strain off the herbs, and transfer the liquid to a spray bottle. Make only 1 cup at a time, because it will not keep long.

The best-known disinfectant herbs are lavender, rosemary, thyme, and sage. Use any one of them or a few in combination. Be careful using them on porous, white surfaces, though, as they might stain. When cleaning white surfaces, use straight white distilled vinegar.

VINEGAR OF THE FOUR THIEVES

Instead of using boiling water, you can steep herbs in white vinegar to take advantage of the disinfectant power of both. There's an old wives' tale that a group of thieves survived the Black Death by cleaning themselves with (or in some versions, drinking) herbal vinegar. This recipe exists in many permutations. Follow the directions below, or switch up the ingredients any way you like:

Combine equal parts of lavender, rosemary, thyme, sage, and peppermint—fresh or dried. Put them in a jar and cover with distilled white vinegar (unheated). Steep the herbs for 4 to 6 weeks, strain off the herbs, and store in a spray bottle.

SCOURING POWDERS

Baking soda scours without scratching. It should be your first choice of abrasives. Keep it in a jar with holes punched in the lid or, if you want to get fancy, in a decorative sugar shaker. Baking soda dissolves in water, so don't try to use it in standing water. It works best when applied to a damp surface or sprinkled on a damp rag or sponge.

Baking soda should take care of 90 percent of your scrubbing needs, but if you need more oomph, pull out the borax. Borax is coarse, but it will not harm fiberglass or porcelain. If faced with a situation that will not respond to baking soda or borax, like a casserole dish caked with burnt-on grease, try soaking and scrubbing with washing soda, but be sure to wear kitchen gloves when you do it. Don't use washing soda on aluminum pans—it will discolor them. It will also scratch fiberglass surfaces.

Here's some special help for the kitchen sink: If stains remain after cleaning with baking soda or borax, dry the sink with a towel, then scrub it with a lemon. You don't need to waste a good lemon on this—set aside lemon rinds when you're cooking. Squish the lemon pieces all over the base and sides of the sink, pressing hard to release every bit of juice and oil. Then walk away and don't use your sink for at least a half hour. Leave it as long as you can, even overnight. When you come back and rinse, your sink will be sparkling.

SOFT SCRUB

Baking soda and liquid castile soap are a great team. Blend the baking soda with a small amount of the liquid castile to make a paste with the consistency of frosting, and use this to attack tough jobs. Try it on everything from bathtub rings to stained coffee cups.

FLOOR CLEANERS

One-half cup white vinegar mixed in a bucket of hot water will clean ordinary dirt from the kitchen or bathroom floor and requires no rinsing. Vinegar is safe to use on tile, vinyl flooring, and linoleum. A strong solution of vinegar might damage stone, so if you have stone floors, check with the product manufacturer. Damp mopping with water alone is usually sufficient to clean wood floors, but you can add a splash of vinegar to the water if they are particularly dirty.

When a kitchen floor is nearly black with grease and grime, special care is needed. Plain old soap and water—about ⅛ cup liquid castile soap in a bucket of hot water—will lift grease more effectively than vinegar and water. Add ¼ cup borax to make it work even better. Scrub tough spots with baking soda or the soft scrub mentioned above. Washing soda cleans grease like nobody's business, but it's so strong it might dull no-wax floors, so it's not recommended for those. For tile floors, use ½ cup washing soda per bucket of water. Follow up with a plain-water mopping to rinse. (To give you an idea of the strength of washing soda, back in the days when floors were waxed, it was used as a wax stripper. If it can strip wax, it's strong enough to strip all the oils from your skin, leaving your hands mummified, so wear kitchen gloves when using it.)

TOILET BOWL CLEANERS

Most of the time, white vinegar is all you need to clean your whole toilet. Use the 50/50 vinegar spray to wipe down the tank, seat, and lid. To clean the bowl, pour a bucket of water in the bowl to force the water level to drop, then pour a generous amount of vinegar all around the edges of the bowl, letting it collect at the bottom. Scrub with a toilet brush. If the area under the waterline is discolored and scrubbing doesn't take off the stain, add more vinegar and let it sit for an hour or so. When you come back, the stain should come off easily. Orange rust stains under the rim can also be removed with vinegar: Soak paper towels or rags with vinegar and tuck them around the rim. Let them sit for an hour or so, then remove them and scrub the area clean.

If the bowl is so dirty that it needs more abrasive power, scrub with baking soda or borax. Baking soda will fizz when mixed with vinegar—this is no cause for alarm. However, baking soda neutralizes the acid in vinegar, making vinegar a less effective cleaner, so don't add baking soda until you've done all the cleaning you can with vinegar alone.

DUSTING AIDS

All you need for dusting is a rag and a spray bottle of water. Scent the water with essential oils, if you want. Mist the rag so it will grab and hold dust; use the damp rag on all surfaces. Fold the rag over and over, remisting as you do, so that you are always wiping with a clean portion. Use as many rags as you need. Old, lint-free T-shirts or kitchen towels are fine for this, but the best dusting cloths are made of wool, because wool attracts dust. Cut rags from wool fabrics or, if you knit, use up leftover wool by knitting dusting squares.

WOOD CLEANERS

In most cases, you can dust wood with a damp rag, as above. If the wood is actually dirty, clean it with a mix of 5 parts vinegar or lemon juice to 1 part olive oil. You only need to make a few spoonfuls of this "salad dressing" at a time because it goes a long way. Combine the ingredients in a bottle and shake well. Rub on with a soft cloth to clean, then buff to a shine with a fresh cloth.

FURNITURE POLISH

Making furniture polish is like making a basic salve. Mix 4 parts linseed oil with 1 part beeswax. See Project 36 for instructions on how to cook it up. Add lemon essential oil for that classic furniture polish scent. Apply the paste with a soft cloth, rub it in thoroughly, then buff with a fresh cloth. Olive oil can be used in the place of linseed oil, but linseed oil dries faster, giving a cleaner finish.

STOVE AND OVEN CLEANERS

The stove is probably the most difficult item to clean in the house. The cooktop, range hood, oven, and broiler all collect grease, and most of that grease is baked on. A mildly dirty stove can be washed with soapy water and scrubbed with baking soda, but if the state of your stovetop and oven make you despair, it's time for a deep cleaning with washing soda.

Put on your kitchen gloves and some old clothes. Wipe down the outer surface of the stove and the range hood with a mix of ½ cup washing soda in hot water. If the wells beneath the burners are filled with baked-on gunk, let them soak in this liquid, or make a paste of washing soda and water, apply to the wells, and let them sit. Meanwhile, wipe down a gas stove's cooking rings. If they're crusty, soak them in the same solution or, in extreme cases, put them in a big pot of washing soda water and bring to a low simmer. That should pry off even the worst baked-on grease. Scrub the inside of the oven with washing soda, or apply a paste and let that sit, if necessary. When cleaning a gas stove, don't apply a paste to the gas burners themselves, as this can gum them up. When cleaning an electric stove, keep the paste off all heating elements. Rinse all surfaces with water when you're done.

> Never use washing soda on aluminum surfaces or aluminum cookware.

SOAP SCUM AND BATHTUB RING CLEANSERS

A combination of soap and abrasive works well to clean ordinary bathtub rings and small amounts of soap scum in the tub or shower. Use the soft scrub described previously, or spray the surface with soapy water, then shake on baking soda. Use something abrasive, like a nylon pad or loofah sponge, to scrub away scum.

If the scum resists these attempts, try scrubbing with borax. If that doesn't work, heat a cup of undiluted white vinegar until it almost simmers, then, wearing gloves, wipe the hot vinegar over the soap scum, wait a minute, then scrub.

For glass doors that are fogged with soap residue, try warm vinegar alone. Or try polishing the glass with cornstarch sprinkled on a damp cloth, then rinse thoroughly.

To prevent soap scum, consider switching soaps. In our experience, castile soaps (i.e., vegetable oil soaps) seem to leave less scum behind, or at least clean up better, than big-brand commercial bar soaps, which are often made with animal fat (sodium tallowate).

HARD WATER SCALE REMOVER

Hot vinegar removes hard water scale almost instantly. If the scale is particularly stubborn, place a rag soaked with hot vinegar on the scale for a few minutes, then wipe clean. Boil vinegar in teakettles to remove the white scale that builds up at the bottom.

DEODORIZER

Baking soda is your go-to deodorizer. Sprinkle it generously on your carpet, go to bed, and vacuum the next morning. Do the same with car upholstery and carpets. If you can't wait overnight, wait at least 15 minutes. Wash stinky hampers and garbage cans with baking soda and hot water. Sprinkle baking soda in the bottom of the kitchen garbage can to reduce odors, and change the powder every week. If plastic containers pick up food smells, soak them in warm water and baking soda. Wash the inside of your refrigerator with baking soda dissolved in water.

MILDEW REMOVERS

To attack mold and mildew in the bathroom, combine 1 tablespoon tea tree oil with 1 cup water in a spray bottle. Shake well before each use. Tea tree oil is a powerful natural fungicide. It's sold in health food stores, near the essential oils. While it's pricey, a little goes a long way. What you don't use for mildew combat can find its way into other cleaning products, like the Almost Universal Spray (page 70), or be used in other projects, like homemade deodorant and mouthwash.

To remove musty mildew smells from a room, wipe the walls with ½ cup borax diluted in a bucket of water.

Suitcases, camping gear, old trunks, and other objects that have developed mildew in storage can be either sprayed with the tea tree oil solution or wiped with the borax solution. Straight vinegar works well, too. If possible, put the items out in the sun.

25› *Laundry Day*

The truth is there is no single universal recipe for homemade laundry detergent. Each household is unique. The variables include whether you have hard or soft water, what type of machine you have, and what kind of clothes you wash.

To create a homemade detergent that fits your needs, you must first understand the basic ingredients of homemade detergent and how they act. To start you off, we'll give a basic recipe. If it doesn't work as well as you hope, customize your blend. The rewards of taking an independent stance on laundry are worth it. You can say good-bye to obnoxious perfumes, phosphates, optical brighteners, and chlorine bleach—and you'll save money, too.

THE PLAYERS AND HOW THEY WORK

SOAP

All store-bought laundry detergent is … detergent, not soap. What's the difference? Soap is derived from animal or plant fats, while detergents are a more modern invention, usually based on petrochemicals, although some have been developed out of plant sources. Water alone actually cleans quite well, especially when combined with agitation, but when you are dealing with oily dirt, water needs assistance. Both soap and detergent work as emulsifiers, allowing water and oil to mix. Dirt in the fabric is agitated out during the washing process and swept away in the rinse water. Both soap and synthetic detergents facilitate this process, but in hard water, soap forms insoluble salts, aka soap scum. Detergents don't form these salts, which is why commercial laundry products rinse clean in all types of water. They've replaced soap in the laundry for this very reason. However, unless detergents are formulated to be fully biodegradable and otherwise environmentally friendly, they are water pollutants.

Homemade laundry formulas are made with grated soap. Pregrated soap flakes used to be available in the laundry aisle, but they seem to have gone the way of the dinosaur, so you have to grate your own. Soaps with enough oil in them to moisturize skin are going to leave that oil on your laundry, so ordinary body bars are *not* good candidates for laundry soap. It's easy to make your own inexpensive laundry soap; see the Coconut Laundry Soap recipe in Project 42.

There are two brands of soap that we know of made specifically for laundry: the somewhat sinisterly named Fels-Naptha and the cheerfully pink Zote. Both are inexpensive and yield very good results, but both contain dyes, perfumes, and other chemical additives. If you're avoiding commercial laundry detergent to avoid chemical additives, you'd want to avoid these two products. The choice is up to you. Dr. Bronner's Sal Suds liquid is an all-natural, all-purpose detergent. While not formulated specifically for laundry, it would be a good green alternative to Fels-Naptha or Zote.

BORAX

Sodium tetraborate is found in the laundry section of supermarkets under the brand name 20 Mule Team Borax. Don't confuse it with expensive pharmaceutical-grade borax or the boric acid powder used to kill bugs. Borax is marketed as a laundry booster, to be used in conjunction with your regular detergent. It enhances the performance of soap and detergent by softening hard water. It also helps deodorize laundry and acts as a mild color-safe bleach. Which is not to say it is a bleach, but it brightens laundry and helps lift stains, especially when used in warm or hot water.

WASHING SODA (SODIUM CARBONATE)

Not to be confused with its cousin, baking soda (sodium bicarbonate), washing soda is a highly caustic cleaning agent. It cuts grease exceedingly well and helps lift stains. Consider it borax's more aggressive big brother. Because it is so strong, it should never be used on wool or silk. It will strip the natural oils from these fabrics, leaving them crunchy. Like borax, it also softens water, boosting the cleaning power of soap.

Sodium carbonate is sold by Arm & Hammer under the name Super Washing Soda. Like borax, it's inexpensive, but it's not as widely available as borax. Look for it in the laundry section of supermarkets. If you have trouble finding it, call Arm & Hammer's customer relations line or visit its Web site for the names of local retailers. You may be able to purchase sodium carbonate at places that sell pool supplies because it is used in the pool business to balance pH levels. Just make sure you get 100 percent sodium carbonate.

> Wear kitchen gloves when handling washing soda, because it dries the skin.

BAKING SODA (SODIUM BICARBONATE)

The primary use of baking soda in the laundry is as a water softener and a deodorizer. It is not a cleaning agent in itself, but like borax and washing soda it helps soap clean, and it is noncaustic and nonirritating. Use baking soda in conjunction with soap for not-so-dirty loads. Buy baking soda in large boxes or bags at restaurant supply stores.

PREPARATION: 10 min

Homemade Laundry Powder

Here is our basic recipe. In this formula, baking soda softens the water, borax brightens, and soap lifts dirt. The ratio of each ingredient goes like this:

* 1 part grated laundry soap
* 2 parts borax
* 2 parts baking soda

If you haven't purchased grated laundry soap, you must begin by grating the soap yourself. See the entry on soap (page 75) that discusses laundry soap options. Some bars of soap are harder than others. Soft ones will form curls of soap; hard ones form powder. Softer soaps can be pared into thin strips with a potato peeler. You can shred soap on a box grater or, if it's not rock hard, chop it into chunks and grind it in a food processor.

Add the borax and baking soda to the soap. You can process them together in the food processor or mix them thoroughly by hand with a spoon. Store your laundry powder in a lidded container. At first, use 2 tablespoons per wash load, increasing the amount only if you find you need more cleaning power.

If you're washing in cold water, there's a chance of undissolved powder bits being left on clothing. You'd only see it in dark loads. To prevent this, put the powder in the washer, turn on the hot water for just a couple of seconds to help the powder dissolve, then return the setting to cold.

This laundry formula doesn't foam much, but it still cleans. Its low-sudsing nature makes it safe for front-loading and high-efficiency (HE) machines.

If the recipe above doesn't work as well as you'd like, break down the elements to find the perfect solution for your home. Play mad scientist in the laundry room. Here are some variations and customizations:

SUBSTITUTE WASHING SODA FOR BAKING SODA FOR GREATER CLEANING POWER. We formulated the Homemade Laundry Powder recipe with baking soda because washing soda can be hard to find. We'd suggest you try baking soda first and move up to washing soda if you have to.

All wash starts with soap, so **KEEP A TUB OF PLAIN GRATED LAUNDRY SOAP ON HAND.** Soap provides the vital service of lifting dirt and allowing it to be rinsed away. In hard water, though, soap can leave behind traces of soap scum, over time resulting in stiff fabric and graying whites. The trick with soap is to use as little as possible. Truthfully, it takes very little soap to make water a more effective cleaner. Start with 1 or 2 tablespoons per load and work up if needed.

BORAX IS PROBABLY THE BEST ALL-AROUND AID FOR SOAP. It won't harm your clothes, and it helps brighten and deodorize laundry. Toss in about ½ cup borax along with the 2 tablespoons of soap, as described above, to make laundry detergent on the fly.

BAKING SODA DOESN'T WHITEN, BUT IT SOFTENS YOUR WATER SO THE SOAP WORKS BETTER. It also deodorizes. Use baking soda alone with soap or in combination with borax. Add both in ¼-cup increments until you find a level that works for you.

WASHING SODA is best employed for washing grease out of clothes—that's where it excels, and that's what differentiates it from borax and baking soda. Add ½ cup to loads that need extra cleaning power.

FLOUR SACK BATH TOWELS

We're all for line drying whenever possible. It saves energy and wear on clothing. One frequent objection to line drying is that terry cloth towels come off the line crunchy. This is true. Heavy terry cloth towels depend on the fluffing action of the drier to stay soft. They're definitely a product of the machine age. Here's an alternative: Try using light cotton toweling in the bath instead. You might be familiar with a breed of kitchen towel called a flour sack towel, those large (around 2 x 3 feet), thin, soft cotton towels often used for drying glassware. They absorb water fast, don't take up much room in the wash, and dry in a wink. One will do for the body, another for the hair. Try it out. If you like it, you can make larger bath sheets out of heavy muslin or similar material.

SPECIAL CONSIDERATIONS

SYNTHETIC FIBERS

These petroleum-based fabrics hold dirt and odors more than natural fibers. They were developed in conjunction with petroleum-based detergents, and these detergents clean them best—though, as always, your results may vary. There's no shame in keeping some regular detergent around for washing your loads of stinky team uniforms, work coveralls, and the like.

WOOL AND SILK

Fine wool and silk items should be washed by hand in cold water. High pH (alkaline) cleansing agents, like washing soda, will damage them, as will regular detergents and soaps, which are also fairly alkaline. Delicates are best cleaned with soap that has been buffered to decrease its pH so that it's neutral rather than base. Use liquid castile soap, like Dr. Bronner's. Acidify it by adding white distilled vinegar to the soap in a 2:1 ratio. For example, mix 1 teaspoon vinegar with 2 teaspoons soap and use this as a hand wash. Add a splash of white vinegar to the rinse water to help remove any soap film and to further restore the acid levels of the fabric.

Soapwort (*Saponaria officinalis*) is a plant with soaping qualities. It's too mild for day-to-day dirt, but it would pamper your most delicate clothing. In fact, some museums use soapwort to wash antique textiles. Add 1 cup soapwort shampoo (made without any of the optional herbal additives, which might stain light fabric) to a sink full of water to hand-wash delicates. Add more if you need additional cleaning power. See the discussion of soapwort in shampoo in Project 5.

Soap nuts, the fruits of trees from the *Sapindus* genus, are another naturally occurring surfactant. They have a neutral pH and thus are gentle enough to use on wool and silk. (See "Soap Nuts, a Natural Alternative" on page 82.)

WHITENERS

Commercial detergents whiten and brighten with a mix of chlorine bleach and optical whiteners. Neither are very friendly to you or the environment. Chorine bleach breaks down into dangerous toxins like dioxin, which accumulate in people and animals, causing cancers and developmental defects. Optical brighteners don't clean fabric, they only give the illusion of cleanliness. They distribute tiny particles all over the fabric that absorb ultraviolet light and reflect blue light, making your clothes *appear* whiter and brighter. You might notice a faint fluorescent glow to your laundry liquid—that's them. The problems with optical brighteners are that they may cause skin irritation, they're not biodegradable, and they're toxic to fish.

There are alternatives to toxic whiteners. First and foremost, wash your whites separately from colors, otherwise you're fighting a losing battle.

FOR GENERAL BRIGHTENING: Borax does a good job of this. It brightens by creating hydrogen peroxide in chemical reaction with water. Increase borax's effectiveness by using it in hot water and/or presoaking your laundry in it.

TO TREAT GRAYED WHITES: Whites that look gray, as opposed to yellow, are probably coated with soap scum created by soap and hard water. Try washing them once or twice in hot water alone, or in hot water and washing soda, to remove this residue. You might notice the wash water suds up from residual soap trapped in the fibers.

TO TREAT YELLOWED WHITES: Nature doesn't make white cloth. Fabric is bleached to whiten it and often rinsed with blue dye in the factory to make it sparkling white. That blue dye washes out over time, leaving whites with a yellow cast. Optical brighteners in modern detergents counteract this yellowing, but so does laundry bluing, a time-honored but largely forgotten product that counteracts yellowing by depositing a tiny bit of blue dye on the surface of fabrics during the rinse cycle. It's nontoxic and has many other odd uses, from turning flowers blue to growing crystal gardens. Look for it in the laundry section, where it is sold in smallish blue bottles, hidden away on the top shelf with other laundry oddities. The biggest brand is Mrs. Stewart's Laundry Bluing. It used to be common but, like washing powder, can be hard to find these days, depending on where you live. We order it online.

To use laundry bluing, follow the instructions on the container. Basically, you dilute a tiny amount of bluing—like ½ teaspoon—in 1 or 2 cups of water and add that to your laundry's rinse cycle. You dilute it first because you'd stain your clothes if you poured straight bluing on them.

FOR SAFER BLEACHING: Store-bought oxygen bleaches are a nontoxic way of keeping your laundry bright when using homemade soap. They often require presoaking and are most effective when used regularly on white loads, as a maintenance measure, rather than after the fabric has become hopelessly dingy. A 3 percent solution of hydrogen peroxide, the sort sold in drugstores for first aid, has a similar chemical makeup to oxygen bleach. It's not cost effective unless you can get it on the cheap, but you can use it as bleach. Use about a cup per load of wash, or concentrate it by presoaking a few items with the same amount of peroxide in a bucket of water.

SUN BLEACHING: The sun is the most powerful bleaching agent of them all. On a sunny day, hang your whites out to dry or spread them on clean shrubbery.

FABRIC SOFTENER

Use ½ to 1 cup distilled white vinegar in the rinse cycle instead of fabric softener to deodorize and soften fabrics. The vinegar scent vanishes when the fabric dries. White vinegar helps rinse soap out of fabric more effectively than water alone and prevents soap buildup in your washing machine. You don't have to use it with every load, but you should definitely use it in your loads of whites to keep soap deposits from turning them dingy. Find white vinegar in inexpensive gallon bottles near the salad dressings in the supermarket.

PERFUMES

It takes a powerful perfume to survive a wash and rinse cycle and to live on to scent dry clothing. That's why the perfumes in commercial detergents can be so obnoxiously strong. Natural fibers washed with plain soap don't smell like much, but the important thing is that they don't smell.

LAUNDRY DETERGENT
FOR GRAY WATER

If you send your wash water to the garden, or plan to someday, kudos to you! Just be aware that you can't use homemade laundry soap or even eco-friendly detergents in your washer. Eco-detergents might be formulated to be harmless in seawater, but they are not good for soil, and homemade laundry soap is similar. It's made up mostly of salts, and salt and plants don't get along at all. Instead, you must use a detergent specifically formulated for gray water, and the only brand we know of is Oasis Biocompatible Super-Concentrated Laundry Liquid by Bio Pac. You might find it in a health food store, or you can order it online. An alternative to Oasis is the soap nut. As of this writing, we've not tested soap nuts in our own gray water system, but we've been told by reliable sources that they are gray water compatible.

Whether you are using Oasis or soap nuts, be sure not to use any laundry boosters (like baking soda, borax, or washing soda) with them, since these boosters are all salts.

Essential oils, the natural alternative to artificial perfumes, don't survive the washing process unless used in huge quantities, and they're expensive. Feel free to put a few drops in your laundry mix just to make it smell good when you open the bottle and when you're loading the wash. It sounds silly, but nice scents can make laundry day more pleasant. Just don't expect the scent to be there at the end.

If you want your clothes to be scented, it's more effective to tuck sachets full of dried herbs and spices, cotton balls soaked with essential oils, cedar chips, perfumed soaps, or boxes of incense in your dresser drawers or in mesh bags in the closet. If you iron, scent distilled water with essential oil and spray it on as you go.

TREATING STAINS

In general, soaking fabrics in cold water prevents stains from setting; hot water sets a stain permanently. Keep the stained garment in a bucket of cold water until washing day. Presoaking in the washer also helps. If you are using borax or washing soda in your laundry mix, let the stained load presoak in the washer for a half hour or more. Both powders will help lift stains. The same is true for commercial oxygen bleaches. But specific stains require specific treatment, as follows:

COFFEE AND TEA: Don't dab these with soap—it may set the stain. Instead, scrub with a paste of borax or washing soda. Or soak in a solution of either borax or washing soda, using a couple of tablespoons in a bucket of cold water. (Remember to use gloves when handling washing soda, and take the time to test the washing soda on an inconspicuous area of fabric, because it is harsh. Don't use washing soda on anything with wool or silk fibers.) When you're out and about, club soda works pretty well on coffee and tea stains because, like borax and washing soda, it's alkaline.

WINE, BERRIES, TOMATO SAUCE: These are acidic stains. Treat the same way as coffee and tea.

BLOOD AND MILK: Protein-based stains respond well to the methods above, especially to washing soda. The real trick with blood is catching it quickly, rinsing it, and then presoaking in cold water until you can do the wash. For stubborn blood stains, soak in 3 percent hydrogen peroxide or an oxygen bleach.

Soap Nuts, a Natural Alternative

Soap nuts are the fruits of trees in the *Sapindus* genus, usually *Sapindus mukorossi* (though all *Sapindus* make soaping fruits), which contain saponins, natural surfactants that can be used as a soap substitute. Soap nuts have been gaining ground in green cleaning circles in recent years, because they are environmentally friendly, non-irritating to the skin, minimally processed, and biodegradable. A handful of these dried fruits, which look somewhat like small dates, are put into a cloth sack and thrown in with the laundry. The same bag of soap nuts can be used up to five times before the nuts are drained of their cleaning power, at which point the fruits can be composted.

Currently, most soap nuts are imported from India, China, and Indonesia, where they've been used for washing for many years. While we're not keen on the fact they must take a transcontinental journey to our washer, we have to remember that the oils we use to make soap are imported as well, borax is mined, and baking soda and washing soda are industrial products, so the environmental calculus is rather complex.

A more pressing concern is how the soap nuts from any given supplier are produced. Are they sustainably harvested? Not all are. Some are harvested by clear-cutting. Practice due diligence when selecting a supplier. Soap nuts are rarely found in stores, even health food stores. It's likely that you'll have to order them by mail. We'd like to see *Sapindus mukorossi* grown closer to home, perhaps in your own backyard. They could be cultivated in the southern parts of the United States, where native trees from the Sapindaceae family, like the western soapberry, already grow. Soapberries are smaller and less soapy than the fruits of *S. mukorossi*, but they can be used in the same way.

As we mentioned, soap nuts are usually deployed in the laundry in a small muslin bag. This is the most direct method, and the one recommended by most soap nut companies. From a DIY point of view, though, it's more interesting to infuse soap nuts in hot water. The resulting liquid is a mild, all-purpose cleanser that can be used as laundry detergent, liquid soap, and shampoo.

TO MAKE A SOAP NUT INFUSION: Place 1 cup soap nuts in 1 quart water, bring to a simmer, and cook gently for 10 minutes. Don't let the mixture come to a hard boil or it will foam all over the stove. You might notice they give off a peculiar vinegary odor when being cooked, but that scent doesn't transfer to the wash. After 10 minutes, let it sit to cool, then transfer the amber liquid to a jar, straining out the fruits. As you're straining, press the cooked fruits with the back of a spoon, or squeeze them with your hands, to release all the juices.

The liquid can sit at room temperature for about 2 weeks before it starts to ferment. For longer storage, keep it in the refrigerator.

TO USE THE INFUSION: Add 2 tablespoons of soap nut liquid to each load of wash. Whether used whole or in liquid form, soap nuts produce few suds and thus are safe for HE machines. They work equally well in hard or soft water, and don't require the use of fabric softeners or vinegar rinses, but do be sure to use an oxygen bleach with every white load to keep fabric bright.

GREASE: Soap and detergent lift grease. Rub grease stains with liquid detergent, wet bars of laundry soap, or even dishwashing liquid. Washing soda also removes grease.

PERSPIRATION STAINS: Try spraying white vinegar on armpit stains and letting the garment sit a few minutes before washing. Ring-around-the-collar is body grease and perspiration combined. Rub this directly with a bar of laundry soap or scrub with dish soap or straight liquid detergent.

GRASS AND RUST: These stains respond best to treatment with acids like vinegar or lemon juice.

In general, make sure stains are gone before you put your clothes in the dryer, or the heat will make the stain permanent.

Basic Mending

Knowing how to sew a little by hand is a useful skill. You can mend favorite garments and sew up simple things like curtains even if you don't have a sewing machine. Mending was traditionally done on laundry day, and it's a good tradition to revive. Inventory your clothes before washing; set aside clothes with loose buttons or small rips that might get bigger during washing.

YOU'LL NEED

NEEDLES. These come in all sorts of sizes for different purposes. In general, you'd use smaller, finer needles for delicate fabric and sturdy needles for tough fabric, but for casual mending you can get by with just about anything.

THREAD. Choose thread that matches the material you're sewing: cotton for cotton, light thread for delicate fabric, heavy thread for coarse fabric, etc. Thread weakens with age, so if you intend to sew with a 10-year-old spool of thread you fished out of your junk drawer, give the strand a few sharp yanks to test its tensile strength. You don't want to waste your time mending with rotten thread.

Gather your garments, needles, and thread. For the strongest stitches, double the length of thread you're using. Thread the needle and knot the two ends together. When hand-sewing, keep your thread short, less than your arm's length, so it doesn't tangle and knot as you sew.

RUNNING STITCH

This is a fast and easy stitch used to join two pieces of material, usually temporarily, because it's not very strong. You can use the running stitch instead of pins to temporarily secure two pieces of material together, which is called basting. The running stitch is also a gathering stitch. If you run it along the length of a piece of fabric and then give the thread a tug, the material will collect into gathers. The wider the spacing of the stitches, the wider the gathered folds.

Sewing the running stitch is just a matter of threading the needle over and under the fabric at regular intervals, as illustrated on the opposite page. It's stitching 101.

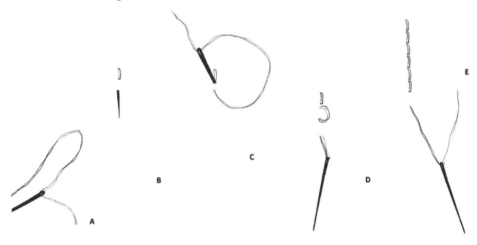

BACK STITCH

This is a strong stitch for general hand-sewing and mending. If you execute it with embroidery floss, you can use it to make decorative patterns on clothing or pillows, to spell names, or to outline simple shapes.

The back stitch is easier to do than to describe in words. Let the diagram be your primary guide. Basically it is a one-step-forward, one-step-backward process. To start, you might want to anchor your stitching securely by taking three tiny stitches, one over the other, at the starting point. That way, you don't have to rely on the knot at the end of your thread. Next, make a stitch that shows on top of the fabric,[A] and bring your needle back up through the fabric one stitch length away from this first stitch.[B] Instead of continuing to stitching forward at this point, you backtrack and plunge your needle back through the fabric at the end point of stitch 1.[C] So this new stitch is stitched backward, rather than forward. Bring the needle up through the fabric one stitch length away from this stitch[D] and, again, stitch backward to fill the space behind your needle. Your goal is to create an even line of stitches with no space between them.[E] Continue in the same manner until you reach the end of your stitching. Then secure your thread by once again taking three tiny stitches at the end point, or tying a knot, or both.

SEWING A BUTTON

Start off by anchoring your thread exactly where you want the button. Lay the button in position, then poke the needle up from underneath the fabric and through one of the button's holes. Set aside the button and take three

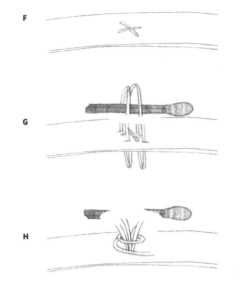

F

G

H

tiny, overlapping stitches at that point to secure the thread.[F] Then place the button into position again.

Flat buttons come with two or four holes. If you have a four-hole button, attach it by sewing parallel loops through opposite pairs of holes rather than crisscrossing your threads to make an X shape. Crossed threads wear against one another and make the button fall off again sooner.

Here's the general procedure for attaching the button: Bring the needle up through one of the button's holes and take a moment to ensure the button is placed properly. Then send the needle back down the opposite hole, looping the thread three or four times between the two holes. If you have a four-hole button, repeat this process for the remaining two holes, so that you end up with the button held down by two parallel sets of stitches, not an X.

But wait!

Before you begin stitching down your button by the general method above, consider the thickness of the button and the fabric you're attaching it to. Every button needs a little "play"—if it's sewn down too tightly, it will be hard to use. The thicker the fabric and the bigger the button, the more play you need. Think of the difference between a coat button and a shirt button. Sometimes you can allow enough play by just remembering to keep your stitches loose when you're attaching the button. For greater play, you need to form a shank.

Forming a shank is a two-step process. Step one is to build in some slack into the stitching process by laying a needle or a matchstick on top of the button,[G] right between the holes. By stitching over this object, you'll guarantee that your stitching will have an even amount of slack. Use a matchstick for heavier fabrics, a needle for lighter fabrics. Stitch the button down as described above. When you're done, remove the needle or matchstick. Now the sewn button should be a little wiggly. For step two, form a secure shank on the underside of the button by winding your needle and thread several times around the button stitches (that is, between the bottom of the button and the fabric).[H] Finish off by taking the needle to the underside of the fabric and making three tiny, overlapping anchoring stitches there to secure the thread.

A QUICK PATCH

Iron-on patches don't hold up under heavy use. Scratch that. They don't hold up too much at all. If you want to repair your favorite jeans, it's not hard to make a simple patch. All you have to do is find a scrap of patching material. Be sure the material is of a similar weight and texture to your garment. For instance, patch denim with denim or something just as heavy. If you patch it with something lighter, the patch won't last, and it will look odd, too.

If the hole you're patching looks like it might rip wider, because it's more of a tear than a worn-out spot, make a few stitches at either end of the tear to stop it from expanding. Those stitches don't have to be pretty, because they're going to be hidden.

Measure the hole you're trying to cover. For the sake of simplicity, we're going to make a square or rectangular patch. Cut the patch about ½ to 1 inch wider than the hole on all sides. Cut a V-shape notch out of each corner[I] so the folded fabric doesn't overlap and bunch on the back side. Fold back ¼ inch of material on all sides of the patch to hide its scraggly edges.[J,K] Use an iron to press down the edges; you want them to lie flat.

Pin the patch into place,[L] or baste it down with a few stitches. Using the backstitch, stitch all around the edges of the patch, keeping within ¼ inch of the edge so that the folded edges underneath are caught by the needle. Make your stitches as small as you can manage, because many small stitches will hold the patch better than large stitches.

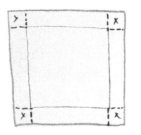

I

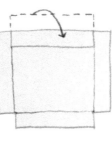

J

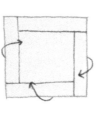

K

L

Month to Month

These are more ambitious projects with longer timelines. Some take a month to make, some yield products that last about a month, some we make on a monthly basis. These projects center around the ideas of preservation and transformation, whether that be transforming cabbage into sauerkraut via the mysteries of fermentation or capturing the power of herbs in homemade medicine.

The Transformational Power of Salt

Salting is the oldest form of food preservation. Unlike canning or freezing, salting transforms that which it preserves, making a new food in the process. Salmon becomes lox. Cabbage becomes kraut. When salt is combined with liquid, it creates an environment ideal for colonization by lactobacillus, a beneficial bacteria. Lactobacillus not only keeps harmful bacteria out, it also makes food more digestible and promotes nutrient absorption. Humans have eaten lacto-fermented foods for thousands of years, until, in the last century, heat processing and freezing became our standard methods of preservation. In just a few years, these lacto-ferments vanished from the average American diet, taking with them their health benefits and a whole world of intense flavors.

27 › *Sauerkraut*

PREPARATION: 20 min
WAITING: 2–4 weeks

The flavor of fresh, raw sauerkraut is a revelation. It's also surprisingly versatile. A classic kraut is fermented into heady pungency. Its sour, tangy flavor is the perfect complement to meats. But you can also make kraut that's crisp and light, more like a cabbage salad than a side for bratwurst, simply by stopping the fermentation sooner.

Store-bought sauerkraut is most often made with vinegar instead of fermented in salt the old-fashioned way. Even if the kraut was fermented, it has probably been heat-processed to make it shelf stable, and heat processing destroys the beneficial bacteria that make kraut such a powerful health food.

All lacto-ferments are living cultures. They are shepherded more than they are "made." Many factors affect the final results, from the quality of the cabbage to the ambient temperatures. Making kraut is not so much a matter of following a recipe as it is understanding a technique. At its most elemental, sauerkraut is nothing but cabbage mixed with salt in a ratio of 1½ generous teaspoons of salt per pound of cabbage. Even the salt ratio is somewhat variable. Less salt makes a kraut that ferments more quickly but spoils more easily. Higher quantities of salt slow down the fermentation but make the product more stable over time. After making a few batches, you'll begin to see these dynamics at work.

YOU'LL NEED

* 3 pounds green cabbage
* 5 tablespoons sea salt or kosher salt (Iodized salt interferes with fermentation.)
* Large mixing bowl
* Ceramic crock, glass jar, or food-grade bucket with a 1-gallon capacity
* Ceramic plate that fits inside the crock, jar, or bucket

PUTTING IT TOGETHER

Remove and discard the outer leaves of the cabbage. Cut each head into quarters and carve out the tough cores. Shred the cabbage using a big knife or a mandoline. Don't use a food processor, because it will chop the cabbage into such small pieces that you'll end up with cabbage soup.

Transfer the cabbage to the mixing bowl, mixing in all of the salt as you do. Toss the cabbage with your hands to distribute the salt evenly.

Put a couple of inches of salted cabbage into the bottom of the crock, jar, or bucket. Pack down the cabbage using your fist or the bottom of a clean beer

bottle or canning jar. The idea is to bruise the cabbage a bit (don't pulverize it) so it releases its juices. You're also compressing the cabbage so it will all fit. The salt draws liquid from the cabbage to create brine. The brine is what transforms cabbage into kraut. The goal is to release so much brine that the cabbage shreds will be submerged beneath the brine.

If you don't have a plate that fits your crock, you can use a zipper-lock bag of salt brine as a weight. It contains brine instead of plain water just in case it leaks—that way it won't ruin your kraut. Put a couple of tablespoons of noniodized salt into a big zipper-lock bag, fill with water, and shake to dissolve. Lay the bag over the cabbage. It should hold the cabbage down. If it doesn't, you need a bigger bag.

Keep adding the cabbage and compressing, layer by layer, until all the cabbage is in the container. At this point, a layer of liquid may be floating at the top, or the cabbage may still look dry. It all depends on the cabbage you used—older cabbages have less liquid in them. Don't worry if it looks dry. The next step might produce more brine.

Weight the cabbage to keep it beneath the brine. During fermentation, the cabbage must always be kept under a layer of brine, because any pieces that float to the top may become colonized with unwelcome bacteria. This is where the clean plate comes in. Put the plate into the crock. It should be just a little smaller than the diameter of the crock so that cabbage doesn't pop up around the sides. Hold the plate down with something heavy, like a big jar full of water or a clean rock.

Applying weight to the cabbage should draw out more brine. If after a couple of hours under weight the cabbage still isn't submerged beneath an inch or so of brine, you'll need to add more liquid. Mix 2 tablespoons noniodized salt in 1 quart water and add it to the crock.

Cover the whole crock and weight apparatus with a kitchen towel or a piece of cheesecloth to keep out bugs. Secure the cloth around the sides of the crock with a piece of string. Put the kraut in a quiet corner of your kitchen to ferment.

Heat speeds up the fermentation process, often to its detriment. If you're making kraut in hot weather, keep the crock in the coolest part of your house.

Check the kraut every day or two for mold. If you see scum forming on the surface, skim it off. Kraut can generate quite impressive blossoms of mold, but the presence of mold doesn't mean it has gone bad. The mold is floating on top of the brine. The brine is protecting the cabbage beneath. Just remove the mold from the surface and carry on. If something goes very wrong, you'll know it. The cabbage will turn slimy, and the smell will be rank.

It takes at least 2 weeks to make traditional, well-fermented sauerkraut. The timing will vary, depending on how much salt you used and the ambient temperature. Taste the kraut as it develops. It's done when it tastes right to you. The longer it sits, the softer and stronger-tasting it will become. When it seems ready, transfer the finished kraut to glass jars and store in the refrigerator. It doesn't need to be weighed down anymore, but try to distribute the juice between the jars so a little juice tops each jar. Kraut lasts several weeks in the fridge.

If you don't think you can eat your sauerkraut that quickly—or if you make a huge batch—then can it. At sea level, heat-process pint jars of kraut in its juice for 20 minutes, quart jars for 25 minutes. Visit the National Center for Home Food Preservation online for complete canning instructions. Yes, heat processing will kill the healthy living bacteria, but the kraut will retain nutrients like vitamin C, and it will taste better than store-bought.

Makes about 3 quarts

VARIATIONS

The recipe above is for sauerkraut in its most basic form. We've been lectured by kraut aficionados that simple kraut is best and that it should always be flavored in the cooking process, not the fermentation process. Other people routinely add spices to their crocks. The most popular kraut spices are whole peppercorns, caraway seeds, and juniper berries. If you add these to your ferment, keep in mind that their flavors will intensify over time, so use them sparingly. To the recipe above, try adding something in the range of 2 or 3 peppercorns or juniper berries or ¼ teaspoon caraway seeds. Also, there's no law that says kraut must be all cabbage. Add grated carrot or other firm vegetables, onion, cloves of garlic, or ginger chunks to the cabbage. The world is your oyster.

PINK KRAUT "SALAD." This makes a blazing pink, crisp, tart side dish or salad. Follow the recipe above, but use red cabbage and add 2 Granny Smith apples, cut into matchsticks, and a pinch of caraway seeds. Let this ferment for about a week, just long enough for the flavor to develop, but not so long that the apples lose their character.

KRAUT QUESADILLAS. The tanginess of kraut pairs well with grease. We often make quesadillas with kraut, cheese and a little hot sauce. It's a tasty clash of cultures.

28›

PREPARATION: 30 min
WAITING: 1–2 days

Kimchi

Packed with nutrition and flavor, kimchi—spicy pickled cabbage—is served with almost every meal in Korea. Traditionally, Koreans used kimchi as a way to preserve the harvest through the cold winter, preparing the cabbage in huge batches and fermenting it in ceramic jars. But kimchi is just as easily prepared in small quantities at home, which is a great way to remember the "fire" of summer during a long, cold winter.

The salt in the brine acts as a filter, allowing the good bacteria (salt-tolerant lactobacillus) to thrive while preventing the growth of molds and other bugs we don't want.

Kimchi is made in many different ways (the Korean Food Academy has identified 100 different types), with varied ingredients depending on region. The common denominator is Korean red pepper powder (*kochukaru*), which is sold in big bags at Asian markets that carry Korean items. We've tried making kimchi with other types of peppers, and it simply doesn't taste as good. If you can't find Korean red pepper powder locally, order it online.

We learned how to make kimchi and kimchi pancakes at Krautfest 2009, a lacto-fermentation event we helped organize in Los Angeles. Kimchi champion and entrepreneur Oghee "Granny" Choe and her daughter Connie Choe-Harikul gave a demonstration on how to make kimchi. This recipe is a variation on the method they taught us.

YOU'LL NEED

* 6 tablespoons sea salt (or other noniodized salt)
* 4 cups filtered or bottled water, cooled
* 1 head Napa cabbage
* 1 bunch scallions, chopped
* 1 cup mustard greens, chopped (optional)
* Handful of shredded daikon radish (optional)
* 1 head garlic, crushed
* 1-inch piece fresh gingerroot, grated
* 1 cup Korean red pepper powder (*kochukaru*)
* 1 tablespoon sugar (optional)

PUTTING IT TOGETHER

Make a brine by stirring 4 tablespoons of the salt into the water. Pull apart the cabbage, stack the whole leaves in a bowl, and pour the brine over them. If the water doesn't cover the cabbage, make more brine at the same salt-to-water ratio. Put a heavy plate on top of the cabbage to keep it under the brine. Let it soak overnight in the refrigerator.

The next day, drain and rinse the cabbage and chop into 1-inch chunks. In a large bowl, combine the cabbage with the scallions and the mustard greens and daikon radish, if using, or with whatever vegetables you have on hand. Season with the garlic, ginger, 2 additional tablespoons of salt, and the red pepper powder. Add the red pepper to taste—but Granny Choe taught us to add it generously, about 1 cup per batch. Sugar is optional—add to taste.

Mix everything thoroughly and transfer to a large jar. Don't screw the lid on tight, as the mixture will begin to ferment and produce gas. Let sit at room temperature for a day or two and then put in the fridge for long-term storage.

Makes about 2 quarts

KIMCHI PANCAKES

Kimchi can be served as a side dish or condiment. It can also be the centerpiece of a meal—like these kimchi pancakes, a spicy favorite at our house. In a bowl, mix together 1 cup kimchi, chopped fine; 1 egg; ½ cup flour; ⅓ cup reserved kimchi juice or water; and a couple of chopped scallions. Add salt to taste. Fry in an oiled pan ¼ cup at a time. Serve with a dipping sauce of equal parts rice vinegar and soy sauce.

Makes 4 pancakes

29›

PREPARATION: 10 min
WAITING: 3–4 days

Gravlax

Lox on bagels is one of our favorite treats, but lox are expensive. We were surprised to learn we could make them at home for a lot less by using frozen salmon fillets.

Lox had always seemed so mysterious to us. Were they smoked? They seemed raw, yet not raw. It was a deli mystery. Turns out they're salt cured, and salt curing is as simple as can be. You just have to trust the salt.

It's a 2- or 3-day process, so start this midweek to enjoy a plateful of bagels on a lazy Saturday. Frozen salmon is usually less expensive than fresh and has the added benefit of being safer, because parasites don't survive commercial freezing. Fresh salmon is lovely, though. Just make sure you use sushi-grade fish.

YOU'LL NEED

* 1 pound frozen salmon or raw, sushi-grade salmon fillets (not steaks)
* 2 tablespoons sea salt
* 2 tablespoons sugar
* 1 teaspoon ground black pepper
* 1 bunch of fresh dill

PUTTING IT TOGETHER

Defrost the fish, if necessary. Rinse and pat it dry. Lay out each fillet on a big piece of plastic wrap. If you feel any bones, pluck them out.

Mix the salt, sugar, and pepper in a bowl. Sprinkle it all over the fillets, making sure to coat the front, back, and sides. Lay whole fresh sprigs of dill over each fillet.

You can adjust these seasonings to taste, just keep the essential proportions of 2 tablespoons salt and 2 tablespoons sugar per pound of salmon. If you'd like sweeter gravlax, add an extra tablespoon of sugar to the mix. If you don't have dill, try other fresh herbs, like parsley. We've even used wild fennel fronds.

Wrap the seasoned fillets in plastic wrap to make little packets. Tuck those into a zipper-lock bag or put them in a deep dish, like a baking dish, because the fish will release juices as it cures.

Refrigerate for 48 to 72 hours. The longer the gravlax cures, the more intense the flavors. Leave it too long and it becomes dark and unpleasantly tough. Some lox fans advocate pressing the fish under weights during the curing process. This results in a denser texture.

After 48 hours or so, discard the dill, rinse off the salt and sugar, and pat dry. Using a very sharp knife, slice the fillets into thin pieces on the diagonal. To store, wrap the fillets well in clean plastic wrap. They'll keep in the refrigerator for a couple of weeks—but they're unlikely to last that long, because they're delicious.

30 ›

Nukazuke

PREPARATION: 30 min
WAITING: 2 weeks

When we hear of an old housekeeping technique that has come to be regarded as too time-consuming or arcane for modern folks, we sit up and take notice. This generally means we're onto something good. NUKAZUKE, or rice bran pickles, are a traditional Japanese pickle. When we heard a Japanese cookbook author wistfully note that she didn't have time to keep a NUKAZUKE crock—a NUKADOKO—like her mother had done, we knew we had to try it.

Nukazuke is the most unusual form of pickle we've ever encountered. Rice bran is soaked in saltwater and various flavorings and kept in a crock to culture. Salt plus time equals lacto-fermentation. In this lacto-fermentation technique, fresh vegetables are buried in the wet salted bran, where they're transformed by lactobacillus into crispy, salty pickles. Each day, pickled vegetables are fished out and new vegetables buried. The miraculous thing about this process is that it happens overnight or, in the case of delicate vegetables, in a couple of hours. Unlike other pickle recipes, this isn't exactly a preservation technique. Instead, it's all about the transformation, taking a raw vegetable and making it into a new food.

The *nukadoko* can be maintained for months, years, even decades. Over time, it takes on its own personality, like an old sourdough starter. Every household's pickles would taste a little different. Like many traditional recipes, the outlines of this are variable. The flavors are a matter of interpretation. What's most important is to set up the correct ratio of salt, water, and bran and to maintain that correct ratio over time.

What could be inconvenient about making pickles overnight, you ask? Nothing. As far as pickles go, these are fast food. The inconvenience arises in maintaining the bed. It has to be stirred every day, without exception, to aerate it. If the damp bran is allowed to sit around clumpy and compressed, it will develop mold. The *nuka* (the salted bran) is best stirred with the bare hands. The bacteria on our hands is said to help the culture. This is interesting, because it also means that the pickles are uniquely yours, that they're tied in subtle ways to your own biology. More practically, it's easier to lift the bran from the bottom of the crock and break up lumps with your fingers than with a spoon. If you're not someone who likes playing with your food, this isn't the project for you.

YOU'LL NEED

* 2 pounds rice bran (Buy it at Asian markets or health food stores.)
* 5 cups water

* ½ sheet dried kombu seaweed, about 3 x 6 inches

* 9 tablespoons sea salt (Never use iodized salt.)

* 1–2 inches fresh gingerroot

* 3–5 small dried chile peppers, any type

* Permanent container for your pickle bed—a Tupperware-type
  container or small food-grade plastic bucket or a ceramic, enamel,
  or glass container (Traditional crocks are made of wood or clay.
  Whatever container you use, it should have a lid, a wide mouth,
  and about a 14-cup capacity. Ours is a bean pot that we found
  at a garage sale.)

PUTTING IT TOGETHER

Toast the rice bran in a wide, hot skillet. It will be easier to do if you break the
bran up into two or three batches. Don't let it burn. Use your nose. As soon as it
starts to smell good, take it off the heat and do the next batch.

Meanwhile, bring the water to a boil. Pour 1 cup of the boiling water into
a small bowl. Break the seaweed into a few strips and place it in the water
to soak.

Pour the remaining 4 cups of boiling water into a larger bowl. Add 6 tablespoons of the salt and stir to dissolve.

Peel the ginger and chop it into rough chunks. Chop the peppers into rings.

By this time, the kombu seaweed should be soft. Holding back the kombu
strips, drain the soaking water into the brine. Now you should have 5 cups total
of brine, give or take.

Transfer the toasted bran to the container you plan to keep it in. Put the
kombu strips, peppers (seeds included), and ginger on top of the bran. Pour the
brine into the container and stir with your hands to make sure all of the bran is
equally wet. Put the lid on the container.

Here we'll stop to say that like barbeque sauce or anything else, different
people make this different ways. The only absolutely necessary ingredients are
bran, salt, and seaweed. Some people make their brine with beer. Other flavorings
that might be used include—but aren't limited to—miso paste; raw cloves of garlic; apple or persimmon peels; crushed, dried eggshells (they're said to clarify the
flavors); and powdered mustard (which is supposed to help preserve the *nuka*).
You can adjust the flavors of your bed as you go along.

OPERATING INSTRUCTIONS

It will take a couple of weeks for the bed to come up to speed. The cultures need
time to develop. You'll notice the smell changing as this happens, becoming less
toasty and more pungent. You can speed its development by offering the bed
fresh vegetables from the very first day. It won't pickle them well at first, but you
might like the way they turn out anyway. Don't be afraid to eat them or add them
to the stockpot.

To pickle, bury any firm, clean vegetable in the *nuka* (the salted bran) and leave it overnight. Really bury it and tamp down the bran, just as if you were laying that radish to eternal rest. Test thin, delicate, or small vegetables after a couple of hours—they may be done that quickly. They're ready when they taste good to you. They become softer and more pungent the longer they sit.

The vegetables are usually buried whole and chopped into pieces before serving. Make exceptions for veggies that won't fit into the bed. Cabbage, for instance, is cut into chunks. Try pickling just about anything that comes to hand—whole red radishes, chunks of daikon, Brussels sprouts, cauliflower florets, even sturdy greens like kale or Swiss chard.

When you take the pickles out, they'll be dusted with bran. Wipe as much as you can back into the crock with your fingers, then rinse the pickles before serving. They are best straight out of the bed, but you can keep them in the fridge for a couple of days if you leave their bran coating on them. Keep a lid on the bed at all times to keep out vermin and help maintain moisture levels.

KELLY: Let's talk about how you killed my pickle bed when I was out of town. You didn't stir it, you didn't love it.

ERIK: It was kind of stinky, and I didn't really want to reach my hands into that funky rice bran. What's wrong with sticking with regular ol' kraut and kimchi?

KELLY: Kraut and kimchi are great, but they're not the same.

ERIK: Meaning they're not a pain in the butt? How's that a problem?

KELLY: This coming from a man who feeds his sourdough starter religiously every single night. You obsess over your starter. You'll get out of bed to feed it.

ERIK: But the starter makes *bread*. That's entirely different.

KELLY (SIGHING): You see, dear reader, we all have different priorities. Even the bonds of matrimony won't ensure that your pickle bed will be tended with the necessary diligence when you're away. Keeping a *nukadoko* is a practice best left to hard-core pickle fans. Pickle fans who don't travel a lot.

MAINTENANCE

Each time you remove a pickle, you're removing bran, so you'll have to add a handful of fresh bran every once in a while. You'll also lose salt, so you'll want to add a little saltwater occasionally, too. The overall proportion of bran to salt by weight is between 5:1 and 7:1. Don't let the bed go dry or turn boggy. You'll get to know the *nukadoko* intimately from stirring it every day, and so you'll know what to do. Sample the flavor of the bran once in a while (it's kind of tasty, really). That way you'll know what it tastes like when it's right, and you can diagnose problems if something goes off kilter. Add new flavorings as the spirit moves you.

If you go on vacation, you must find someone trustworthy enough to tend your bed. As this can be difficult, it may be better to trust no one and put the bed in suspended hibernation. Take any vegetables out and smooth the surface. Pour ¼ inch of sea salt over the entire surface and put the crock, covered, in the fridge. When you return, pour off as much salt as you can and mix in the rest.

Signs of a sick crock are pretty obvious. A healthy crock should always smell like a ferment, which encompasses a range of interesting smells, but it should not smell rotten. Rotten is dead. Ferments smell alive. You should never see any mold or slime. If you do, it's best to start over.

Indoor Gardening

Vegetables are sun hungry. This makes it difficult to grow food indoors unless you have a sunny, south-facing window. Even then, it's tricky. It takes a lot of solar energy for a plant to set fruit (like a tomato) or to generate a starchy, edible root (like a carrot). The best crops for indoor gardening are those where the leaves are the edible parts. Potted herbs, like chives and parsley, do well on a windowsill and are a great starting point for your indoor garden. The next two projects are a little more ambitious than potted herbs but are lots of fun. Both translate well to outdoor growing, too, if you have the space.

31›

PREPARATION: 30 min
WAITING: 2+ weeks

Microgreens

With a couple of flats, potting mix, and seeds, you can run a real minifarm, indoors or outdoors. Not to be confused with hippie sprouts, microgreens are baby plants—seedlings grown until they produce one or two sets of leaves. Then they are cut to make salads. Their delicate shapes and bright flavors have secured them a place as trendy restaurant fare.

To grow microgreens indoors, you need a sunny, south-facing window. If you don't have one, you can grow the greens under fluorescent lights. (See Project 48 to learn how to put a grow-light system together.) Microgreens also make ideal patio or balcony crops.

YOU'LL NEED

* Standard 10 x 20-inch seedling flats from a nursery; homemade flats (see Project 56); or, for small batches, clear plastic clamshell containers that hold takeout food
* Clear plastic covers for the flats (Lids are usually sold with nursery flats. Clamshell containers come with lids. For homemade wooden boxes, you'll need to improvise a plastic lid, perhaps by foraging one from a catering tray.)
* Potting mix
* Seeds (See the lists in the table below.)

PUTTING IT TOGETHER

Make sure the seedling flats have drainage holes—seedlings don't like wet feet. If a container doesn't have holes, punch some with a sharp knife. Work very carefully so you don't split the plastic.

Fill the flats with soil, level it, and compress it ever so lightly.

Sprinkle the seeds over the surface of the soil, about an inch apart. You can mix different kinds of seeds, but choose types that mature at roughly the same time. In the table on page 115, we've divided seed types by growing times. Otherwise, sow different seeds in separate flats. Small seeds should be barely covered with a light sifting of soil. Large seeds, like peas or corn, should be pushed in.

Water gently with a watering can or a hose with a soft sprinkle setting. We like to use a Haws watering can, which has a particularly gentle water flow, perfect for seedlings.

Put the clear plastic cover on each flat. This creates a minigreenhouse where moisture and heat will speed germination. In hot weather, you may need to remove the cover to avoid cooking the microgreens. Watch for signs of wilting.

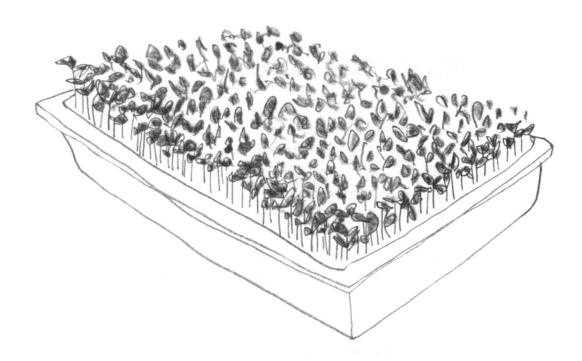

Keep the soil moist but not too moist. Don't overwater. If you're growing seeds in front of a window, turn the flats around every couple of days to keep the plants growing straight. They'll lean toward the sun.

Harvest no later than the appearance of the first set of true leaves. "True leaves" are leaves that look like miniature versions of the plant's mature leaves. They are the second pair of leaves a seedling produces. The first set of leaves a seedling produces are called cotyledons. These are rounded, generic-looking leaves. You can harvest after the cotyledons appear or after the development of the first set of true leaves, depending on your preference. How long it takes a seedling to develop two sets of leaves depends on the type of plant you're growing and the light conditions, but the time frame is usually around 2 weeks. Use scissors to harvest at soil level, as if you were giving your seedlings a haircut.

Seed Sources for Microgreens

As you'll be using a lot of seeds for this project, consider ordering in bulk. Many seed suppliers have sections in their catalogs devoted to microgreens. Health food stores often sell seeds for sprouting, and many of these are good candidates for microgreens. And speaking of health food stores, we've even grown microgreens from seeds sold in bulk bins. Surprisingly, we've actually had good germination rates with bulk bin seeds, but there are no guarantees. If you have an outdoor garden, you might have leftover seeds from planting. Many of these could be used as microgreen seeds as well.

Leave the roots in the soil. Microgreens are best eaten right after harvest, but you can keep them in plastic bags in the fridge for a day or two.

When the harvest is done, put the roots and spent soil in your compost pile and start again. Clean out the flats for their next go-around. Toss your harvest in a salad or stir-fry and enjoy.

TROUBLESHOOTING

The most likely problem you'll have growing microgreens indoors is insufficient light. The signs of this are seedlings that become "leggy," meaning they develop long stems because they're struggling to reach the light. Leggy seedlings will delay growing leaves or may never reach harvest size. If your seedlings turn leggy, try to find a spot with more light or grow them under fluorescent lights. See Project 48.

If the seeds don't sprout at all, they may no longer be viable. Seeds have expiration dates. Double-check the package.

For other hints about growing seedlings, see Project 46.

Seed for Microgreens

FAST-GROWING SEEDS	SLOW-GROWING SEEDS	SEEDS FOUND IN BULK BINS AND ETHNIC MARKETS
Broccoli	Amaranth	
Cabbage	Arugula	Amaranth
Cilantro	Basil	Cilantro
Cress	Beet	Fenugreek
Endive	Carrot	Green chickpea
Hon tsai tai	Celery	Mustard
Kale	Chard	Popcorn
Kohlrabi	Ice plant	Sunflower
Mizuna	Komatsuna	
Mustard	Magenta spreen	**SEEDS THAT FORM EXTRALARGE GREENS, CALLED SHOOTS, THAT ARE USUALLY COOKED**
Pac choi	Orach	
Radish	Red purslane	Pea
Tatsoi	Scallion	Popcorn
Tokyo Bekana	Shungiku	Sunflower
Waido	Sorrel	

32 ›

Sweet Potato Farm

PREPARATION: 10 min
WAITING: 1–2 months

An edible houseplant is an urban farmer's Holy Grail. Traditional food crops require at least 6 hours of direct sunlight a day, making them tricky to grow inside. Houseplants do well indoors because they are jungle dwellers that have evolved to grow in low light. But they are also prima donnas, expecting you to water, mist, and dust them while offering you nothing in return but their fabulous looks. This rubs against our general gardening rule number one: If you water it, you have to eat it. A worthwhile houseplant would give back—imagine sautéing a spider plant!—but as far as we knew, no such thing existed. Then, one day, we experienced the Filipino Epiphany.

Our neighbor Julia basically has a Filipino produce section growing in her front yard. One day, we asked her about a nice patch of greens she had going, and she said, "It's sweet potato. You eat the leaves." This freaked us out because we erroneously associated sweet potato foliage with potato foliage, which is poisonous. But Julia handed Kelly a leaf and Kelly ate it, because she'll eat almost anything. It was a tender green with a mild, pleasant flavor.

Turns out that sweet potato greens are indeed a favorite in the Philippines and are eaten throughout Asia and Africa. They're nutritious, too, rich in vitamins C and A and a good source of calcium and protein. You know what else a sweet potato vine is? A houseplant. A novelty houseplant last popular in the 1970s. We'd found our Holy Grail: a houseplant that feeds you. And because it's a relative of the morning glory, it's a good-looking plant, too. It may even flower for you.

YOU'LL NEED

STAGE 1

* At least 1 sweet potato. Organic is better, to be sure the potato hasn't been treated to prevent it from sprouting. If it's been around your kitchen a while and has some buds on it, all the better. Just as long as it isn't withered or moldy.

* A pot/vessel large enough to lay your potato sideways. It doesn't have to be pretty. It could even be a box lined with a plastic bag.

* Potting soil. Pure sand or peat moss would also work for this first stage.

STAGE 2 (A FEW WEEKS LATER)

* Containers to hold the mature plants. Basically, you can grow a plant in just about anything, from expensive designer ceramics to an old milk jug. These vines would look great in a long trough or in hanging baskets. Just remember that plants need drainage. If your pot doesn't have a hole in the bottom, drill one. Or put the plant in a plastic nursery pot and tuck that pot inside whatever decorative container you choose. Be sure to put a layer of rocks at the bottom of your pot so the drainage hole doesn't get clogged.

* Good quality potting soil

PUTTING IT TOGETHER

STAGE 1: THE VINE NURSERY

It's easy to grow a sweet potato vine. All you have to do is bury the tuber under soil, keep it moist, and wait. It will sprout. What we're going to do here is a little different. We're going to encourage a potato to send up many sprouts—called "slips"—and transplant those slips to other pots. In this way, one sweet potato will yield many plants. This is important, because to make your sweet potato vines a viable food source, you're going to need a lot of vines. Otherwise you'll use up your whole plant in your first stir-fry.

You could opt to just sprout the potato and consider that your finished plant. If so, you'd probably want to plant several potatoes, or halves of potatoes, each in its own pot. That works. The advantage of the transplant method is economy and flexibility. One sweet potato yields many slips, and you can plant those slips anywhere you want.

YAMS OR SWEET POTATOES?

In the United States and Canada, different varieties of sweet potatoes (*Ipomoea batatas*) are referred to interchangeably as yams and sweet potatoes, with the darker-fleshed ones often being sold as yams. True yams are members of the Dioscoreaceae family—big, starchy things generally found only in Africa and Asia. Any yam/sweet potato you find in the supermarket or farmers' market in North America, whether it be dark or light skinned, pointy or rounded, will work for this project.

PLANTING THE MOTHER POTATO: Plant a whole sweet potato lengthwise under 2 inches of soil or sand. That is, you want the sweet potato lying so the long side is facing up. Think of it as a submarine. If there are any buds present, plant them facing up.

Feel free to lay more than one potato in each container, if you can fit them in. Just keep them about 1 inch apart. These potatoes are the mamas that will produce slips for transplanting. The potatoes are planted sideways to maximize the surface area available for sprouting.

Don't pack down the soil. All you need is a loose covering. Leave a few inches of headroom between the soil and the rim of the pot. This will make watering easier.

Add water. During the sprouting period, keep the soil lightly moist but never soggy. Soggy conditions could cause the potato to rot. The sprouts aren't killed by lack of water, because they get moisture from the mother potato. It's better to let the soil go dry than to keep it too wet.

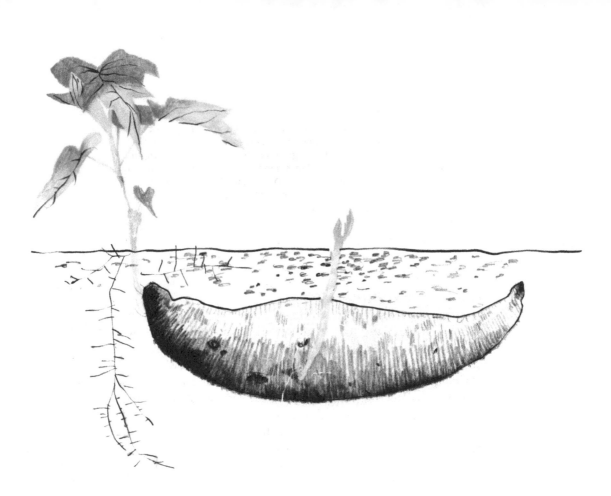

If your house is cold, store your nursery somewhere warm—in the kitchen, near the radiator, or on top of your electronics. You don't want to bake the mama potatoes, but they will sprout best if the ambient temperatures are between 70° and 80°F. It may take a long time for the sprouts to appear—even months. It depends entirely on the starting state of the potato. Be patient. If you can't be patient, gently push the soil away from the potato and check for signs of life. You'll probably see nubby sprouts and roots forming. Cover up the spud again and go find something else to worry about.

STAGE 2: ESTABLISHING YOUR NEW PLANTS

HARVESTING THE SLIPS: Rejoice when the first sprouts appear above the soil. They're ugly at first, but they unfurl into pretty leaves. Let them grow until they have at least three sets of open leaves. Then they're ready to move.

Gently twist 'n' pull the slips off the potato. Yep, just pop them off. They come off with a tiny set of roots attached. Leave the mother potato in the soil. It will keep producing sprouts for you until it has withered down to nothing.

PLANTING THE SLIPS: How many slips to pot and where to pot them is up to you. It depends on your living situation. For instance, if your only available space is a narrow windowsill, you could line the whole sill with lots of small pots. In that case, you would put one slip in each container. If you have room for a few big pots, you could put several slips in each pot.

This is intensive agriculture. Plant the slips fairly close to each other—much closer than they'd ever be planted out on the farm. Try planting them about 3 inches apart. That would translate to about four slips in a 9-inch pot.

When you plant the slips, bury them up to their chins. In other words, the whole long stem goes under the soil, leaving just the leaves above the soil. That way, each slip will sprout more roots along the stem and make the plant strong. Be sure to leave at least two sets of leaves above the soil. It's okay to bury the lower sets.

Note: All this applies to planting your slips in the ground as well. Just remember that sweet potatoes like warmth, so if you're planting outside, do it during warm months.

CARING FOR THE PLANTS: Keep the slips moist and be kind to them while they're rooting and establishing themselves.

Put them somewhere sunny. More sun equals more leaves. If you suspect they're not getting enough sun indoors, place them under fluorescent lights. (See Project 48.) Potted plants lose nutrients each time you water them, so feed your plants to keep them luxuriant. If you keep a worm bin (Project 61), tea made from worm castings is a fantastic soil supplement. You can buy organic fertilizers at the nursery. Follow the directions on the fertilizer container and feed the slips about once a month.

To keep the plants bushy instead of long and straggly, pinch or cut off the long ends of the vines, making your cut right before the next set of leaves or leaf buds. This will cause side shoots to form.

Like any houseplant, sweet potato vines are subject to common houseplant pests. Spider mites appear on our vines once in a while. These are teeny bugs, just dots to the naked eye. If you notice them, rinse or wipe them off the leaves immediately, and keep checking to make sure no more appear. Simple vigilance should be enough to suppress them within a couple of weeks. Spider mites thrive in dry conditions, so if you mist your plants or rest the plants on trays of wet gravel to increase the local humidity, you may prevent them from ever appearing.

CONTINUING PROPAGATION: As you eat your plants, you might add more pots to your collection or fill holes in your current pot with new slips. If the mother potato stops offering slips, start a new one. You can also clip small portions of the mature vine and stick them directly in moist soil. They'll root.

Your indoor plants will never bear potatoes. They won't get enough light inside to make that big, energetic push. Outdoors, they might develop tubers, but you must have a long growing season—roughly 100 frost-free days.

HOW TO EAT THEM: The leaves and the stem bits attached to the leaves are the best parts to eat. The newest shoots are the most tender. Prepare these as you'd prepare spinach or any green.

Herbal Medicine and Beauty

Some of the most common culinary herbs, like rosemary, sage, and peppermint, have potent healing properties. This dual nature has made them beloved garden mainstays for centuries. Other traditional healing plants, like chickweed, plantain, and yarrow, grow wild and are considered weeds. The following projects highlight the uses of these plants in homemade medicines and beauty products. It's well worth growing a few herbs in your garden or learning to forage beneficial weeds around the neighborhood. If that's not possible, you can always buy herbs in bulk at health food stores or online.

33 ›

PREPARATION: 5 min
WAITING: 1+ days

Medicinal Honey

Unpasteurized (raw) honey, which you can buy at the farmers' market from beekeepers—or, better yet, produce in your own hive—is one of nature's great gifts. Not only is it delicious, but it has potent antibacterial and antifungal properties. As we noted in Project 13, it can be used to treat wounds and to soothe sore throats and coughs. It is also a fine vehicle for herbal medicine.

When you get a new jar of honey, invest a little time in making a few small jars of medicinal honey. You'll be glad you have them when you need them. If you can't find raw honey, use regular honey.

All you have to do is fill a clean, dry jar—a small one, like a jam jar—with chopped fresh herb or roots and cover the herb with honey. If the honey is too thick to pour, try stirring it or, if you must, warm it gently in a bath of warm water. Whatever you do, don't overheat raw honey, and definitely don't put it in the microwave. You want to keep those healing properties active.

Put a cover on the jar, label it, and let it sit for a while. You can start using honey infusions after a day, but they become more potent over time. After 4 to 6 weeks, strain out the plant matter to make the honey more palatable. Each infusion will last a long time in the cupboard, or you could opt to keep it in the fridge. Take herbed honey by the spoonful, stir it into hot water or tea, or apply it to the skin.

Here are some variations you may want to try, but you should also experiment with any herbs you like to create both medicinal and culinary honeys.

GARLIC HONEY

Fill a jar halfway with whole, peeled garlic cloves and cover with honey. Take garlic honey when you suspect a cold is coming on, to combat throat infections, or to treat wounds. Garlic honey is also a tasty glaze on meat or vegetables.

GINGER HONEY

Peel gingerroot and cut into thin coins. Cover the pieces with honey and let steep. Ginger honey makes a nice, aromatic addition to tea or hot water for general use or for sipping when you have a cold. A spoonful will help settle an upset stomach.

SAGE HONEY

Fill a jar loosely with chopped fresh leaves and cover with honey. Sage is a strong antibacterial herb. Combined with honey, it makes a powerful healing syrup for coughs and sore throats or a salve for wounds.

CHAMOMILE OR CATNIP HONEY

Fill a jar almost to the top with fresh chamomile buds or chopped catnip leaves. Cover with honey. Both herbs work to soothe and relax an overactive mind. Take a spoonful at bedtime or stir it into tea.

PEPPERMINT HONEY

Fill a jar with fresh peppermint leaves and add as much honey as will fit. The cooling properties of peppermint make this a good honey for cold and flu symptoms, like sore throat, congestion, and coughs. A spoonful might help soothe your stomach if you've overeaten.

ROSE HIP HONEY

Rose hips, the small red fruits that appear on rosebushes in the fall, are packed with vitamin C. Rose hip honey is a delicious vitamin C supplement and a sweet-tart condiment for general use. You can pick rose hips from plants that you know haven't been sprayed with pesticides or buy the hips dried. Sample the fresh rose hips before you pick them: Some varieties of rose make tastier hips than others. The best time to harvest hips is after the first frost, when the hips turn sweet and go slightly soft.

The good parts of the hips are the skins and the pulp that surrounds the inner core. The core is filled with seeds, and the seeds are covered with tiny hairs that are skin irritants. Kids used to collect the seeds and deploy them as itching powder. Needless to say, you want to avoid eating the seeds. There are two ways to manage this. The first is to use the pods whole. The second is to chop the hips, extract the juice, and then strain off the seeds and solids. Both methods are described below.

ROSE HIP SYRUP #1: Pick fresh rose hips. Wash them and trim off the stem and blossom ends, but leave the hips whole. Submerge them in honey or layer them with dry sugar. In the case of the sugar, the juices of the hips will leach out and turn the sugar into a syrup. The honey will thin into a syrup. After about a month, strain off the solids.

ROSE HIP SYRUP #2: Chop fresh or dried rose hips in a food processor. Put them in a saucepan, cover with water, and simmer for about 20 minutes. Strain through cheesecloth or a coffee filter. Measure the juice and add an equal amount of honey to make a syrup.

34› *Foraging Feral Greens*

We consider the wide world of weeds our second garden. Anytime we're out walking, we've got an eye out for food and medicine. Wild greens supplement our garden produce and fill in the gaps between harvests. They're the ultimate in local cuisine.

To learn to identify feral plants, seek out wild food experts in your area who offer guided walks. Field books help, but firsthand experience is the best way to learn. While every region has its own distinctive wild edibles and medicinal plants, there are a few ubiquitous weeds that can be found all over North America. Here we describe a few of our favorites and give you some hints on hunting them.

If you do go hunting, always be certain of your plant identifications. If you're not sure about your identification, just pass the plant by. If you taste a plant and don't like it, don't eat it. This might sound obvious, but sometimes new foragers eat foods they don't like out of misguided machismo (or masochism!). A large part of working with the wild ones is learning to trust your palate and your instincts.

CHICKWEED (*Stellaria media*) is a low-growing, pretty little green that grows in cool weather, so you'll find it in early spring and autumn but not in midsummer. It grows just about everywhere. Look for it on shady slopes, under trees, and as an undergrowth among taller weeds. Chickweed grows in masses rather than as single plants. It has small, smooth, pointed green leaves that grow in opposing pairs and tiny white flowers. Distinguish it from similar-looking plants by its distinctive flowers, the single line of hairs running down its stalk, and by the *absence* of milky sap. Chickweed's mild flavor makes it an excellent addition to salads. It's also a plant with cooling and soothing medicinal properties, and so it's often used in oils, salves, and poultices for irritated skin.

MALLOW (*Malva parviflora*). Also called cheeseweed, this not-so-attractive and all-too-common weed is quite edible. The leaves can be used in salads or as a cooked green. It doesn't have much flavor, so we usually cook it with lots of garlic and hot pepper. What it lacks in flavor, it makes up for in availability and reliability. While many of the more tasty and delicate weeds don't outlast the spring, mallow produces reliably well into the summer. It might be a little bland, but it is never as bland as supermarket greens. And like most weeds, mallow is very nutritious. Look for it in any sunny, untended urban or suburban space, such as median strips and vacant lots.

MuLLEIN

MULLEIN, COMMON (*Verbascum thapsus*). Mullein plants are attractive if you like bold, untamed things. Their leaves are distinctive: huge, soft, velvety, and gray green in color. They grow in a rosette pattern from a single point, piling upward to become taller and taller. When the plant matures, it sends up spectacular stalks covered with small yellow flowers. These stalks can be over 6 feet tall. In the spring, look for the large leaves growing low to the ground in sunny spaces with disturbed soil, like vacant lots. If you have trouble finding mullein, just wait, because mullein is hard to miss once it puts up its huge flower stalk.

Mullein leaves have demulcent, expectorant, and anti-inflammatory properties. Make them into teas and tinctures for coughs and respiratory problems—just be sure to filter the tea before drinking to remove any of the leaf fuzz, which might be irritating to the throat.

PLANTAIN, COMMON (*Plantago major*). This is a low plant with broad, veined leaves that grow from a central point, from which it throws up pencil-like seed stalks when mature. This useful plant is widely derided as a weed. Like the dandelion, it's the bane of lawn owners, but it's not as flashy as the dandelion, so you may have never noticed it. Yet it's there, waiting for you. Look for it starting in the early spring in any open grassy area (where you're sure people haven't been spraying chemicals).

Plantain can be eaten as a salad green when it's young—older leaves are too tough. However, its best use is as medicine, as a topical treatment for bites and boils and other skin eruptions and irritations. In herbal speak, it's a "drawing herb." Chew on a plantain leaf and rub it on bug bites to make them stop itching. It's also an astringent plant, meaning it will help stop bleeding. Use oil infused with plantain to make a skin salve.

STINGING NETTLE (*Urtica dioica*). These plants can be foraged in most parts of the country and are in no danger of being overharvested. Most people have some experience with their sting. Perhaps nettles are wicked because they know they are so good. Nettles are one of the most nutritious greens we know of—if not *the* most. Prepare young nettles as you would any green. The stingers cook off with even a light steaming. Nettles are not superflavorful, but they can be tricked up with spices or combined with more flavorful greens. When they get too big and tough to eat, dry them and make them into a nutritious tea. Nettle teas have long been enjoyed as spring tonics. Drink nettles or eat them when you feel malnourished and depleted. Nettle infusions are also good for the hair and scalp. The nutrients in nettles can be transferred to your garden by composting the plants or by making a strong nettle brew to use as fertilizer.

In the spring, we eat nettles fresh, and we gather and dry nettles whenever we can so we always have lots on hand. Search for stinging nettles in shady, damp places—though sometimes they set up camp in unlikely spots. They're

stinging nettle

easy to recognize once you know what to look for: leafy plants that grow straight up, with rounded, matte, serrated, slightly textured leaves that terminate in points. They look a little like spearmint. In the early spring, they are quite small and tender; later in the year, they can grow shoulder high. Harvest the upper parts (the newer growth) using shears and work gloves or kitchen gloves. It's wise to wear long pants and closed-toe shoes, too. Nettles never give up without a fight. If you do get stung, apply a paste of baking soda and water.

OXALIS OR WOOD SORREL (Oxalidaceae, the wood sorrel family, including *Oxalis stricta, O. montana,* and *O. pes-caprae*). These low-growing plants have distinctive, shamrock-shaped leaves and pretty flowers that may be white, purple, or yellow, depending on the variety. The flowers, leaves, and stems are all edible and have a bright, tart lemon flavor that makes them an excellent garnish or addition to salads. Oxalis is high in vitamin C.

For all its delicate beauty, oxalis is a tough, invasive plant. Here in our home turf of California, buttercup oxalis (*O. pes-caprae*) swamps yards and median strips every spring, then dies back as soon as the weather heats up. To us, oxalis is the first taste of spring, and we crave it all winter long. We've heard plenty of complaints from people who claim oxalis is taking over their yards—to which we'd reply they're obviously not eating enough of it. Any edible plant that volunteers in our yard is more than welcome to make itself at home. A plant with similar flavor and uses is ordinary garden sorrel (*Rumex rugosus*), which can be found growing feral in many places, as well as its wild sister, *R. acetosella,* known as sheep sorrel or sour grass.

Note: Oxalis is rich in oxalic acid and thus should be approached with caution by people suffering from kidney problems, gout, and rheumatoid arthritis as well as by those who are prone to kidney stones.

Other edible weeds you might like to try, if you can find them in your neighborhood, include purslane (*Portulaca oleracea*), lamb's-quarters (*Chenopodium album*), miner's lettuce (*Claytonia perfoliata*), garlic mustard (*Alliaria petiolata*), and various wild mustards, like wild white mustard (*Sinapis alba*), and of course, dandelion (*Taraxacum officinale*).

Drying, Infusing, and Tincturing Herbs

Herbal preparations are the backbone of the home pharmacy. Infusions, decoctions, and tinctures capture the power of herbs, transforming them into anything from a simple cup of tea to a healing salve. Below we'll discuss the different types of preparations and how they're used.

DRIED OR FRESH?

This is always the first question that comes up when it comes to making herbal preparations. The answer depends on which type of preparation you're making.

INFUSIONS IN WATER: Fresh or dried herbs can be used in water infusions.

INFUSIONS IN OIL: Dried herbs are best for oil infusions because the water in fresh leaves may encourage bacteria to breed in oil. If you do use fresh plants, spread them out on a table and let them wilt for a day or two. This allows much of the water to evaporate from their leaves.

TINCTURES: Tinctures can be made with either fresh or dried herbs.

HOW TO DRY HERBS

To dry fresh herb leaves for future use, gather them into small bundles, tie the ends with string, and hang them indoors and out of the sun. They are officially dry when the leaves crumble rather than bend between your fingers. At that point, strip the leaves from the stems and transfer the leaves to a lidded glass jar. The easiest way to strip the leaves is over a piece of newspaper. Newspaper captures all the bits and then can be folded to direct the dried herb neatly into the jar.

To dry flower heads, spread out the flowers on a screen or piece of newspaper. Remove petals from larger flowers to speed drying. When all parts are crispy dry, transfer them to lidded glass jars.

Store dried herbs in the dark to keep them potent. Use them within a year.

KELLY SAYS... Be sure your herbs are truly dry before you transfer them to jars. Last summer, I painstakingly accumulated a quart of fragrant dried chamomile flowers from our garden, but one day I was in a rush to clean up the kitchen and added a last handful of flowers that weren't completely dry. Dried chamomile should smell like heaven. Imagine my dismay when I cracked open the jar a month later and smelled mold.

WATER INFUSIONS

These are simply herbs soaked in hot water. Herbal tea is an infusion, but for medicinal and cosmetic purposes, the infusions are made strong by using a high percentage of herbs to water and by letting the herbs steep longer. Water infusions can be consumed as drinks, used as a skin wash or hair rinse, or blended into facial creams. Infusions of cleansing herbs like sage and thyme or even gentle chamomile can be put to service around the kitchen as mild disinfectants and deodorizers.

The proportion of herb to water depends on its final use. As a rule of thumb, 1 ounce of herb in 1 quart of water makes a very strong infusion. An ounce is about a cup of dried, chopped herb, though this varies by type of herb.

Don't overthink measurements. It doesn't matter much if the infusion ends up slightly strong or slightly weak. It's all good. With experience, you'll develop a feel for the correct proportions. To start, just put 2 to 3 inches of dried herb in a clean, quart-size jar, or fill it ¾ full with fresh herbs.

Set a kettle of water to boil. If your water is heavy with minerals or smells like a swimming pool, you may want to use filtered water or rainwater instead. Take the kettle off the stove just as it reaches a boil, because it's best if the water isn't scalding. Fill the jar with the hot water, cap it, and leave it to sit about 4 hours. Overnight is good, too. If you're in a huge hurry, you'll have something useful enough in 20 minutes or so. When the steeping time is over, strain out the herbs. Squeeze or press the steeped herbs to extract every bit of liquid.

Keep the water infusion in the fridge for short-term storage. It's best to put the infusion to use immediately, while the herbs are at their most potent.

DECOCTION

This is a water infusion made with roots, bark, or seeds. These plant materials are tougher than leaves and flowers, so you have to simmer them to extract their active properties. Place 1 or 2 ounces of plant material and 2 cups water in a saucepan or double boiler. The pan should not be aluminum, which might react with your herbs. Bring the water to a bare simmer and keep it there for 30 minutes. Strain and bottle. Use the decoction quickly, as you would with ordinary infusions.

OIL INFUSION

Oil infusions are the basis for medicinal salves. They can also be used in creams and lotions, lip balms, body scrubs, and body oils. They are not practical for soap making, because the chemical processes of saponification will probably "eat up" any of the herbal benefits.

TRADITIONAL OIL INFUSION: The traditional method of oil infusion involves filling a clean, dry jar halfway or so with dry or well-wilted herbs and filling it the rest of the way with good-quality oil. Olive oil is stable and inexpensive and well suited to beauty applications. Never put wet or fresh herbs in oil. With oil

SAFETY NOTE

Whenever plant matter is steeped in oil for a long period of time, there's a chance of botulism developing in the oil. Botulism is a rare but serious illness caused by botulinum toxin, which is produced by bacteria that grow in anaerobic settings—like oil. It's commonly associated with improper canning, but it doesn't have to be passed through food. The toxin can enter the body through open wounds as well. We infuse herbs by this traditional oil infusion method, and we've not heard any tales of herbalists dropping by the droves because they, too, used oil infusions, but you may want to take this safety issue into account, particularly if the oil will be used on cuts or on the lips. To minimize this risk, use the alcohol and oil infusion method instead.

infusions, your goal is always to minimize water content. Cap the jar and put it in a dark, warm place for 4 to 6 weeks, then strain out the plant matter through cheesecloth or other fine strainer and store the oil in a dark place or in the refrigerator. Use it as soon as possible, meaning within a few weeks instead of several months, because eventually the oil will turn rancid.

OIL INFUSION USING ALCOHOL: Alcohol can speed up the oil infusion process. This method is more work than the traditional long infusion—requiring about an hour of your time—but it produces infused oil in about 24 hours instead of 4 weeks. There are other benefits to this method, too. We've noticed that oils prepared this way have more complex, delicate scents. Also, sometimes long-soaked infusions turn rancid, either because of water content in the herbs, because the oil itself was old, or because the jar was forgotten and left to steep far too long. Finally, because the plant matter doesn't spend much time in the oil, the botulism concern mentioned at left is lessened if not eliminated entirely.

To start the infusion, put dried or fresh herbs in a glass jar and cover with grain alcohol, like Everclear. Don't use vodka, because it has too much water in it. The best kind of Everclear to use is the 190 proof form, but some states only allow the sale of a diluted 151 proof version, and that will do. Pack down fresh herbs; weigh them down, if necessary, to keep them below the surface of the alcohol. To do this, nest a smaller jar or glass full of water in the mouth of the jar. Let the infusion steep for 24 hours. Give the jar a shake whenever you pass by.

The next day, put the herbs and alcohol in a blender. Give it a whirl to chop the herbs up a bit, then note the quantity of herbed booze in the blender. Add about five times as much olive oil (or another high-grade oil, like sweet almond oil or sunflower oil). Mix on high speed until everything is very finely blended, then keep blending for another minute for good measure. Strain the herb solids out of the oil using cheesecloth, a stocking, or a coffee filter, squeezing the herbs as you go. It's okay if a little bit of green matter gets through, because you'll strain it again later.

Next, cook the alcohol out of the oil mixture. The trick is to do this at the lowest temperature possible so you don't destroy the delicate aromatics in the oil. Pour the mixture into a saucepan and heat it very gently over the lowest heat setting on your stove. The alcohol evaporates at relatively low temperatures. You'll be able to see and smell the alcohol fumes rising from the pan. This process takes a good while, perhaps an hour, depending on quantity. Don't be tempted to rush it by raising the heat. Check to see if the alcohol is gone by passing a lit match over the surface of the oil. If it crosses a pocket of alcohol, it will flare up, then extinguish on its own. Keep warming. When you can't light the surface on fire anymore, you'll know the infusion is done—and in the meanwhile, you'll have been well entertained by the pyrotechnics. If any scum forms during this process, spoon it off the surface. Pass the finished oil through a coffee filter or a piece of cheesecloth. Store the oil in a clean, lidded jar out of the light or in the refrigerator.

TINCTURES

Tinctures are alcohol-based herbal medicines. Soaking herbs in alcohol (*tincturing*) extracts their active healing properties. Oil infusions are used for topical applications, like salves. Water infusions are used both topically and ingested (in the case of tea), but they are weaker than tinctures because water doesn't do as good a job at extracting herbs as alcohol. Tinctures are usually taken orally, though sometimes they are applied to the skin. Because they are so concentrated, they must be considered medicine. Therefore, before you use any tincture, you must study the herb you're using and fully understand its proper uses and dosages—or consult an herbalist.

If used correctly, tinctures give you convenient access to the healing properties of plants. For instance, it's inconvenient to simmer up a pot of willow bark tea at the office, but you can keep a small bottle of willow bark tincture in your desk drawer in case you get a headache. Tinctures are used in small quantities—the dosage is measured in drops—applied directly on the tongue or stirred into liquid. Another advantage of tinctures is that if properly stored, they will keep for at least 2 or 3 years.

Alcohol is the most effective medium (*menstrum*) for tincturing, but tinctures can also be made by soaking herbs in food-grade vegetable glycerin or vinegar for use by people with objections to alcohol. Neither glycerin nor vinegar performs as well as alcohol, though, and neither keeps as well, either. Keep in mind that a typical dose of tincture contains less than a teaspoon of alcohol, less than you'd probably get in a dose of cough syrup.

In common practice, the alcohol used for tincturing is 100 proof vodka, which is actually composed of 50 percent pure alcohol and 50 percent water. Eighty proof vodka (40 percent alcohol and 60 percent water) does not work as well with most herbs. All that matters is the proof, not the brand, so buy cheap vodka. In advanced practice, alcohol levels are customized for each tincture, because the precise amount needed varies somewhat from plant to plant. Pure grain alcohol, like Everclear, can be diluted with water to the correct proportions. But for the backyard herbalist, 100 proof vodka will do splendidly. The majority of herbs tincture well in a 50 percent alcohol/50 percent water medium.

Other high-proof alcohols, like rum or brandy, can be used in tincturing. Never use isopropyl alcohol or other industrial alcohols. Only use alcohol made for human consumption. In other words, shop at the liquor store, not the hardware store.

MAKING THE TINCTURE

The directions below are for alcohol tinctures, but the same procedures are followed when working with glycerin and vinegar.

DRIED HERBS OR ROOTS: Combine 1 ounce dried herb or root with 5 ounces 100 proof vodka in a lidded glass jar. Use this 1:5 ratio in any quantity.

FRESH HERBS OR ROOTS: Put what fresh herbs or roots you have in a jar. Don't pack them down. Pour enough 100 proof vodka over them to barely cover. You may have to put weight on fluffy herbs to keep them in the vodka. One way to do this is to put a smaller jar or drinking glass in the mouth of the tincturing jar. Or avoid the problem by filling the jar completely so there's no headspace left after you add the vodka.

Whether you're using fresh or dried herbs, after you've combined the plant matter and vodka, cover the jar and put it somewhere out of the light. Label and date it so you don't forget what it is and when you made it. Every day, or as often as you can remember, give the jar a shake. Let it steep like this for 6 weeks.

Strain out the herbs using a coffee filter or cheesecloth. Transfer the tincture to blue- or brown-glass dropper bottles. Store out of sunlight. Alcohol-based tinctures last for years. Use vinegar or glycerin tinctures within a year.

A STARTER TINCTURE

In Project 13, we talked about how to source willow bark to make a pain-relieving tea. Try tincturing willow bark as described in this section: i.e., steep willow bark in vodka at a 1:5 ratio for 6 weeks. The standard dosage for willow bark tincture is ½ teaspoon mixed in water or juice, taken up to 3 times a day for the relief of headache and muscle pain. Remember to follow all precautions generally given for aspirin when using willow bark.

Making Salves

Salves (balms, ointments, unguents—whatever you want to call them) are easy to make and endlessly versatile. Using one simple technique, you can make lip balm, healing salves, deep moisturizing balms, aromatherapy preparations, and even deodorant.

Salves can be made with anything from goose fat to petroleum jelly, but we make them with vegetable oils and beeswax. Beeswax binds and thickens oils and also soothes, protects, and hydrates skin. We consider it an indispensable ingredient in any healing salve, but if you're a vegan, you can use candelilla wax, derived from plant sources, as a substitute.

First, we're going to give some general tips for making any salve. Then we'll give recipes that illustrate some of the many different ways salves can be used. We hope you'll soon be inventing your own salves.

TIPS FOR MAKING SALVES

BASIC RATIOS: To make a salve, all you have to do is melt enough beeswax in oil so that the oil turns solid when it cools. The ratio of oil to wax varies from 3:1 for a hard salve to 8:1 for a loose salve. The ratio you choose depends on what kind of feel you want for the final product.

MEASURING INGREDIENTS: For some recipes, we're sticklers for exactness and ask that everything be weighed. For salves, though, the measurements can be casual, by volume instead of weight, using measuring cups and spoons or even eyeballing it. Since salves are often made in small quantities, measuring by the spoonful is a straightforward way to compare volumes. To measure solid oils, like coconut oil, pack them into measuring spoons. Beeswax comes in blocks and in small beads, also called pastilles. Solid beeswax can be grated and packed into a spoon; the beads measured as they are.

HEATING SALVES: Oil and wax should be combined over a water bath or double boiler, instead of over direct heat, to prevent scorching and possible combustion. If you're making a small quantity of salve, just a few tablespoons' worth, all you need to make a water bath is a Pyrex (heatproof glass) liquid measuring cup and a saucepan. Combine the wax and oils in the measuring cup. Put the cup in a saucepan of gently simmering water and stir until the wax melts. The lip of the measuring cup makes it easy to pour the salve into containers.

A water bath *(left)* and an improvised double boiler *(above)*.

TESTING DURING COOKING: If you wish, test the salve while it's hot by putting a few drops on a chilled plate. It will set up fast, giving you a preview of the final texture.

TROUBLESHOOTING: If the finished salve comes out too soft or hard for your liking, just scoop it out of the containers, return it to the water bath, and melt it down again. Add a touch more wax to thicken, a touch more oil to soften, or a few more drops of essential oil to up the scent.

Skin-Healing Salve

Once you begin making herb-infused oils, as described in Project 35, you can put them to use in healing salves. Different herbs bring different properties to the salves. Half the fun of keeping a home pharmacy is learning the properties of different herbs and how to apply them to your specific needs. It's particularly satisfying to use herbs you've grown or foraged yourself. When you *know* a plant, when you've read about it, when you've raised it in your garden or located it growing in the wild, when you've take the time to harvest it and transform it into medicine, your relationship to that medicine becomes both intimate and profound. The difference between a jar of homemade medicinal salve and some anonymous tube of drugstore ointment can be likened to the difference between fast food and a meal cooked with the freshest ingredients and lots of care. There's power in the *intention* and *attention* you put into making your own medicine.

This general-purpose salve speeds healing of minor cuts and scrapes, rashes, burns, bug bites, and sores. To make it, you will first have to make oil infusions of calendula (*Calendula officinalis*) and common plantain (*Plantago major*). Both are renowned for their skin-healing abilities, and either one would make a fine salve on its own. Their medicinal uses overlap in many ways, but they're combined here to take advantage of calendula's skin-regenerating properties and plantain's astringent qualities.

YOU'LL NEED

* 2 ounces calendula-infused olive oil
* 2 ounces plantain-infused olive oil
* 1 ounce organic beeswax (½ ounce for a softer salve)
* 5 drops lavender essential oil (optional)
* 4-ounce jar or 4 (1-ounce) tins

PUTTING IT TOGETHER

Combine the oils and wax over a water bath. Bring the water to a low simmer to heat the oil, stirring occasionally to speed the melting of the wax. When the wax is entirely dissolved in the oil, take the mixture off the heat.

Stir in the lavender essential oil, if using. The lavender won't contribute to the healing qualities of the salve, but the calendula and plantain oils don't have much scent on their own, and the first thing everyone does when they open a jar of salve is sniff it. Lavender is a soothing scent that most people like, and lavender essential oil won't irritate the skin.

While the oil-and-wax blend is still hot, pour it into clean containers. We recommend that you keep this salve in a few small containers rather than one large one. Small tins stay more hygienic, and spares can be kept in the fridge for long-term storage or given as gifts. This recipe will fill one 4-ounce jar or four

1-ounce tins. After pouring, let the salve cool until solid. Then put the lids on the tins and label them.

Makes 4 ounces

Note: Other herbs that make excellent skin salve ingredients are comfrey (*Symphytum officinale*), chickweed (*Stellaria media*), and chamomile (*Chamomilla recutita*).

PREPARATION: 10 min

Headache Balm

Pleasant scents don't relieve pain, but they do help you relax. Rub this salve on your temples, nape, wrists, and sternum; take a deep breath; and let go of the tension of the day. The scent of lavender is relaxing, and rosemary has long been associated with both clearing the mind and soothing headaches. The peppermint helps you breathe easier and also makes the skin tingle slightly, which distracts you from the pain. If you're not a fan of menthol sensations, reduce the amount of peppermint.

Since the scents of essential oils fade over time, it's best to make this balm in small quantities. Therefore, this recipe is presented in spoonfuls.

YOU'LL NEED

* 4 tablespoons organic sunflower or extra-virgin olive oil
* 1 tablespoon organic beeswax
* ¼ teaspoon lavender essential oil
* ¼ teaspoon rosemary essential oil
* ⅛ teaspoon peppermint essential oil
* Jar with a 2-ounce capacity, or smaller containers with a total capacity of 2 ounces

PUTTING IT TOGETHER

Measure the sunflower or olive oil and wax into a Pyrex (heatproof glass) liquid measuring cup. Set the cup in a small saucepan of gently simmering water. As the oil heats, stir it once in a while to speed the melting of the wax. When the wax melts in the oil, take the cup out of the saucepan.

Stir in the essential oils while the oil is still liquid. Then pour the finished balm into clean containers to cool. Once cool, cap the containers and label them.

Makes 2 ounces

Note: Substitute any of the essential oils with other types if you wish, using any scent you find soothing. You might want to try eucalyptus, lemon balm, or chamomile essential oils.

No-Nonsense Lip Balm

Lip balm doesn't "wear off"—we eat it off. What we don't consume by licking our lips is absorbed into our skin. Most commercial lip balms are made with ingredients we wouldn't otherwise eat on purpose and may not even want on our skin: things like petroleum products and artificial scents, flavors, and preservatives. Homemade balms are truly edible, truly nontoxic, truly natural. They're also easy to make. Just melt and pour.

Most lip balm tins hold ¼ to ½ ounce. Lip balm tubes hold less than ¼ ounce— 0.15 ounce, to be precise. A little lip balm goes a long way, so this recipe makes only 1 ounce. It can be scaled up easily, but, in general, it's better to make a fresh batch every few months. Olive oil stays sweet longer than most cooking oils, and beeswax never goes bad, but this is a preservative-free recipe, so spoilage is possible.

Olive oil and beeswax are a fantastic healing combo. Use the recipe for your lips, but it will also soothe angry cuticles and cracked, dry skin.

Balm intended for tubes should be made stiff, at a 3:1 or 4:1 oil-to-wax ratio. For use in pots or tins, it can be made anywhere from 4:1 to 8:1, depending on how soft you like it. This recipe is formulated at 4:1.

YOU'LL NEED

* 2 tablespoons extra-virgin olive oil
* 1½ teaspoons organic beeswax
* Clean lip balm tubes or tins, enough to hold 1 ounce of balm total (You can repurpose old tubes and tins or order new ones online. See the note below.)

PUTTING IT TOGETHER

Combine the oil and wax in a Pyrex (heatproof glass) liquid measuring cup, then set the cup in a saucepan filled with 2 or 3 inches of gently simmering water. Heat, stirring occasionally, until the wax melts. Take the mixture off the heat and, while it is still liquid, pour it into tubes or tins. Let the balm cool, then cap the containers.

Makes 1 ounce

If you're planning to recycle lip balm tubes, you should know that the mechanisms in the tubes are delicate—we learned this the hard way. Don't clean them in the dishwasher or even with hot water. Instead, wipe them out as well as you can and disinfect with rubbing alcohol or white distilled vinegar.

LIP BALM VARIATIONS

For scent and/or flavor, stir in a tiny amount of essential oil when the balm comes off the stove. If you choose to use peppermint essential oil, just remember that too much of it will make your lips burn. Start with no more than 3 or 4 drops in the preceding recipe. Test the balm by cooling it a bit on a chilled plate while the rest of the mix stays in the water bath.

FOR SCENT, COLOR, AND HEALING PROPERTIES, use herb-infused oils, as described on page 116, in place of all or part of the olive oil. Our favorite lip balm is made with chamomile oil. It has a lovely applelike fragrance. Also try peppermint-, rosemary-, lavender-, and calendula-infused oils. Just be sure that the herb you choose is edible. And if it's medicinal, be aware of its medicinal properties.

FOR A CHOCOLATE SCENT, add organic cocoa butter to your balm recipe by replacing one-third the volume of olive oil with cocoa butter. Add peppermint essential oil to make peppermint-chocolate balm.

FOR A HEAVIER, RICHER FEEL, add in a solid oil like cocoa butter, coconut oil, or shea butter. Substitute any solid oil for one-third the olive oil. To put it another way, the recipe would be 2 parts olive oil (or more for a softer balm), 1 part solid oil, 1 part beeswax. Be sure to use organic and minimally processed solid oils. Other rich, high-quality liquid oils can also be substituted for all or part of the olive oil.

FOR TINTED LIP BALM, the easiest thing to do is melt a chunk of your favorite lipstick into the heated oils. We experimented with adding beet juice and pomegranate juice, and the results were disastrous. The pigments in beet juice oxidize, slowly turning the balm from beautiful magenta to the color of old liver. Pomegranate juice attracts mold. The best natural red dye for cosmetics comes from the root of alkanet (*Alkanna tinctoria*), a plant related to borage. You can order it from herbal suppliers in root and powder form, then infuse it in oil to make wine-red oil, which you then use to make rosy-tinted lip balm.

PREPARATION: 15 min

Cocoa Puff Skin Butter

This recipe starts like a salve, but at the end we add a little water. This creates a hybrid between salve and cream with a thick, buttery texture. It's a superrich moisturizer meant for elbows and feet and gardeners' hands. The cocoa butter gives it both a heady chocolate scent and a silky feel on the skin. Jojoba mimics the oils in our own skin and is absorbed readily. Meanwhile, the olive oil and beeswax, both stalwart healers, work their magic in the background.

Pure cocoa butter, sans additives, is hard, even dry. It has to be warmed to be applied to the skin. To measure it for this recipe, scrape at it with a spoon to shave off cocoa butter shavings or dust.

YOU'LL NEED

* 2 tablespoons organic cocoa butter shavings (Find cocoa butter at health food stores or order it online.)

* 2 tablespoons extra-virgin olive oil

* 1 tablespoon jojoba oil

* 1 tablespoon organic beeswax

* 1 tablespoon water (Optional; omit the water if you'd prefer a solid salve.)

* Clean 2-ounce jar

PUTTING IT TOGETHER

Combine the cocoa butter shavings, olive oil, jojoba oil, and beeswax in a Pyrex (heatproof glass) liquid measuring cup. Place the cup in a saucepan filled with 2 or 3 inches of gently simmering water. Heat, stirring occasionally, until the cocoa butter and beeswax melt in the oil.

Take the mixture off the heat. Pour into a small bowl. Stir in the water and keep stirring like crazy as it cools (a regular spoon is fine for this purpose), whipping until the texture turns to that of thick pudding. Transfer to the small jar. It will thicken a little more as it sets.

Makes 2 ounces

37› *Moisturizing Cream*

Moisturizing cream is made with a combination of oil, beeswax, and water. The water changes the texture of the oil, making it lighter, fluffier, and easier to apply than body oil or salves. The oil and water combine to provide light and lasting moisture to the skin. Under normal circumstances, oil and water do not mix. Fortunately, beeswax is an emulsifier.

Both of the following moisturizers are ideal for sensitive skin, precisely because they are so uncomplicated. In general, we believe that the fewer ingredients in any personal care product, the better. None of the ingredients in these creams are skin irritants, which is more than most commercial moisturizers can say. Olive oil doesn't block pores or interfere with the skin's natural processes. It is also a humectant, meaning it attracts moisture out of the air and draws it to the skin. Beeswax moisturizes and protects the skin from the elements. The addition of coconut oil gives our Silky Cream its rich, buttery texture.

All-natural moisturizers, ones that don't contain any objectionable chemicals (like artificial scents and preservatives), are expensive and hard to find. Making your own is surprisingly easy and costs only pennies. You'll quickly get addicted to the luxury of slathering yourself from head to toe in rich, gentle, nourishing cream.

Homemade moisturizers contain no drying agents, so when you first put them on, they may seem shiny compared to their commercial counterparts, but the shine fades in a few minutes. After you go through one batch and get used to the slightly different feel, we bet you'll never buy face cream or body lotion again.

We're offering two variations here, one rich, one light.

PREPARATION: 15 min

Silky Cream

This rich, supermoisturizing cream is almost a butter and is suitable for face and body.

YOU'LL NEED

* ✳ **6 ounces olive oil (See "The Right Olive Oil for the Job" on page 128)**
* ✳ **2 ounces coconut oil**
* ✳ **1 ounce organic beeswax (about 4 tablespoons), chunks or pastilles**
* ✳ **10–20 drops essential oils of your choice (optional)**
* ✳ **1 cup tepid water (Distilled water, filtered water, or rainwater is best.)**
* ✳ **Clean, dry jars; enough to hold 2 cups of cream**

THE RIGHT OLIVE OIL FOR THE JOB

Extra-virgin olive oil is unrefined and the best-quality olive oil for skin care overall. However, it usually has a strong color and olive scent, and that will transfer to the skin cream to some extent, depending on the individual oil. Lower-grade oils have little color and scent and thus make white, scent-free cream. However, they have been chemically processed. That said, they're still perfectly acceptable for this recipe. We use whatever olive oil we have around. If you choose to use extra-virgin olive oil, seek out brands that aren't strongly scented.

PUTTING IT TOGETHER

Measure and combine the oils and wax in a Pyrex (heatproof glass) liquid measuring cup. Begin by pouring in the olive oil until you reach the 6-ounce line, then add the coconut oil bit by bit until the oil level rises to the 8-ounce line. Add the beeswax until the liquid reaches the 9-ounce level. Then place the cup in a saucepan full of simmering water.

Note: If you don't have a Pyrex measuring cup, measure the oils and wax by weight on a kitchen scale, then combine them in a double boiler.

Heat the oil and wax over gently simmering water, stirring occasionally, until the wax melts completely. Take the pan off the heat and stir in the essential oils, if using. If you're not going to start mixing immediately, let the melted oil and wax sit in the water bath, off the heat, so the mixture stays warm.

While the wax is melting, pour 2 cups or so of boiling water into a blender or mixing bowl to prewarm it. This will prevent the wax from solidifying on the walls. Measure 1 cup of water. It should be tepid—not chilled and not hot.

The next step has to happen quickly, so have everything at hand. Empty the boiling water out of the blender or mixing bowl. Pour in the hot oil. Start the blender or mixer running, and pour in the tepid water in a steady stream.

The oil will turn to cream almost instantly. More than likely, some water will remain unincorporated, and this will make the blender or mixer choke. Just stop the machine, scrape down the sides, and start the machine again. Repeat until the water is incorporated. It should turn thick and smooth. Before you stop mixing, poke down to the bottom to make sure there's no standing water hiding there. Stop as soon as it all comes together. Don't overmix.

Transfer the cream to clean, dry jars. You might be able to pour it, you might have to scoop it. If you see air pockets in the filled jars, stir to remove the pockets—the cream will keep better that way. Leave the lids off the jars until cool. It should set into a heavy, silky cream. It may even set thicker, more like butter.

Makes about 2 cups

VARIATIONS

Experiment with the recipes by trying different blends of oils, replacing the olive oil in whole or in part with other rich liquid oils, like avocado oil, grapeseed oil, or sweet almond oil. Replace the coconut oil with shea or cocoa butter. Or make the cream with oil infused with herbs beneficial to the skin, like calendula.

PREPARATION: 15 min

Olive Oil Whip

Olive Oil Whip has a lower oil content and more water than Silky Cream. While it's thick in the jar, it's light and cool on the skin and is suitable for face and body.

YOU'LL NEED

* ½ cup olive oil
* 2 tablespoons (½ ounce) organic beeswax
* 10–20 drops essential oils (optional)
* 1 cup tepid water (Filtered water, distilled water, or rainwater is best.)
* Clean, dry jars; enough to hold 1½ cups

PUTTING IT TOGETHER

Combine the oil and wax and warm over indirect heat. Either place the oil and wax in a Pyrex cup and rest the cup in a saucepan of gently simmering water, or combine the oil and wax in the top portion of a double boiler. Either way, warm gently until the wax melts. As soon as it does, take the mixture off the heat and stir in the essential oils, if using.

While the wax is melting, pour a couple of cups of boiling water into a blender jar or mixing bowl to prewarm it. This will keep the beeswax from solidifying on the walls.

Measure out the tepid water. Have everything ready so you can do the following steps quickly. Empty the boiling water out of the blender or bowl. Pour in the warm oil and start the blender or mixer. Add all the tepid water in a steady stream. The oil will thicken to cream instantly, but there will be extra unincorporated water. Don't be fazed by this. Just stop the blender or mixer, scrape down the sides, then start it again. Repeat until all of the water is incorporated and the cream is smooth. Don't overmix.

Immediately transfer the cream to clean, dry jars. You should be able to pour it, but if it has cooled some, you will have to scoop it into the jars. If you see any air pockets on the sides of the filled jars, stir to eliminate them. This will help the cream keep better. Let the cream cool before you put the lid on the jars.

Makes about 1½ cups

TROUBLESHOOTING

If, after cooling, water rises to the surface of the jar or the cream turns grainy or develops a crust, it has separated and needs more blending. Scoop it all back into a double boiler and gently warm it, then blend again.

NOTE ON STORAGE

Since these moisturizers contain no preservatives, it's best to use up an unrefrigerated jar in 4 to 6 weeks or so. Store extra jars in your fridge for about 6 months, or give them to friends. If you add anything "foody" to this basic recipe—like aloe, tea, or oatmeal water—you increase the risk of spoilage. Make creams with those sorts of ingredients in small quantities and use them quickly.

TIPS FOR CLEANUP

Scrape as much cream out of the blender or mixer as you can with a rubber spatula and dispose of it in the garbage. Then fill the blender jar or mixing bowl with boiling hot water and use the spatula to stir and scrape away the rest of the waxy residue. Pour off the oily water. If there's lots of yellow wax floating in it, pour it through a strainer so the wax doesn't go down the drain. While the blender or bowl is still warm, wipe it down with a rag or paper towel to remove any remaining grease, then wash as usual. If any clouding remains after washing, polish with baking soda.

38 ›

Deodorants

Below are two simple and natural deodorants. The first is a stick deodorant, which is made like a salve. In essence, it's a giant lip balm. The second is a cleansing spray that could be used alone or in conjunction with the stick.

PREPARATION: 15 min

Herbal Stick Deodorant

Homemade deodorants can take many forms, but we make it this way because it can be applied like a commercial stick deodorant. That familiar shape fits into our routine, travels well, and goes stealth in public situations, like the gym. Note that this is a deodorant, not an antiperspirant. The olive oil lets the skin breathe and will not stain clothing when used in reasonable quantity. The essential oils repress bacterial growth.

Before you make this recipe, you'll need to find an old deodorant applicator, the stick sort rather than the roll-on, and clean it out. Don't subject it to heat while you do this, just wipe it out well and then sanitize with vinegar or rubbing alcohol. While cleaning, take a moment to measure the capacity of your stick. Roll the platform down as far as it will go and add water a tablespoon at a time to see how much it will hold. Factor that into the recipe. We're assuming your stick holds 5 tablespoons.

YOU'LL NEED

* 4 tablespoons olive oil
* 1 tablespoon organic beeswax
* ⅛ teaspoon tea tree oil
* ⅛ teaspoon rosemary essential oil
* ⅛ teaspoon lavender essential oil (optional)
* Stick-type deodorant applicator

PUTTING IT TOGETHER

Combine the oil and wax over a water bath and heat the water to a gentle simmer. Stir occasionally until the wax melts in the oil. Take the mixture off the heat and stir in the tea tree and rosemary oils. Add the lavender oil for a sweeter scent, if desired.

Make sure your applicator is clean and dry. Roll it down to its lowest position. Add just enough hot oil to cover the platform. Wait a moment while it cools slightly. Some applicators have tiny holes in them—this step will block the holes. Add the rest of the mixture. Let it cool before capping.

Baking Soda Cleansing Spray

Sweat doesn't stink. Odors set in when old sweat forms a breeding ground for bacteria. To stay odor free, all you have to do is keep your armpits clean. Use this deodorizing wash between showers and after exercise. The cleansing spray can be used instead of the Herbal Stick Deodorant or in conjunction with it.

YOU'LL NEED

* 1 cup water
* 1 tablespoon baking soda (sodium bicarbonate)
* 4 drops tea tree oil
* Small bottle fitted with a spray pump

PUTTING IT TOGETHER

Mix the water, baking soda, and tea tree oil in the bottle. You'll probably have to use a funnel to get the baking soda inside. You can improvise one with a piece of paper. Shake the mixture to blend, and shake before each use. Use this spray to freshen armpits, neck, and chest. Pat dry afterward. If you don't like the scent of tea tree oil, replace it with lavender or rosemary, or just use plain baking soda and water. And yes, this is basically the same recipe as our mouthwash. What can we say? The best things serve multiple purposes.

39 ›

Keeping the Bugs Away

Old folk wisdom says you can dissuade insects from biting you by eating raw garlic or drinking vinegar. The most palatable way to drink vinegar is by enjoying our old-fashioned vinegar-based beverages in Project 23. We've found these drinks protective—against lazy California mosquitoes, at least. In Minnesota, the story might be different. It can't hurt to try. For further protection, you can make a skin spray that confuses mosquitoes and other biting insects.

Strong scents like citronella, lavender, peppermint, rosemary, cedar, and lemongrass repel mosquitoes. You can mix essential oils of these herbs in vodka to make a spray or in olive oil to make insect repellent body oil. However, herbal scents like these may attract bees. In fact, lemongrass, a very effective mosquito repellent, is used as a bee *lure*. This may or may not be a problem, depending on where you live and when you're going to be outside. Bees go to bed at twilight, when the mosquitoes come out in force, but there is some morning crossover. We love bees and want to keep bee-human relations positive, so we offer an alternative mosquito repellent that bees don't like as much: common yarrow.

PREPARATION: 5 min
WAITING: 4–6 weeks

Yarrow Mosquito Repellent

This repellent calls for the white flowers of common yarrow (*Achillea millefolium*). Yellow- or pink-flowered varieties don't work as well. Common yarrow grows wild and in many gardens. Harvest the flowers yourself, or buy dried yarrow flowers from online herbal suppliers.

YOU'LL NEED

* * Fresh or dried yarrow flowers (It's okay to include the little flower stems, but don't use the main stalk or leaves.)
* * 100 proof vodka

PUTTING IT TOGETHER

Fill a clean, dry glass jar with the yarrow flowers. Cover the flowers with the vodka and put a lid on the jar. Let the jar sit for 6 weeks. Give it a shake every day, or as often as you can. After 6 weeks, strain out the flowers and transfer the liquid to a spray bottle. To use the spray, apply to the body every hour or so. Unlike DEET, yarrow's insect-repellent qualities are short-lived. The liquid itself, however, keeps indefinitely.

40 ›

Curiously Homemade Peppermints

Empty tins were beginning to pile up around our house, dusty little memorials to our mint habit. Sure, they can be repurposed, but that only goes so far. Hit with a bolt of DIY inspiration, we asked, "Why can't we make our own mints and refill these tins?" After some pretty sticky rounds of R&D, we decided that the closest homemade approximation to Altoids would be peppermint-flavored fondant.

Fondant is the stuff they use to make the roses on wedding cakes. There are many ways to make fondant, but this recipe is so simple it's almost magical. The resulting mints are not as hard as commercial mints, their texture being more akin to buttermints, but they hold up fine in a tin.

Note: The best days for candy making are dry, clear days.

YOU'LL NEED

* 2 cups white sugar
* ⅛ teaspoon cream of tartar
* ½ cup water
* ½ teaspoon peppermint extract (in the baking section of the supermarket)
* 4–5 drops (or more) peppermint essential oil (optional)
* Confectioners' sugar
* Candy thermometer (optional)

PUTTING IT TOGETHER

In a small saucepan, combine the sugar and cream of tartar. (The cream of tartar acts to retard crystallization, making the fondant smoother.) Add the water and stir just until the sugar is dissolved. Bring the sugar water to a simmer over medium heat. Do not stir. Just watch it. You may notice sugar crystals forming on the sides of the saucepan. Most candy books will tell you these must be washed down with a wet pastry brush or else crystals could end up in your fondant. We've stopped bothering and have not noticed any difference.

Your goal is to heat the syrup to between 235° and 240°F, which signals it's reduced to 85 percent sugar. If you don't have a candy thermometer, you can use the cold-water candy test. As sugar heats, it goes through several transformational plateaus, each of which yields a different sort of candy: fondant, taffy, hard candy, etc. These stages are signaled by the behavior of the sugar syrup in cold water. To make fondant, you need to take the sugar off the heat at the stage called soft ball. It will only take a few minutes of simmering to reach 240°F, or soft ball. So pay very close attention to the syrup. Don't leave the kitchen while it's cooking.

To test for the soft ball stage, keep a small bowl of cold water by the stove. As the sugar simmers, take a bit out with a spoon every minute or so and drop it into the water. At first, the syrup will vanish or settle to the bottom. You won't be able to pick it up. Eventually, the sugar will congeal. At the soft ball stage, you'll be able to pick up the sugar and manipulate it into a squishy lump that won't hold its shape. As soon the syrup reaches 240°F or the soft ball stage, take the pan off the heat. If the sugar heats up past 240°F, or to the point where the syrup makes a firm ball, the sugar is overcooked and you'll have to start over again.

TO WORK THE CANDY BY HAND

Pour the hot syrup onto a clean cookie sheet, a big baking dish, or a big platter: anything smooth and heatproof with a lot of surface area and a raised edge (so the syrup doesn't spill over the sides). Let the syrup cool for a few minutes. You can tell it's cooling if the surface wrinkles when you poke at it. Then, using a spatula or a wooden spoon, start stirring the syrup in a slow figure-eight pattern. By stirring, you are helping the syrup cool and working air into the mix. As it cools, it will thicken and turn opaque. When it's thick enough, you can use a spatula (or two) to scrape up the congealing sugar and fold it over and over on itself. Eventually it will turn white and become very stiff. If you stir too enthusiastically, it may turn crumbly. This is fine. It will come together again when you work it with your hands.

Keep moving the candy mixture until it's cool enough to work with your hands. It shouldn't stick to your fingers much, but wet your hands if it does. After a minute of kneading, the texture will be smooth and cohesive. The dough should look like white playdough and be about the size of a tennis ball. Congratulations. This is fondant.

TO WORK THE CANDY WITH A STAND MIXER

It was a happy day when we realized we could process the syrup in our KitchenAid. Just pour the hot syrup into the mixing bowl. Attach the mixing paddle, turn the mixer on the lowest setting, and let it go. The agitation will cool the sugar quickly. It will turn creamy, then solid white, then break into crumbles. This takes only a couple of minutes. Scrape down the sides to make sure it's mixed evenly. Dry white crumbles indicate the end of the line. Turn the mixer off. Let the crumbles cool a little before you try to work with them: Go do something for a few minutes and come back. Gather the crumbles in your hands and squish and knead them until you have a ball of cohesive dough.

CURING

However you mixed your fondant, you need to let it rest overnight to cure. Put the dough in a covered container and leave it on the countertop for 12 to 24 hours. If you put a little confectioners' sugar on the bottom, the dough won't stick to the container—or you can wrap it in plastic wrap. If you can't get to it the next day, don't worry, it won't go bad. It can stay out at room temperature a good while. For long-term storage, put it in the fridge.

FLAVORING AND SHAPING

The next day (or when you are ready to move to the next step), sprinkle a cutting board with confectioners' sugar and knead the fondant until it has a nice, smooth texture. Wet hands will help moisten the dough if it feels dry, and powdered sugar will dry it if it's too sticky. When it turns smooth, flatten it into a pancake. Sprinkle the peppermint extract over the dough. Fold it over and knead some more to distribute the flavoring. Taste it. You can add more extract or, for a stronger mint punch, add a few drops of peppermint essential oil. If you use the essential oil, be sparing. Start with 4 or 5 drops. Too much is unpleasant and can actually make you sick. You might also want to try flavor variations using anise or cinnamon extracts. One ball of dough could be divided to make a few different flavors.

Shape your mints any way you want. Roll them into balls, press them into candy molds, or sculpt each one into a tiny rose—it is fondant, after all. Chilling the dough makes it stiffer and easier to shape. All we do is roll the dough into snakes and then use a sharp knife to cut the snakes into rough, oval-shaped slices. It's not fancy, but it works for us.

Spread the mints out to dry on a plate or tray dusted with confectioners' sugar. It will take a few days, maybe as much as a week, for the mints to harden. If it's humid, you may want to put them in front of a fan. Don't put them in the oven, whatever you do—they'll melt!

Cloth Pads

We couldn't resist putting this project in the Month to Month section, though, unlike the results of other projects here, these pads are made to last for years. Cloth menstrual pads are really, truly, genuinely pleasant to use. Until you try one, you can't know what a relief it is to feel natural fabric against your skin, to be free of bleach, perfumes, creepy gel cores, and those fiddly little plastic strips.

Cloth pads aren't made from trees, they ease the burden on landfills, and they can be made inexpensively. In short, by using cloth pads, you'll save money while you're saving the world. Best of all, if you have a set of these, you can say good-bye to emergency trips to the drugstore.

Pads can be made out of luxurious specialty fabrics, inexpensive remainder material from the fabric store, or repurposed fabric from around the house. The basic pattern we provide can be altered to make pads of all sizes to meet your specific needs. They wash well and don't wear out quickly.

You'll need a sewing machine for this project and some basic sewing skills. Nothing fancy, just enough competence to cut a simple pattern and steer the machine. If sewing isn't possible for you, but you're curious about cloth pads, look online for pads to buy. While there are a few national brands of cloth pads, making and selling homemade pads online has become a cottage industry. You'll find all sorts of different styles of pads made by individuals for sale through private Web sites and on sites like Etsy.com.

To start, let's look at the kinds of materials you could use in constructing your pads. Every pad is made up of three basic parts: a top layer, an absorbent core, and a backing material. You can make a pad with almost any kind of fabric, but here are suggestions:

THE TOP

The top layer should feel good against your skin. It should be absorbent, so moisture passes through it. If you want fancy pads, this is where you get to choose fun colors and patterns.

COTTON FLANNEL is soft and absorbent and easy to find. It's a favorite among pad makers and can be used to construct the entire pad. The only downside is that cotton flannel can pill and look a little worn after long use.

FLAT COTTON, like percale or pima cotton (think sheet and dress shirt fabric), is cooler than flannel against the skin and shows less wear. Moisture will pass through it and into the core easily, but it doesn't add any absorbency to the

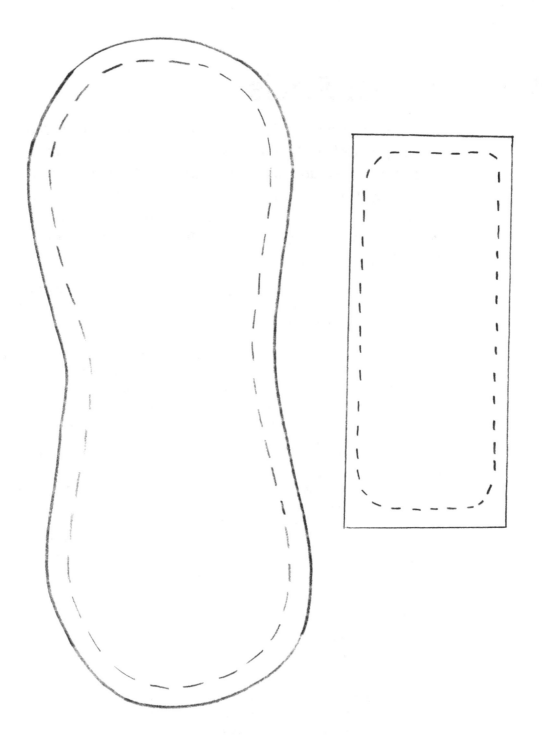

Enlarge by approximately 150% until the pad shape measures
10½ inches in length and the rectangle measures 6 inches in length.
The rectangular piece will form the two wings.

pad, so you have to factor that in. It's easy to find flat cotton in different weights and patterns.

NATURAL VELOUR OR VELVETEEN is a luxurious option. The pile makes the surface of the pad feel drier. Natural velour (made of cotton, hemp, or bamboo) is hard to find in stores, though. You'll probably have to order it online. Synthetic velour is easier to find but not as absorbent.

THE CORE

The core of the pad can be thick or thin, filled with many layers of thin material or one layer of thick material, depending on the type of pad you wish to build. You can mix fabrics in the core.

COTTON FLANNEL makes a good basic core. One or two layers of flannel make a light pad or panty liner. Add more layers for greater absorbency. The only limit is how thick you wish the pad to be.

TERRY CLOTH (toweling material) is very absorbent, if thick. Cotton terry is the easiest to find, especially if you're working out of your rag bag, but bamboo and hemp terry are more absorbent. One or two layers of toweling are usually all you need.

FLEECE MATERIAL is also absorbent. Bamboo and hemp fleeces must be ordered online, but they are thinner than cotton fleece and hold more moisture, so your pads can be thinner.

THE BACKING

The backing material has a couple of functions. The first is that it is a last line of defense between blood and your clothing, so some women prefer to use a water-resistant backing. But this comes at the cost of breathability. It's a trade-off. Pads made with natural fibers do a very good job of wicking the moisture along their length and holding that moisture in. A moisture-resistant backing isn't really necessary for an average menstrual flow, but it's a nice backup feature.

Another consideration is fabric texture. To minimize sliding of the pad, it's best if the backing has a bit of a tooth. This pad is designed to be made with or without wings. Wings help hold it in place. If you opt for the no-wing style, the backing choice becomes more important. We'll talk about wings later on.

FLANNEL is a good choice. It has a slight tooth to it, so it doesn't slide much. It's breathable, but moisture can pass through it.

CORDUROY is an excellent no-slip material and darn sporty looking, too. It does not form a moisture barrier, though.

PUL (POLYURETHANE LAMINATE) FABRIC has been laminated to be truly waterproof. It comes in natural and synthetic varieties. PUL is thin. It can stand up to hot water and dryers, too. It's unlikely that you'll find this fabric in local stores. Your best resource would be online sellers of diapering fabrics.

FLEECE (synthetic or natural) is water resistant (not waterproof) and doesn't slide around much.

We've heard of some women crafting pad backs out of repurposed crib liners and plastic-coated tablecloths and the like. These things would make waterproof pads, but because of their plastic content, they can't be washed and dried like normal fabric.

REGARDING WINGS

This pattern includes optional wings that snap together. Wings help hold the pad in place. You may or may not want wings. The hourglass shape of the pad helps keep it in place, as does the backing material. If you wear close-fitting underwear, these pads won't slide much. The one thing you do have to remember when using wingless pads is to be careful when you visit the toilet. The pads can fall in. And that is not pretty. The disadvantages of wings are few, mainly they take extra effort to sew, and if you bike (or ride horses or straddle bar stools, etc.), you might feel the snaps.

REGARDING FASTENERS

You can use different fastening methods for the wings, snaps being the most common. There are several different types of snaps and corresponding ways to attach them, from inexpensive sew-on snaps to expensive snap presses. Examine the offerings at your local fabric or craft stores, and don't forget to ask your crafty friends if they have a snap setter you could borrow. If you know how to make buttonholes, you can use buttons on the wings. Or you can buy Velcro tabs and sew them to the wings.

Web sites devoted to homemade diapers offer a wealth of information about suitable pad fabrics. The same principles apply, after all. Many of these sites sell high-end diapering materials and may be your best source for absorbent bamboo and hemp fabrics.

PREPARATION: 1 hour

A Pad of Your Own

These instructions show you how to make one basic, medium-weight pad. We encourage you to make one out of fabric you have around the house—an old flannel shirt, perhaps—and give it a test run. Then you can customize the pattern to your liking. For instance, you might prefer a longer or shorter pad or one with a slightly different shape. It's your call. Once you alter the pattern, you can make a whole bunch of pads in different weights for different phases of your cycle.

YOU'LL NEED

* 11 x 5-inch piece of fabric for the top of the pad
* 11 x 5-inch core material of your choice (for instance, 1 piece of toweling or 4 pieces of flannel)
* 11 x 5-inch piece of backing fabric
* 7 x 7-inch piece of fabric for the wings, probably the same type of material as the top
* Pins
* Chalk or pen
* Sewing scissors
* Sewing needle
* Spool of cotton thread
* 1 set of sew-on snaps, any size (optional)

PUTTING IT TOGETHER

PREWASH THE FABRIC

Prewash and dry your fabric if it's new. Iron if it's wrinkly.

ENLARGE THE PATTERN

Hand copy or photocopy the pattern (page 138), enlarging the pattern pieces by approximately 150 percent, so that the pad shape measures 10½ inches long and the rectangle 6 inches. Copy onto cardstock if you prefer a stiff pattern.

CUT THE FABRIC

Stack your top, core, and backing fabric in a neat pile. Pin all four corners of the pile together so the material doesn't move around. Next, either trace the pad shape onto the top piece of fabric or pin down the pattern on the cloth.

With the sewing scissors, cut around the trace marks or the edges of the pattern piece, cutting all layers of fabric at once so that the pieces match as much as possible. If this is difficult because of the thickness of your stack, separate the stack into two parts.

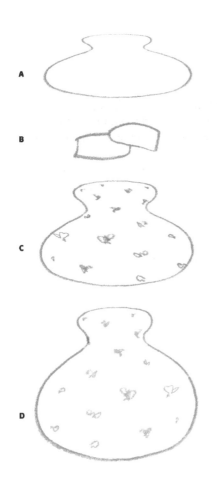

A

B

C

D

OPTIONAL: MAKE THE WINGS

You'll need two matching pieces of fabric, so either cut the 7 x 7-inch piece of wing fabric in half and stack the pieces, or fold it in half. Either way, arrange the fabric so the two good sides face each other. Trace the shape of the wing on the wrong side of the fabric, then cut it out.

Sew a single line of stitching all around the wing, following the dotted line on the pattern, so that you have a ¼-inch seam allowance and slightly rounded corners. (You could cut the shape out after sewing, if that's easier.)

Cut this rectangle in half across the short side so you have two pieces. Turn the two cut pieces right way around. You'll have two wings (or two finger puppets) about 2½ inches long. The raw edges will be sewn into the pad, so don't worry about them for now.

ARRANGE THE PAD LAYERS

Stack your pad fabric in the following order and pin the pieces together. The sequence may seem counterintuitive, but the pad will be turned inside out after sewing.

From top to bottom:

* Backing, face down[A]
* Wings (if using)[B]
* Top material, face up[C]
* Core fabric, one or more layers[D]

POSITION WINGS

If using wings, position the two wings between the backing and top material, equidistant between the two ends of the pad. They'll be sewn into place when you sew the rest of the pad. Lay them so one wing crosses on top of the other[B] and so their raw edges line up with the raw edges of the pad fabric. (Imagine the pad has its arms folded, rather than outstretched.) This way, when the pad is turned, the wings will be in the right place. You could attach them later by sewing them to the back side of the pad once it's turned, but that doesn't look as neat.

SEW THE PAD

Stitch together the layers, following the contour of the pad, allowing a ¼-inch seam allowance all around. Leave a 2- to 3-inch opening at one end.

Turn the pad inside out through the opening: Reach between the top material and the backing material and pull from there. After turning, the core fabric should end up hidden, you should see only the material you intended for the front and the back, and the wings should be in place.

A SHORTCUT
Stitching and turning create
a clean-edged pad. If you
don't mind a frayed edge,
you can assemble all of the
pieces in their final order
and topstitch them together
using the zigzag setting on
your machine. Just stitch all
around the edges. If you have
a serger, the edges could be
serged all the way around.

Close the opening by tucking the raw edges under to match the seam you've already made. Pin the edges into place or iron them flat, then hand-sew the hole closed or topstitch with the machine.

TOPSTITCH THE PAD

Topstitch the entire pad. This keeps the layers from puffing or slipping around, and the resulting channels can help direct menstrual flow. You can stitch it any way you like, really. If your top fabric has a pattern on it, you can stitch along the pattern to give the pad a fancy quilted effect. Or you could be more utilitarian and sew a simple 5-inch line straight up the middle. Or trace all around the edges of the pad, placing the needle ½ to ¾ inch in from the outer edge.

ADD THE SNAPS TO THE WINGS

Add sew-on snaps to the wings, if using. The snap halves should be placed to meet at the center of the pad. Fold the wings against the pad and put a little mark on both to mark the center point. One half of the snap is the ball and the other half the socket. It doesn't matter which half goes on what side, but they do have to be sewn on opposite faces of the wings so they'll meet when the wings are folded under the pad. In other words, when the pad is flat and the wings are outstretched, one part of the snap faces up and the other faces down.

Both halves of the sewn-on snaps will be ringed with four or more small holes on the edge. Using a needle and thread, hand-stitch the snaps to the wings by looping the needle in and out of the first pair of holes five or six times. Then move on to the next hole. The more anchoring stitches, the stronger the snap.

The wings are very forgiving regarding placement of the snaps. Don't worry too much about precise centering or if the snaps shift around a little when you sew them.

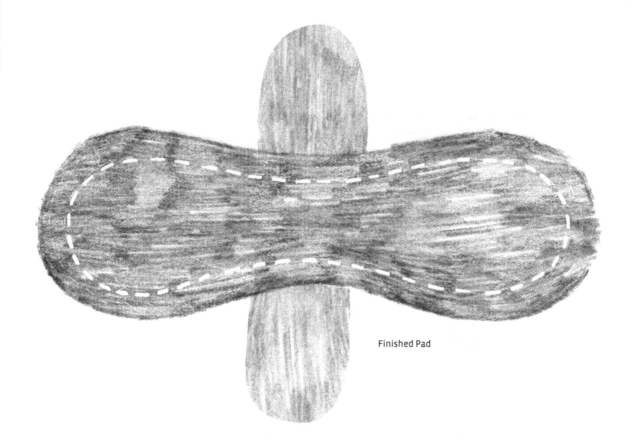

Finished Pad

USING YOUR PADS

WASHING

The best way to prevent stains from setting is to soak pads in cold water, preferably from the moment you take them off, though this is not always possible. Leave the pads soaking until you have a chance to wash them. Designate a bucket or covered container for this purpose. We've heard of watering cans being used for soaking. This is a great idea, because bloody water is an excellent fertilizer. Plants love it. Sure, the idea may seem a little strange at first, but if you think about it, it's nice to know all that blood is going to good use.

If it will be several days before you launder, switch out the soaking water for fresh every other day so funky smells don't develop. Just pour off the water onto a grateful plant, then add fresh water to the bucket. On wash day, drain the water and toss the soggy pads straight into the machine.

WHEN YOU'RE OUT AND ABOUT

Carry a clean pad in a little bag, like a pencil case. Swap it for a used pad when you need to. Don't worry about carrying a used pad around with you. We promise, packs of dogs won't follow you down the street. *No one will ever know.* Take the used pad home and drop it in the soaking bucket.

HOW MANY PADS DO YOU NEED?

Depends on you. Keep count of how many disposable pads you go through each month and which types you use. That will be a good approximation of what to make, though you might find that you use fewer cloth pads. They hold a lot of blood and don't crumple and twist with wear, like disposables do.

You'll probably add to your collection over time and experiment with designs. For instance, you might decide you want an extralong pad with a flaring back for overnight use or a set of petite panty liners made out of some fabulous fabric.

In general, panty liners are about 6 to 8 inches long, regular pads are in the 9- to 10-inch range, maxipads are around 11 inches, and overnight/postpartum pads can be as long as 13 inches.

If you're just not a pad kind of gal but are interested in reuseable protection, investigate menstrual cups, like the DivaCup or the Keeper, or try sea sponge tampons. Menstrual cups last for years, sponges for 4 to 6 months. Both are more economical and environmentally friendly than regular tampons.

Section Four

Season to Season

The projects in this section are things we do a few times a year. Some of them follow the course of the seasons, like preparing a garden bed for planting, while others yield results that we use for months, like hand-crafted soap or a stockpile of home brew. Here, ambition and rewards are directly correlated.

Making Soap the Easy Way

You might have heard that it takes a long time to make soap. Or if you've ever looked at a typical soap-making book, you might have been put off by the long list of exotic vegetable oils, expensive fragrance blends, and other daunting ingredients involved in the recipes. What if we told you that you could make soap in your countertop blender in 15 minutes, and that all you needed was a bottle of olive oil and a can of drain opener?

It really is that simple. The resulting soap is a rich, gentle castile soap suitable for both body and hair. This is kitchen alchemy at its best.

BLENDER SOAP

Most soap-crafting books assume that you want to make a lot of soap at once. Standard recipes make 20 bars or more at a time, so they have to be made in a big pot and stirred laboriously with a spoon or a stick blender. One batch of our blender soap yields about a pound of soap, which is about 3 cups in its liquid form, which yields four or five large bars. To us, this is an advantage, because it allows for experimentation and minimizes material losses if something goes wrong.

The major objection to making soap in a blender is the risk of a blender disaster occurring. Say the lid pops off during the blending process, or the base comes loose, and hot, caustic soap spills everywhere. This is a real risk, but one that can be counterbalanced by taking the proper precautions. Any type of soap making must be performed with all due caution, and that caution can be applied to blender soaps as easily as any other method. To us, the advantages of making soap in a blender—the speed and flexibility—outweigh the risks. These instructions have to be long, because there are lots of warnings and "explanifying," but once you have the steps down, you'll find you can make a batch of blender soap faster than a batch of cookies.

REGARDING LYE

Soap is created through a chemical process called saponification, in which acid (in the form of fats and oils) reacts with a strong base, an alkali of a metallic salt. The alkali used to make bar soap is sodium hydroxide. The common term for sodium hydroxide (or similar alkalis) mixed with water is *lye*. "Lye soap" has become a misleading synonym for harsh soap, but the truth is that all soap is made with lye. Saponification is a chemical transformation. Once the process is complete, there is neither fat nor lye present in a bar of soap—soap is the product of their reaction. The relative harshness or mildness of any soap is determined by both the quality of the fats used and the proportion of fat to lye.

Pure sodium hydroxide is sold in hardware stores as drain opener. This is the easiest way for a home crafter to find it. Read the label. It should say 100 percent sodium hydroxide. Drano is not sodium hydroxide. If you have trouble finding sodium hydroxide at the hardware store, order it from soaping or chemical supply companies.

REGARDING TEMPERATURES

There are two basic types of soap making: hot process, where the soap is made over heat, and cold process, where the lye and the oils are brought into a certain temperature range and combined off the heat. Blender soap is a variant of the cold-process method. In the cold-process method, saponification is guaranteed to occur if the oils and the lye are mixed when each is in the temperature range of 90° to 110°F. The temperatures of the two don't have to match; they just have to fall somewhere in that range.

Measuring the temperature of the oils and lye is considered a critical step in traditional soap making. However, the blender soap enthusiasts claim that in their method, the oils and lye do not have to be mixed at any particular temperature, that it all works, no matter what. The crazy thing about this is that they seem to be right. We've made batch after batch of soap this way without taking temperature readings, and they've all come out fine. This might be because of the small quantity of materials or the violence of the mixing. If, however, for some reason your blender soap doesn't set up, use the temperature guidelines above in your next batch, and success will be guaranteed. If you decide to make a *large* batch of soap in a pot, definitely use those temperature guidelines.

SOAP-MAKING EQUIPMENT

Use the following tools and equipment for all our soap recipes.

COUNTERTOP BLENDER WITH A GLASS MIXING JAR. Why glass? When sodium hydroxide is combined with water, a chemical reaction occurs that heats the mixture upward of 180°F. Lye is also quite caustic. Under such extreme conditions, plastic containers, unless heatproof, can become dangerously flexible. We believe it is safer all around to use glass containers. We use our everyday glass blender and Pyrex mixing cups to make soap and have found that the ingredients do not damage them or leave residue behind. Some people choose to have a complete set of equipment used solely for making soap. The call is up to you.

DIGITAL KITCHEN SCALE. Precise measurements are important.

HEATPROOF GLASS CONTAINER to mix the water and lye, like a Pyrex measuring cup.

SPOON FOR MIXING THE LYE. Lye is hard on spoons, so you may wish to use a designated spoon for this purpose. Don't use an aluminum spoon, because it will react with the lye. Plastic, rubber, and wood are all good choices, though wood will degrade. We use disposable chopsticks.

INSTANT-READ COOKING THERMOMETER. This is optional for blender soap but imperative for other kinds of soap making.

KITCHEN GLOVES.

EYE PROTECTION, like shop goggles (or ski goggles or a diving mask or a motor-cycle helmet…).

MOLD FOR THE SOAP. For your first outing, we recommend an empty quart milk carton. It's the easiest solution and makes nice square bars. Wash out the carton and open the top completely to facilitate pouring. When the soap sets, you just peel away the carton. Don't use any sort of foil-lined carton, because the lining might react with the soap. Alternatively, you could use any container with a 3-cup volume, like a small box or baking tin, lined with plastic wrap or cut-up plastic bags. Leave enough extra plastic dangling over the sides to serve as handles for unmolding the soap later. The disadvantage of plastic is that it leaves impressions of wrinkles in the soap unless you are preternaturally skillful at laying it out. If you get into soaping, you can buy specialized soap molds from craft stores or soaping suppliers or make your own wooden breakaway molds.

Genuine Castile Soap

PREPARATION: 15 min
WAITING: 4 weeks

Castile soap has become a catchall term for any soap made with vegetable oil. The original castile soap came from Spain and was made with pure olive oil. It's hard to find pure olive oil soap anymore. This is a shame, because pure olive oil soap is exceptionally mild and rich, if a little more slippery and less lathering than modern soap. We like it a lot and use it for both body and hair. It's also easy to make on a whim, because all you need is lye and olive oil.

Don't be intimidated by the length of these instructions. There's a lot of detail, but the actual process of mixing up the soap takes only a few minutes. Make sure to read the entire project first—maybe read it twice, just to be safe. After you make this recipe once or twice, you'll be a pro.

YOU'LL NEED

* 2 ounces sodium hydroxide
* 6 ounces distilled, filtered, or bottled drinking water
* 16 ounces olive oil (Not extra-virgin; lower grades work better for soap. Be sure to buy pure olive oil, though, not a "light" mix of olive oil and other vegetable oils.)
* 1 teaspoon essential oil for scent (optional)

SAFETY WARNING

Lye (sodium hydroxide) is not only
hot when mixed with water, it's
also caustic. Any splashes will burn
your skin and damage your eyes. Put
on your goggles and gloves before
you start working. You should also
wear long sleeves, long pants, and
closed-toe shoes. Secure infants or
pets somewhere for a few minutes,
so they're not underfoot.

If you spill liquid lye on your skin,
rush to the sink and flush your skin
with cold water for several minutes,
then wash with soap. If you spill
dry lye crystals on yourself, remove
them carefully. Even perspiration
can activate the crystals, so use a
hand broom or something similar
to brush them off. If you feel any
itching, which is the precursor to
burning, flush with cold water as
above. If lye gets in your eyes, flush
with cold water and go straight to
the hospital. Never apply vinegar to
a lye burn.

PUTTING IT TOGETHER

STEP 1: MEASURING THE LYE AND WATER

Place a small bowl on a digital kitchen scale, turn on the scale, and set the weight to zero. Add the sodium hydroxide crystals until the scale reads exactly 2 ounces.

Fill a heatproof glass container with 6 ounces water. You can measure the water on the scale as you did with the sodium hydroxide or use a liquid measuring cup.

STEP 2: MIXING THE LYE AND WATER

Perform this step either outdoors or near an open window. Sprinkle the lye crystals *into* the water. Do not pour water *over* the lye crystals, because it might create a volcanic effect. Stir until the crystals are dissolved. The reaction will create both heat and odor, so don't hold the container in your hands.

The mixture will be cloudy. Let it sit until it turns clear, about 5 minutes.

STEP 3: MIXING THE OIL AND LYE

While the lye is settling, weigh out the 16 ounces of oil on the scale the same way you did the sodium hydroxide.

Do a "preflight" check of your blender. Make sure the bottom ring is threaded correctly and secured tightly. Pour the oil into the blender. If you're using essential oil, measure it and set it to one side. Make sure the soap mold is ready to go.

As soon as the lye mixture turns clear, add it slowly and carefully to the oil in the blender. Be sure to wear gloves and goggles as you do this.

Put the lid on the blender. Cover the lid with a kitchen towel as an extra safety precaution. Holding the lid down with one hand, set the blender to the lowest possible speed. Start mixing.

After 10 seconds, stop mixing. Let the contents settle, then carefully remove the lid. The liquid in the blender will already be opaque. From here forward, you will alternate short bursts of blending, no more than 30 seconds at a time, with pauses to check progress. Watch for signs that the soap has reached the stage called "trace," which is the point of no return in saponification. Recognizing trace is the trickiest part of soap making. The liquid will turn creamy first, then thicken. Once it starts to thicken, it will turn solid quickly. You need to pour it into the mold before it becomes too thick to handle easily. The total time this takes varies with different sorts of soaps. For this olive oil soap, it will probably take about 5 minutes of blending.

Here's how you watch for trace: Monitor progress by dipping a spoon into the blender and dribbling a few drops off the spoon on the surface of the soap.

USING TEMPERATURE TO
DETERMINE TRACE

If you have an instant-read thermometer, you can verify the visual clues that your soap is about to reach the trace stage. Take a baseline reading of the temperature of the oil and lye when they are first mixed, then measure the temperature each time you stop to check progress. Saponification releases heat, so the temperature of the mix will rise when saponification occurs. When the temperature has increased by 2° or 3°F, the mixture is ready to mold. Any higher than that, and the soap is already setting up.

At the early stages, the surface will not hold any memory of these drizzles or any traces of the spoon's path as you stir. However, you will notice that it is getting thicker, turning from an opaque but thin liquid into something more the consistency of eggnog. When it gets to this stage, pay very close attention when you test. When you see even the *slightest* sign of the surface displaying a memory, it's reached "trace" and is ready to be molded. Add essential oil, if desired, at this point and blend it for a couple of more seconds. Don't lollygag, because time is short.

If the swirls don't reincorporate at all but sit on the surface, as they would in pudding, the soap is setting up and you need to rush to get it into a mold.

STEP 4: MOLDING THE SOAP

Pour the soap into the mold. If the soap has just reached trace, it should be pourable. If it's too thick to pour, ladle it into the mold with a spoon and tap the mold on the counter to remove air pockets. Then smooth the surface of the soap with the back of a spoon. The surface might be lumpy, but that's only a cosmetic flaw.

If you're using a milk carton as a mold, pinch the top back together after you've poured in the soap and secure it closed with a clip or tape. If you are using another kind of mold, lay a piece of cardboard or something similar over the top to keep foreign matter out while the soap sets up. Many soaping books say that soap has to be wrapped in blankets or otherwise insulated at this point. We haven't found this to be necessary. Just put the mold somewhere it won't be disturbed and leave it alone for at least 24 hours. If you touch it during this period, you might find it quite warm. This is normal.

After 24 to 48 hours, the soap should be solid. (If it doesn't turn solid within 2 days, something is wrong.) Different types of soap harden faster than others. Fast-drying soaps should be removed from the mold and cut into bars as soon as they are hard to the touch—usually in the first few days after pouring. Pure olive oil soap will tend to stay sticky to the touch longer than any other type of soap. If you touch the soap and a fingerprint remains on the surface, let it dry a day or two more before unmolding. You may not be able to unmold for a week or so. When it's ready, peel the milk carton away carefully, because the soap will still be soft enough to damage. If you used a lined mold, carefully lift the soap out of the mold using the long ends of the plastic wrap.

Using a very sharp knife or a cutting wire, slice the soap into bars. The bars can be sized any way you like. At this point, the olive oil soap will have a soft, smooth consistency, similar to American cheese. It will continue to harden as it dries.

TESTING YOUR SOAP

New soap can't be used immediately because its pH levels are too high—it will dry the skin. If you're curious about the pH of your soap, you can chart its progress as it cures and verify the pH of the final product by using our Cabbage Patch pH Indicator as described on page 163. Wet a portion of one of the bars and put a few drops of cabbage juice on it. Do the same with a similar type of soap that you know is finished. The color reaction should be similar. See Project 44 for more details.

Lay the bars somewhere to dry where they'll get plenty of air but not be in the way, like on a shelf. Cover them with a light piece of cloth to keep the dust off. If they're soft and tacky to the touch, hold off on covering them for a couple of days. This drying process is called curing. The soap is still chemically active inside and too harsh to use immediately. It will become milder over time. Let all homemade soap cure 4 weeks before using. Also, the longer you let soap dry, the harder it will become, which will make it last longer in the bath.

As the soap dries, you might notice changes in color or texture. That's normal. After you slice it, you can often see the outer edges drying first, becoming lighter and harder than the center portions. Sometimes a thin white coating will appear on the surface of the bars, a coating thin enough to remove with a fingernail. That's called "ash" and is a harmless cosmetic flaw. If you molded the soap a little late and had to spread it into the mold with a spoon, it will likely crack on the surface. This is also a cosmetic flaw. Just slice off the unattractive bits. A vegetable peeler is a good tool for trimming flaws. Signs of genuine soap failure include refusal to set up or pockets of liquids or solids in the soap. Throw away any batches like this and try again.

STEP 5: CLEANING UP

Wear gloves while cleaning your equipment. Raw soap isn't nearly as caustic as pure lye, but it's still harsh, and you might run into stray lye crystals. Using a rubber spatula or a paper towel, scrape as much of the raw soap out of your blender as you can and put it in the garbage, not down the sink. Then wash all of your utensils and containers in soap and hot water. If you happen to spill your lye crystals, sweep them up thoroughly with a hand broom and dustpan. The crystals activate when exposed to water, so be careful as you wipe up any remaining residue.

ADDITIONS AND VARIATIONS

As you've seen, soap making is a hot, caustic process. Anything you add to the soap is subjected to these brutal conditions: Dried flower petals are stripped of their color, and essential oils lose much of their fragrance, which is why you have to use a whole teaspoon of essential oil in this recipe. Because we are cheap, we tend to leave our bath soap unscented, both because of the quantity of essential oil necessary for scenting, and the fact that essential oil scents fade over time anyway. If you want to make fancy soap with lasting perfumes, colors, and/or colorful bits of dried flowers, you'll need to use a secondary process called *rebatching* or *hand milling*, where finished soap is melted down, additions stirred in, and the soap remolded. Look up these terms in soap manuals. However, exfoliating ingredients are sturdy enough to stand the heat. If you wish, you can stir in 1 or 2 ounces of finely ground oatmeal to your soap when it reaches trace.

Almost Castile Soap

This particular combination of olive, coconut, and palm oils is a classic formula for a good all-purpose bath bar that cleans well, moisturizes, sets up hard, and makes lots of lather. It's mild, but it's not quite as gentle as our Genuine Castile Soap.

Coconut oil and palm oil can be found in ethnic markets and health food stores. (Palm oil is sold as vegan shortening in health food stores.) Both oils are often less expensive when purchased through soap-making supply companies.

YOU'LL NEED

* 7 ounces olive oil (Not extra-virgin; lower grades work better for soap.)
* 5 ounces coconut oil
* 4 ounces palm oil
* 2.3 ounces sodium hydroxide
* 6 ounces distilled, filtered, or bottled drinking water
* 1 teaspoon essential oil for scent (optional)

PUTTING IT TOGETHER

Measure and weigh all three oils on a zeroed scale. Then heat the oils together to melt the palm and coconut oil into the olive oil. The safest way to do this is over a water bath, but you can use a saucepan if you keep the temperature low and are careful not to scorch the oil. Overcooked oil will make your soap smell like the bottom of a deep fryer. Take the blended oils off the heat.

Proceed to measure and mix the sodium hydroxide with water, as described in steps 1 and 2 of the Genuine Castile Soap recipe. Then follow Genuine Castile Soap steps 3 through 5.

Peppermint-Rosemary Shampoo Bar

The common denominator in all shampoo bar recipes is castor oil, a rich, viscous oil that lends excellent moisturizing and lathering qualities to soap. Castor oil can be found at health food stores or ordered online. This simple recipe makes a bar that will clean your hair without stripping its natural oils, eliminating the need for conditioner. We've added a generous quantity of rosemary and peppermint essential oil, scents guaranteed to wake up sleepyheads, but of course you could scent this soap any way you want, or not at all.

YOU'LL NEED

* 6 ounces olive oil (Not extra-virgin; lower grades work better for soap.)
* 5 ounces coconut oil
* 5 ounces castor oil

* **2.2 ounces sodium hydroxide**
* **6 ounces distilled, filtered, or bottled drinking water**
* **1 teaspoon rosemary essential oil**
* **½ teaspoon peppermint essential oil**

PUTTING IT TOGETHER

Weigh the oils on a zeroed scale and heat them together over a water bath until the coconut oil melts. You could heat them in a saucepan, but be careful not to scorch the oils. After the coconut oil melts, measure and mix the sodium hydroxide and water as described in steps 1 and 2 of the Genuine Castile Soap recipe, then combine the sodium hydroxide and oils in the blender as described in step 3.

This recipe reaches "trace" rapidly. Do the initial 10-second mix in the blender, then take a close look for any signs of thickening. Your soap could reach trace that quickly! If not, it will probably come together in a couple of minutes. Make sure your essential oils are premeasured and ready to add.

Then follow steps 4 and 5 of the Genuine Castile Soap recipe.

Coconut Laundry Soap

PREPARATION: 20 min
WAITING: 4 weeks

Soap used for laundry is formulated differently than body soap. It should not contain any excess oils that will build up on fabric. All-lard soap is a traditional favorite for laundry. This is a vegetarian alternative. Coconut oil makes a hard bar of soap with good cleaning and lathering properties, but it is drying to the skin when used alone, without other oils to buffer it. This recipe is made with 100 percent coconut oil and a stout percentage of lye. The resulting soap is hard to the point of being crumbly and too drying for the skin, but just the ticket for cleaning.

Coconut oil is sold in health food stores, ethnic markets, and some supermarkets as a cooking oil, often in high-grade, virgin form. It's a bit of a waste to use such a nice oil for soap. You can buy lower-grade coconut oil in bulk less expensively from soap-making and herbal supply companies. See Project 25 to learn how to use soap in the laundry.

YOU'LL NEED

* **16 ounces coconut oil**
* **2.8 ounces sodium hydroxide**
* **6 ounces distilled, filtered, or bottled drinking water**

PUTTING IT TOGETHER

Follow the instructions for Genuine Castile Soap, with the following exceptions:

Scoop the coconut oil on a scale to measure it, then melt it into liquid form. The safest way to do this is over a water bath, but you can melt it in a saucepan if you keep the temperature low and are careful not to scorch it.

Coconut oil reaches trace quickly. In the blender, it takes about 1½ minutes of total mixing time. It also hardens fast in the mold. Unmold the soap and cut it into bars within 24 hours of pouring. Otherwise, it will be difficult to cut. If you have trouble cutting it neatly, that won't matter much—laundry soap is ultimately grated anyway.

MAKING YOUR OWN SOAP RECIPES

You can experiment with any oil or fat to make your own custom soaps. Jojoba oil, avocado oil, and wheat germ oil, to name a few, make luxurious moisturizing bars. However, soap making isn't easy to improvise. There's some pretty advanced chemistry behind it. Different oils give different characteristics to soap, and each oil requires different amounts of lye to saponify properly. For this same reason, you should never simply double or halve a soap recipe. Miscalculations can result in soap that is too harsh or in soap that never sets up. Fortunately, there are all sorts of free online soap calculators. Just search "soap calculator" or "lye calculator." Enter the kinds of oil you want to use, and the amounts you want to use, and the calculator will generate the amount of lye and water necessary for the recipe.

Homemade Liquid Soap

Genuine liquid soap, the thick, rich sort, requires long cooking over very low heat in a large slow cooker. It also requires potassium hydroxide instead of sodium hydroxide, and potassium hydroxide cannot be found in stores but must be special ordered from chemical or soaping supply companies. It is true that you can extract potassium hydroxide from wood ash, as seen in Project 43, Making Soap the Hard Way, but it is difficult to adapt a standardized liquid soap recipe to the vagaries of homemade lye. For these reasons, we've not tackled liquid soap ourselves yet, so are not including a recipe for it in this book. If you want to try making liquid soap, most soapmaking manuals will include at least one recipe.

If you're hankering after the tidiness of pumped hand soap, it's easy to make watered-down liquid castile soap (like Dr. Bronner's) work for that purpose—you just need to use a foaming pump. They can be bought new or easily reused. See, these newfangled foam pumps require the soap inside to be highly diluted in order to function properly. They're ideal for the purpose. Just fill one with diluted liquid castile soap or even throw some chips of bar soap in the container and fill the rest of it up with water. The soap chips will dissolve into a dilute solution ideal for making foam. Of course, you can use diluted soap in nonfoaming pumps too, it's just a little runny.

43›

Making Soap the Hard Way

What if you couldn't get nice vegetable oils to make soap? What if you had no access to sodium hydroxide? We like to mull over hypothetical apocalyptic scenarios like this, because it leads to interesting discoveries.

As you learned in the last project, soap is made with fat and lye. These days, vegetable oils are inexpensive and widely available, but if that weren't the case, the oils would be hard to make at home because of the sheer volume of plant matter necessary to extract oil in quantity. It is far easier to collect fat from animal sources. Homemade soap was once made entirely with animal fat, either tallow from cows and deer or lard from pigs. Better soap was made with high-grade fats, but workable soap could be made with scraps and cooking fats saved from the kitchen. Lye was made by filtering water through wood ashes. Ashes from the stove and fireplace were put aside for this purpose. Wood ash lye (potassium hydroxide) does not make hard soap. It makes a sort of soap paste, which years ago was kept in crocks and scooped up for washing.

Having made this soap, we'd say that we're mighty grateful for blenders, olive oil, and sodium hydroxide in a jar. But we also like knowing that we *can* make soap from absolute scratch, if we have to.

Making truly homemade soap is a three-part process:

1. Collecting wood ash and making lye
2. Collecting fat and rendering it
3. Combining the fat and lye over heat to make soap

Part 1: Making Lye

PREPARATION: 1 hour
WAITING: 24 hours

Folks used to save all their ashes in a wooden barrel with a drain built into the bottom or in a trough-shaped ash hopper. The lye barrel or hopper was left open to the rain, and the rainwater leached through the ashes and became lye, which dripped out into a small receptacle bucket. The weak lye in that bucket was collected for general household cleaning. Clothes were washed in lye water, too, as opposed to soap and water, in a process called bucking. To make soap, people needed to make a stronger lye solution. To do this, they either passed the weak lye through ash again and again, or they boiled it down until the solution became strong enough to float an egg. Egg floating sounds bizarre, but it is a primitive test to determine, in chemistry terms, the relative density or specific gravity of the solution.

While you could make your own leaching barrel by packing a 5-gallon plastic bucket with ashes, we're going to share a faster method with you.

YOU'LL NEED

* 1 gallon (16 cups) white ash*
* Old pillowcase
* 3- or 5-gallon bucket
* 2 gallons rainwater, filtered water, or distilled water, brought to a boil
* Protective gear: kitchen gloves, shop glasses or goggles, long sleeves
* Cabbage Patch pH Indicator (page 163)
* 1 fresh egg
* Stainless steel or enamel soup pot (It must not be aluminum, because it will react with the lye and discolor. Lye will not harm stainless steel or enamel, though, so it's okay to use your usual cookware.)

*Note on ash: Ash for lye making must always be the white, feathery ash that comes from a hot fire. Charcoal will interfere with the lye's effectiveness, so use a colander to sift out black charcoal chunks. The best wood ash lye is made with burnt hardwood (oak, hickory, maple, etc.) or fruitwood (apple, cherry, etc.). Don't use softwood, like pine, because it is too resinous. The ash of dried seaweed, bracken fern, and even palm fronds can be used as well.

PUTTING IT TOGETHER

SOAK THE ASH

Scoop the 16 cups of ash into the pillowcase and knot the top. Put the pillowcase in the bucket and pour the 2 gallons of boiling water over it. You don't have to add the water all at once—you can add it in kettle-size increments as you heat it. Put the bucket somewhere safe, out of the way of children and pets. Let it sit overnight. Anytime you think of it, put on a pair of kitchen gloves and slosh the pillowcase up and down a few times, like a tea bag. Be careful not to splash your skin as you do this.

The next day, don gloves and goggles and raise the pillowcase out of the water. Let the first rush of water drain out, then contrive some way to suspend the pillowcase over the bucket to finish draining. You want to collect every last drop of that ashy goodness, so leave the ashes suspended until they stop dripping entirely—several hours or overnight.

TEST THE LYE

When it's all drained, you'll probably have a gallon of lye, and this lye will probably need to be cooked down to reach soap-making strength. Test it two ways.

First, we recommend you do a preliminary test with our Cabbage Patch pH Indicator, just to make sure you're on the right track. The lye should turn the indicator yellow or green, meaning it's highly alkaline. If the reaction is blue to blue green, that's not a good sign. Those colors indicate a lower pH, meaning the

SAFETY NOTE

At this point, the solution is not caustic enough to burn your skin outright. It's milder than the sodium hydroxide solution you mix up for regular soap. Still, it will dry your skin severely, and you definitely don't want to get it in your eyes, so be sure to wear gloves and goggles. Later, when the solution is reduced to full strength, be extra careful.

solution is not alkaline enough to make good lye. Be sure you are using ash from the right kind of wood and that you haven't mixed lots of charcoal in with it. It's unlikely that this low-pH lye will ever be strong enough to make soap, even after it's boiled down. We've been there and done that. It might be best to try again with a new batch of ash.

If the liquid tests yellow or green, move on to the egg test. If the lye solution is dense enough to float an egg, this means it's strong enough to make soap. Start with a fresh, raw egg. (It must be fresh, because rotten eggs float in water. If you're not sure how old your egg is, put it in a bowl of water. It should sink to the bottom.) Then lower the egg into the lye water—wear gloves when doing this. If it sinks to the bottom, the lye is too weak and must be cooked to reduce the water content. If the egg floats high enough that a little circle of shell the size of a nickel or quarter breaks the surface of the water, then it's just about perfect. Some people will also accept the lye if the egg floats just below the surface but does not quite break it. If the egg floats high on the water, the lye is too strong and must be watered down with rainwater until the egg floats correctly.

Set the egg aside for subsequent rounds of testing. Don't eat this egg! It is a sacrifice to the cause.

REDUCE THE LYE

Most likely, the egg will sink at this stage and you'll have to cook down the lye. We've found the quantity of lye usually needs to be reduced by half. Pour the lye into a large stainless steel or enamel pot and heat it to a steady simmer. Take note of the water level early on so you can gauge how much water has cooked off. At any point, transfer a couple of cups of lye into a bowl and let it cool (so it doesn't cook the egg) and test again. Test, cook, and retest until the egg floats. You'll find it takes surprisingly large amounts of water and ash to make small quantities of soap-worthy lye. This project will probably yield 1 or 2 quarts.

If you notice ash sediment in the finished lye, strain it through a finely woven piece of cloth, like a dishtowel or a coffee filter. Store the lye in a lidded glass jar until ready to use.

PREPARATION: 2 hours

Part 2: Rendering Fat

Both tallow and lard are used in soap making. Lard is pure pork fat. Tallow comes from the fat of any grazing animal, like cows, sheep, or deer. Of the two fats, lard makes the better soap, because of its cleaning abilities and its gentleness on skin, but both types of fat are used for soap, alone or in combination with other fats and oils. Lard is also a high-quality cooking fat, which is enjoying a renaissance after years of undeserved scorn. You might want to render lard just to have it on hand in the kitchen. Tallow can be used to make candles as well as soap.

YOU'LL NEED

* 3–5 pounds animal fat
* Big, heavy-bottom pot
* ½ cup water
* Colander or sieve lined with cheesecloth

PUTTING IT TOGETHER

The best days to render fat are mild days when you can open all the windows in your kitchen, because this is a stinky process. If you have a range fan over your stove, turn it on when you start cooking.

Chop the fat into 1- to 2-inch chunks to facilitate melting. If you can grind it, things will go much faster. As you cut the fat, trim away as much meat and tissue as practicable. The rest will be separated out later. The processes of melting lard and tallow are a little different, so the directions branch off here.

SOURCES OF ANIMAL FAT

In an apocalyptic scenario, the fat would come from animals you've hunted and butchered yourself. But while civilization holds, you can get fat from a butcher. Butchers are few and far between these days, but if you have a meat seller you deal with regularly, such as someone you know from your local farmers' market, he or she will be able to provide fat for you if you give a little advance notice. It shouldn't cost much. If you're using pork fat, use fatback, not the fine fat from around the kidneys that is used to make leaf lard for pastry cooking. Such high-grade fat is wasted in soap. Some supermarkets sell packaged ground suet, which you can use to make tallow. You can also buy premade lard at the supermarket, near the shortening. However, it's usually hydrogenated and full of preservatives.

TO MAKE LARD

Put the pork fat in a heavy-bottom pot. Add the water. The water's only purpose is to protect the fat from burning until it begins to melt, so you need very little. Cook over low heat, letting the fat melt slowly and the water evaporate. Stir occasionally to keep the fat from sticking to the bottom of the pot. How long this process takes will depend on how much fat you have and how finely it is chopped. Count on about an hour. Keep the heat as low as possible so you don't burn the fat. It should barely bubble.

When the fat chunks have completely dissolved into liquid, it's time to strain the fat. Put a large bowl in the sink and rest a cheesecloth-lined colander over it. Working very carefully (hot fat = ouch!), pour the hot lard through the colander and into the bowl. The cheesecloth will catch all the little fried meat bits. These are called cracklings, and they can be eaten as a snack.

The strained lard should be clean enough to use at this stage, meaning it looks like fat and nothing but fat—you should see no crumbs, chunks, or discoloring. If it looks good, pour it into clean containers for storage.

If it seems a little dirty, you can "wash" it. While the lard is still warm, stir in about a cup of water for every pound of fat and put the bowl in the refrigerator overnight. The clean fat will rise to the top, leaving impurities behind in the water. The next day, just lift the disk of fat off the surface of the wash water. Use a knife to scrape off any gelatin or impurities that might be clinging to the back side of the disk, then pack it into a clean, covered container.

Lard will keep in the refrigerator for about a month. Freeze it for longer storage.

TO RENDER TALLOW

Put the chopped fat in a heavy-bottom pot. Cover it with an equal amount of water (e.g., 1 quart of water per 1 quart of fat scraps). Bring it to a low, steady simmer. Skim off any foam or blood that rises to the surface. Watch for all of the fat to liquefy and the meat bits to separate out and become free floating. This should take about an hour.

When the fat chunks have melted into the water, so the only solids you see are bits of gristle, put a large bowl in the sink and rest a cheesecloth-lined colander over it. Pour the hot tallow/water mix through the colander and into the bowl. The cheesecloth will catch all the little meat bits. Unlike lard cracklings, these are not considered a tasty treat for humans, but birds like them.

Let the tallow/water mix cool to room temperature in the bowl, then refrigerate the bowl overnight. The tallow will harden into a disk of solid white fat, leaving beneath it a layer of nasty water and gelatin. The next day, carefully pry the disk of solidified tallow or lard out of the dirty water. Turn it over and check its underside. If there's gelatin or anything else clinging to it, scrape that off with a knife. Cut the fat into pieces and transfer to covered containers.

Store tallow in the fridge, where it will keep for about a month. Freeze for longer storage.

PREPARATION: 2–3 hours

Part 3: Making Soap

Soap made with wood ash lye (potassium hydroxide) is always soft soap, its texture ranging from jelly to paste, its color from cream to dark caramel. It may retain a faint animal scent. In some circumstances, it will dry into something firm enough to cut into bars, but it won't have the consistency or staying power of real bar soap. In the old days, white, sweet-smelling bars of hard soap were a store-bought luxury.

For the purposes of demonstration, the following recipe makes only a couple of cups of soap. Your ancestors probably made soap in quantity once a year, because between making the strong lye, rendering the fat, and cooking the soap, the whole venture was a major undertaking. You're welcome to increase the size of this recipe, but we suspect that until the zombies come, you'll prefer making soap in a blender. If you would like to increase the recipe, just remember to always use twice as much fat by liquid volume as lye water.

ERIK SAYS... If you ask me, they didn't make the soap very often because cooking it makes your house smell like a rendering plant. When the zombies come, I'll just stay dirty, thanks, and hope my BO drives them off.

YOU'LL NEED

* 2 cups clean, rendered fat (any sort)
* Saucepan (for heating the fat)
* 1 cup lye water
* Heavy-bottom, nonreactive pot with a minimum capacity of 4 quarts
* Wooden spoon, wooden stir stick, or silicon spatula for stirring

PUTTING IT TOGETHER

Start by melting the fat over low heat in the saucepan. Melt it very gently, so it doesn't scorch. Meanwhile, heat the lye water in the larger, nonreactive pot, until it just simmers. Keep the heat as low as possible.

Ladle the liquid fat into the hot lye water bit by bit, stirring in between additions. The lye will turn creamy with the addition of the fat. You'd imagine that it would keep thickening from that point, turning creamier and thicker. What it actually does is more distressing: The creaminess breaks, and you'll end up with a transparent liquid layer on the bottom and an oily foam on top. Cook this unlikely looking brew over the lowest heat possible for at least 2 hours. If you're making a larger quantity, the cooking time will be at least 3 hours.

You don't have to stir constantly, but you should keep an eye on it. Stirring will cause the mix to foam up. You might have to take the pot off the heat for a moment if it foams too violently and looks ready to overflow. The texture of the foam will range from cappuccino fluff to pond scum. Just keep stirring and cooking.

At some point in the second hour, the transformation will occur. First, you'll probably notice a thick, soaplike substance clinging to the neck of your spoon or the sides of the pot. Start stirring steadily. The liquid in the pot will thicken rapidly, acquiring a texture like grits or mashed potatoes. Beat it thoroughly to make the texture as homogenous as possible.

Transfer the soap to a bowl, crock, or whatever storage container you prefer. Because the soap is cooked for so long, the saponification process is completed in the pot. You can use the soap immediately.

SAFETY NOTE

Since you're working with lye, you should wear gloves and eye protection, at least until the lye is incorporated with the fat.

44

Cabbage Patch pH Indicator

It's useful to be able to test the pH of homemade soap, cleaning solutions, and beauty products. Sure, you can buy pH testing strips, but you can get a general idea of the pH of any substance using nothing but a red cabbage. You may have a hazy memory of doing this when you were in school.

All you need are the outer leaves of a red cabbage—the leaves that you'd normally discard before cooking. Save the rest of the cabbage for dinner or a batch of sauerkraut.

YOU'LL NEED

* ½–1 cup chopped red cabbage (Exact proportions are not critical.)
* Distilled, filtered, or bottled water

PUTTING IT TOGETHER

Put the cabbage in a saucepan and cover it with water. Bring to a simmer and cook over low heat for about 10 minutes to extract the pigments from the leaves. The water will turn deep purple. Pour off the water into a jar. It will keep in the fridge for a couple of weeks. You'll know it's gone off when it turns cloudy and loses color.

This liquid is your indicator. Its pH is about 7, which is neutral. While this test will not give you a specific pH number, it will help you compare like to like and give a general sense of the nature of whatever you're testing.

TO ESTABLISH A BASE-ACID RANGE

Pour a spoonful of indicator in a small, clear glass. Choose a substance you know to be acidic, like lemon juice or vinegar. Add it to the glass until the cabbage juice turns color. The color should shift toward red, depending on the acidity of the substance you're testing. Hold the glass up to the light to see the color shift better.

Now find a substance you know is base (alkaline). Washing soda is alkaline, and lye would be one of the strongest bases found around the house. Stir in washing soda or a few grains of lye to the liquid. Handle lye carefully! Washing soda should turn the indicator acid green, while lye should produce yellow. A mild base, like liquid laundry detergent, would turn it blue.

Red is acid, yellow is base, and purple is neutral. All reactions happen along the spectrum of red to magenta for acids, and from blue to green to yellow for bases. Knowing this, compare your homemade solutions with store-bought equivalents. Test shampoo, laundry soap, lotion. Most soaps test in the blue range. Milder soaps lean toward purple; harsher soaps lean toward blue green.

TO TEST HOMEMADE BAR SOAP TO SEE IF IT HAS CURED ENOUGH

Wet a portion of the soap with water and rub it with your finger to liquefy a small circle. Drip the indicator on it. It will turn color on contact. Compare this reaction to one on soap that you know is fully cured. When your homemade soap is ready to use, the color reaction should be similar to the control bar—probably blue. If the color leans toward yellow, turning turquoise or spring green, you'll know that its pH is still high and it needs to cure for a couple more weeks.

45·

How to Slaughter a Chicken

PREPARATION: 1 hour

At this peculiar junction of place and time, few of us know where our food comes from, and fewer still have any hand in its production. Food comes from the store. It appears on the shelves by magic, picked, washed, and wrapped, devoid of any context. If we are what we eat, what we are is dislocated. Eating should be highly temporal, regional, specific, intimate, and reverential. Anyone who has raised his or her own food, even just a little, knows its true value. Food is not a unit of exchange. It is life itself.

All of our food production systems need reform, but the way we raise and slaughter animals on the industrial scale is particularly troubling. If you eat meat, you know how difficult is to be a conscientious carnivore. It's difficult to have any assurance that the animal you consume for dinner was treated with kindness and respect unless you know a farmer personally or raise animals yourself. Among the many urbanites who are keeping backyard chickens for eggs, there are people who will quietly cull a chicken for dinner every now and again. In doing so, they take full responsibility for the life of that animal, and its death, and so know the value of what is on their plates.

For those of us who are new to keeping chickens, the line between pet and livestock can be fuzzy. We start out thinking we'll keep hens for eggs only, never intending to slaughter one, but we might come face to face with the choice anyway. Hens lay fewer and fewer eggs as they age. What do you do if you'd like to bring in a few young hens but there's no more room in the coop? Or say one of your new chicks, which you believed were all female, grows up to be a rooster? Or what if one of the hens in your flock develops cannibalistic tendencies and is becoming a danger to the other hens? Perhaps you'll be able to pawn off your unwanted chickens on some kind-hearted soul. If not, and if you eat meat, it might be time to make a clear distinction between livestock and pet.

We put this project in the book to give you a solid overview of what's involved in slaughtering a chicken. However, we are not fans of what we call dilettante slaughtering. The animal shouldn't suffer because of your ineptitude. If you plan to raise chickens for meat, we encourage you to find someone else who slaughters poultry regularly and apprentice with that person. Visit on culling day and lend a hand. Watch and learn. Read up on chicken anatomy, paying particular attention to the placement of the veins in the neck, the location

of the crop, and the arrangement of the internal organs. Have your mentor over as backup the first time you go solo. If you don't plan to make a practice of it, find someone experienced who will do it for you, quickly and competently.

BEFORE YOU START

Identify a work place outdoors. You'll need some sort of sturdy overhead support for the bird to hang from—this might be a tree branch, a swing set, a laundry line, or something you rig up for the occasion. It's best to work in the shade and to have easy access to a hose or tap.

Twelve to 24 hours before you intend to harvest, withhold food from the bird you've chosen so it will have time to clear out its crop and bowels. Waste matter in the bird can contaminate the flesh during evisceration.

If you're new to this, you may not want to eat immediately before the slaughter, either. The sights and smells are a little intense. You should anticipate that you may not have a big appetite that night and—unless you're made of stronger stuff than we are—you definitely won't feel like eating chicken.

YOU'LL NEED

LENGTH OF ROPE OR A KILLING CONE. The rope should be affixed to an overhead support and finished with a slipknot, the length of the rope calculated to the height at which you want the chicken to hang. The chicken will hang by its feet. Some people prefer to work sitting down, others standing up. An alternative to hanging is to use a killing cone, an open-ended metal cone fastened to a wall. The chicken is placed in the cone, head down, so its head and neck pokes out the bottom. The advantage of the cone is that it restrains flapping. The disadvantage is that blood will end up on the wall. The slaughtering method is the same. Killing cones can be purchased from poultry suppliers.

EYE PROTECTION. This is necessary only if you're hanging the bird instead of using a killing cone. You don't want to get poked in the eye by the tip of a flapping wing. Ordinary glasses are fine.

APRON

PLASTIC WASTEBASKET OR BUCKET to catch the blood and later to use for feathers and viscera.

VERY SHARP SCALPEL, OR 2 FRESH RAZOR BLADES (one for slaughtering, another for butchering) per bird.

LARGE POT for scalding, big enough to submerge an entire bird, filled with water heated to 130° to 150°F. It's most convenient to have this set up outside on a portable gas burner, but it could be done indoors on the stovetop.

WHAT ABOUT GLOVES?

Note that we don't include gloves on our list of tools you'll need. It's hard to do this work in gloves, though you could use them if you like. Your bare hands should be very clean and washed frequently as you go. Use hand sanitizer between steps, if you'd like.

STURDY WORK SURFACE for butchering, covered with a clean plastic tarp or butcher paper or similar. A waist-high table is most comfortable. The table need not be wide if you're only doing one bird at a time.

CLEAVER to remove the head.

CHEST FILLED WITH ICE WATER to hold finished birds if you're doing more than one at a time.

SMALL COVERED BOWL if you want to save organs.

BUCKET OF CLEAN WATER so you can rinse off your hands.

PUTTING IT TOGETHER

It's not easy to kill. It shouldn't be. It's okay to be sad, but for the sake of the bird, you need to be clearheaded and steady. If you're not, postpone. Remind yourself that this killing is the kindest killing a chicken can have, and that all of those other factory-raised chickens you've eaten throughout your life lived poorly and died brutally. By doing this, you are taking responsibility for your food, accepting that dinner involves sacrifice, and committing to seeing this bird to its end in the most dignified and humane way possible.

Acknowledge your feelings and make your apologies, but once you begin, you must be businesslike.

CATCHING THE BIRD

This is no time to panic the bird. You want it as calm as possible. So you must be calm yourself when you go to collect it, and through speed or guile you need to capture it quickly and quietly. Hold it in your arms, stroking the breast, neck, and beak to calm it. If you cradle it like a baby and tilt the head down, it will calm even more.

HANGING THE BIRD

Take the bird by the legs, gripping it with one hand just above the feet, and turn it upside down. If it's calm, it will accept this with remarkable ease and hang quietly with its wings slightly spread. Being upside down has a tranquilizing effect on chickens.

Bind the feet with the hanging rope, using a simple slipknot. The bird should now be hanging upside down from your overhead support. Again, the chicken should be calm at this point. If it's a little agitated it might flap a bit, but not as much as you'd expect, and it should quiet down quickly. In the very unlikely event the bird has a total freak-out, release it and try another day. It's imperative that both of you remain calm, for many reasons.

Position the wastebasket beneath the bird to catch the blood.

THE KILLING CUTS

At this point, some people take off the bird's head with sharp shears. The method we describe is not as direct. In it, the bird's jugular veins are cut neatly and quickly. It takes more skill and requires your continued presence with the bird as it dies. When you do it, you'll understand why the proverbial chopping block is more appealing to us humans: It's over fast, so it's easier on us. But the method we were taught, and we're sharing with you, kills the bird with the least pain if done correctly.

Gently stretch out the bird's neck and brush its throat feathers downward so you can see the bare skin on the neck. You need to identify the two jugular veins that run on either side of the throat. They are usually visible as blue lines beneath the skin. They may be harder to see in older, fatter birds. Feel for the pulse with your fingers.

You are going to make two cuts, opening the arteries on either side of the neck. Stretch the chicken's head downward while you do this, to keep it still and to expose the veins. You must cut both veins, not one, or the bird will die slowly. You should make the cuts deep and sure, one immediately after the other. Once you cut off blood circulation to the head, the bird will be brain-dead. So locate those veins, and when you act, act decisively.

The scalpel or razor will part the flesh with frightening ease. The bird will not struggle against you at this point. Your only worry is positioning the cut. The incision should be about an inch long and deep enough to sever the vein. A fast, copious gush of blood over your hand, or sometimes an arterial squirt, will let you know you've hit a major vein. If you do both sides successfully, you can take a big sigh of relief.

If there's only a little, slow-pooling blood in the wake of your cut, you've probably missed the jugular. Don't panic. Take a breath and deepen the cut. Don't be afraid to get in there with your fingers and find the vein if you have to. Once this begins, it needs to end fast, for the chicken's sake.

As the chicken bleeds out, it will usually go through two rounds of physical struggle, which shows as wing flapping. The first round comes soon after the cuts, and the second signals death. Remember, you've cut off the blood supply to the brain, which means the bird is brain-dead at this point and these struggles are the final throes of the nervous system. Still, out of respect for the bird, you should sit with it as it dies, holding its head so that it doesn't move much when it flaps. This also keeps the cuts open and the blood flowing freely.

Let the chicken continue to hang and bleed for about 5 minutes after it dies. Five minutes is all it takes to drain the blood from the body. There's not as much in there as you might expect.

SCALDING

Scalding loosens the feathers to make plucking easier. Immediately after the bleeding is complete, untie the bird and grasp it by its feet. Using the feet as a handle of sorts, dunk the bird upside down in the scalding pot. The temperature should be at least 130°F. This temperature is suitable for young, tender chickens. For older birds, the temperature should be 150°F. The difference is cosmetic. The higher temperature results in looser skin but is necessary to loosen the feathers of older birds. Keep the bird under water for 60 seconds.

PLUCKING

Take the carcass to the work surface. Enjoy the distinctive odor of scalded chicken. Move the wastebasket from beneath the bleeding site and position it by your work surface to catch feathers and guts.

Begin plucking. Don't be afraid to be forceful. Start with the wings, because they are the hardest part and best done when the body is fresh out of the hot water. Yank out the wing feathers. It takes considerable force. Pull them straight out, in the direction of growth. Use pliers if you have to. Once that's done, the rest is easier. Pull out the smaller feathers on the breast and back using raking motions of your hand, pulling against the grain of the feathers. Grab as many feathers as you can at once and rip them out. Some force is necessary here, as well. Toss the feathers in the collection bin, but they'll inevitably end up everywhere.

The tiniest feathers are called pin feathers, and they can be hard to remove. Sometimes its easier to squeeze them out than to pluck them. You might want to do as much plucking as you can quickly do outdoors, then do the fine work inside later, in the sink and under running water.

As you pluck, the chicken begins to take on the familiar appearance of a grocery store chicken, and that is something of a comfort. It's difficult for the mind to process the changes the bird undergoes in a very short time. It goes from being a beautiful, bright-eyed creature to a bloody, dangling corpse (though still magnificent, in a way) to an anonymous piece of flesh—a plucked chicken.

At some point, you need to chop off the head. Some people do it before plucking, some after. It's best to pluck while the bird is hot out of the water, so unless you can do this part fast, wait until you're done plucking. Just stretch out the neck and bring your cleaver down with considerable force, aiming right above the shoulders.

The tail stub also has to come off. It doesn't have to be chopped off with the cleaver. Instead, tease it off with the scalpel. You might notice the yellow oil gland that sits at the base of the tail. This should come off along with the tail.

A Esophagus
B Trachea
C Crop
D Heart
E Gall Bladder
F Spleen
G Liver
H Gizzard
I Small Intestine

J Large Intestine
K Cloaca
L Oviduct
M Kidney
N Ovary
O Ceca
P Lungs

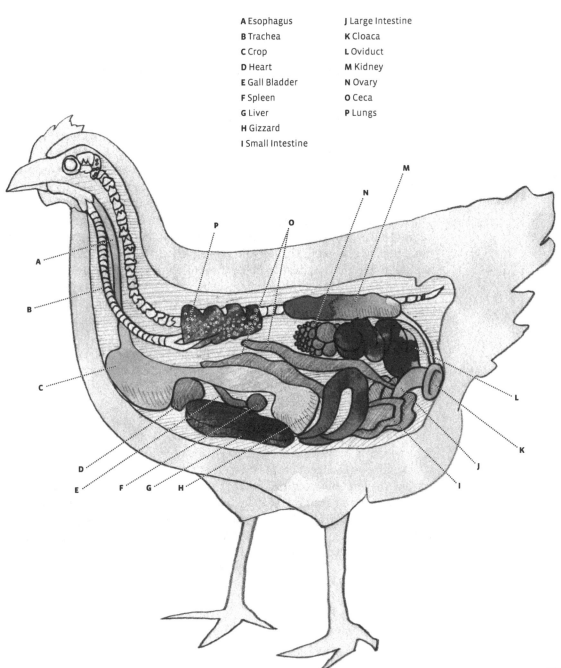

GUTTING THE CHICKEN

Turn the chicken on its back and face the hind end toward you. Using the scalpel or razor blade, cut a circle around the chicken's cloaca, or vent, so you can remove it like a plug. Attached to the back of the cloaca is a ropelike tube, which looks like a colon, but which is actually the bird's intestinal, urinary, and reproductive tract combined. There may be poop in there, especially if the bird did not fast, and that will leak out as you manipulate the organs. You don't want any waste spilling into the body cavity, so handle with care. Tug on the cloaca. All of the intestines attached to it will slither out in a group. This is definitely the stinky part of this business. Use your scalpel to cut away any clingy membranes or connective tissue. Push all that into the wastebasket.

After this, you will be working blind with your hand far up the chicken. You might want to enlarge the first hole you cut to accommodate your hand. Feel around—gently—and find the liver, gizzard, heart, and lungs. Pull them out as best you can, again using your blade to cut connective tissue. The liver will come out with the green bile sac attached. Don't puncture that green sac. You can't eat any flesh that bile spills on, so if you want to eat the liver, cut the bile sac away carefully. The gizzard is the largest organ. It should be cut in half and cleaned out if you plan to eat it. The lungs are the most difficult to remove. They sort of adhere to the ribs. You have to fiddle them off with your fingers. Bits that you miss can be rinsed away later. When you're moving your hand inside the carcass, don't be surprised if you force air through the larynx and inadvertently cause the carcass to give a sorry crow. Put any organs you wish to save in a covered container and put it in the cooler.

Turn the bird around so you are facing the neck end. Using your scalpel, cut out the neck muscle and the remains of the larynx and esophagus. At this point the main body cavity should be clean.

The last thing to do is find the crop. This is the grit-filled sac that chickens use to help digest their grain. It is located high on the breast, near the base of the neck. If the chicken hasn't fasted, it might be swollen, full of grain. If it's empty, it's just a little tissue that needs to be cut away.

Finally, you will cut off the lower legs, the feet, and the scaled portion of the leg. The joint between this part of the leg and the drumstick is where feather meets scale. Using the scalpel, delicately carve your way around that joint. You don't have to saw through the leg. All you have to do is pare away the cartilage until the lower leg works free. You'll recognize the rounded end joint of the drumstick when you see it.

You're almost done!

WASHING

Take the bird inside, wash your hands well, and give the carcass a thorough rinsing in the sink, inside and out. Pluck out the remaining pin feathers and rinse again.

Wrap the bird well and put it in the fridge or freezer—or brine it.

BRINING

Brining makes fowl taste good and can help tenderize a bird that is a little past its prime. It takes a day to brine a bird, which is conveniently about how long it may take you to recover from butchering the bird.

Submerge the bird in a stainless steel or enamel stockpot (never aluminum) and cover it with brine mixed to these proportions: ½ cup sugar and ½ cup salt for every gallon of water. You can liven up your brine by adding citrus wedges or spices. Place the pot in the refrigerator and soak for a maximum of 14 hours, then take out the carcass. Rinse well and pat dry, then prepare as you usually would.

Projects for the Garden

Starting seeds, preparing the soil, planting the bed, tending the plants, and saving seeds when harvest is over: This is the basic rhythm of gardening, played out season after season.

46›

Starting Seeds and Planting Your Garden

The best way to guarantee a thriving garden is to start with good soil and healthy seedlings. Prepping the soil requires some work, but it pays off tenfold in the long run. Growing vegetables from seed also requires more time on the front end, but that effort is also well rewarded.

WAITING: 4-6 weeks

We start most of our plants from seeds these days, for the following reasons:

VARIETY

Growing from seeds offers you a greater selection of vegetables, and isn't that why you garden? Seeds give you access to rare, heirloom vegetables never seen in the supermarket. Nurseries and garden centers usually offer only standard varieties as seedlings.

COST

Seeds are much cheaper to buy than seedlings. Get together with some friends and go in on an order of seeds, since one packet will likely produce more plants than you can grow in a small space. Most seeds last at least a year or two, so you can use them over multiple seasons.

SAFETY

Purchased seedlings can bring diseases into your garden. In 2009, a soil pathogen called late blight fungus (a strain of which was responsible for the Irish potato famine) was spread throughout the Northeast and Mid-Atlantic states of the United States in the soil of tomato seedlings propagated by a wholesale gardening company and sold at big-box retailers. Soil pathogens are hard to eradicate, so we like to minimize our chances of bringing them into our yard. For this reason alone, we now grow all of our vegetables from seed.

YOU'LL NEED

* Plastic nursery flats or homemade wooden flats (Project 56)
* Commercial potting mix or a 50/50 blend of garden soil and finished compost
* Seeds
* Chicken wire mounted in a wooden frame (optional)
* Humidity dome (optional)
* Heating mat or cold frame (optional)

**WHAT'S THE BEST CON-
TAINER FOR STARTING
SEEDS?**

There are a lot of gimmicky products touted for starting seeds.
We've tried multicelled trays,
newspaper pots, and peat pots,
but we have had much better
luck with simple flats made out
of scrap wood. See Project 56
to learn how to build your own
flats. The second-best alternative would be a standard plastic
nursery flat.

PUTTING IT TOGETHER

STEP 1: PLANTING THE SEEDS

Make sure that your flats have drainage. Wooden flats drain
between the slats. If the plastic flats lack drainage, poke
several evenly spaced holes in them.

Choose your soil mix. In our experience, seeds sprout
more readily in commercial potting mix. But later on, after
transplanting, seedlings grown in a garden soil/compost mix
acclimate more readily to the garden bed. So each choice has
its advantages and drawbacks. If you buy potting mix, be
sure the package says it's for starting seeds. If you want to
make your own mix, combine equal parts of soil from your
vegetable bed with well-decomposed compost. Make sure you
only use good garden soil for this—dark, loose soil filled with
organic matter. This kind of soil only comes out of an active
garden bed. If you don't have one yet, use potting mix. Keep in
mind that what seeds and seedlings like best is light, fluffy soil. If your homemade mix is dense because you have clay soil, lighten it up by adding a few cups
of sphagnum moss or coconut coir from the nursery.

Fill the containers with your chosen soil mix, flatten, and lightly compress—
don't pack it in. The soil should be just below the top of the container.

The seed package will state how deeply to plant your seeds. A good rule of
thumb is to plant the seed to a depth twice the diameter of the seed. Poke the
seed down into the soil and cover it. If the seeds are tiny, just sprinkle them
over the surface of the soil and then, using a colander, sift a thin layer of soil on
top of them.

Use the seed-spacing guidelines on the seed package as your primary refer-
ence for spacing the seeds in the tray. If the directions say the seeds should be
1 inch apart, try to sow them approximately that far from one another. Each plant
is a little different. Some make delicate seedlings; others grow big and brawny.
Ideally, the seeds will be spaced so that the leaves of the seedlings just touch
when ready to transplant. In other words, not too close, but not so far apart that
you're wasting space. The more you do this, the easier it will become. Don't worry
about it too much, though. If the seedlings look crowded when they come up, you
can always pinch off the extras.

When sprinkling really small seeds on top of the soil, there's no need to
plant them in rows. Just cover the designated area of your flat with a scattering
of seeds, doing your best to follow the spacing recommendation on the seed
package. Again, any stray seeds can be thinned out later when they sprout. Larger
seeds should be poked into the soil in offset rows at the distance recommended
on the seed packet. Offset rows means the spacing is staggered, the way cookies
are positioned on a baking sheet. That way each seedling has more elbow room.

MAKE A
PLANTING GUIDE

A handy suggestion we've taken from gardening guru John Jeavons is to make a planting guide using a piece of chicken wire attached to a frame. The frame should be the same size as an average seedling flat. Each cell of chicken wire is 1 inch wide. Lay the frame on the soil and plant one seed in the middle of each open cell: You'll have perfect staggered 1-inch spacing. Plant in every other cell and you'll have 2-inch spacing, and so on. It's worth the little trouble it takes to make the guide to be able to plant seeds so quickly and easily.

Mark what you planted. Trust us, you'll forget what's in the tray otherwise. We like to save plastic forks, knives, and spoons and use them as plant labels. Use a permanent marker to write on them. You could also use popsicle sticks or plastic containers (like yogurt containers) cut into strips. Mark on your calendar what you planted and when you planted it. Also take note of when you transplant the seedlings and when you get your first harvest. These notes will be valuable when you plant your seeds next year. Knowing how long it takes to get to harvest can help you keep a constant supply of veggies in the garden.

Be prepared for gardening surprises: Always plant more seeds than you need to transplant and keep some in reserve. If some critter goes on a rampage in the vegetable bed or the weather turns against you, you can use the extra seedlings as backup. Many types of unused vegetable seedlings can be enjoyed in salads as microgreens. Compost all the leftover soil. Don't reuse it until it has had a go-around with mother nature.

STEP 2: SPROUTING THE SEEDS

Whether starting seeds indoors or outdoors, you need to pay attention to the ambient temperature, because it's critical for getting good germination rates. The seed package should tell you the temperature range at which your seeds will germinate. Starting seeds indoors in the winter usually provides enough warmth for seeds to sprout, but if your house is especially cold, or the seeds are housed in a cool room, like a basement, you may need to purchase special seedling warming mats that you place under the flats. When starting seeds outdoors, cold frames (basically mini greenhouses) may be needed to get seeds off to an early start. Clear plastic lids for flats, called humidity domes, may offer just enough protection from the cold and enough additional solar heat by day to sprout your seeds outdoors in the early spring.

Too little light will produce weak, leggy seedlings—but too much will bake them. Aim to split the difference. When growing indoors, consider using florescent lights to make sure seedlings get enough light every day (see Project 48). Light from a south-facing window should be enough, but if the weather is gray, that light might not be sufficient. When starting seedlings outdoors, position the flats where they get partial sun exposure. In the summer, when shade is hard to find, protect seedlings from the intense sun with shade cloth, a lightweight mesh cloth that you can buy at the nursery. It comes in different grades of protection.

The number-one mistake beginners make when starting seeds is overwatering. Heavy watering can compress the soil and starve your seedlings of the oxygen their roots need to thrive. It can also create conditions that cause "damping-off," a general term for the effects of a group of pathogens that thrive in wet soil and kill seedlings. Seedlings suffering from this condition either fail to thrive or rot through the stem. Aim to keep the soil as moist as a wrung-out sponge. Even when the soil is wet, it should still be a little springy. Letting the seedlings dry out is obviously a bad thing, too, but easier to recognize and correct. Water gently. We recommend you buy a hose attachment with a gentle shower setting. Or use a Haws watering can, which has an upward pointing nozzle that generates a delicate shower perfect for seeds and seedlings.

STEP 3: TIMING YOUR PLANTING

We wish we could tell you when to plant your veggies, but the right timing varies greatly from place to place. Consult local gardening experts to get vegetable

An appropriately sized triangular template makes planting a snap.

planting schedules. In climates where the growing season is short, there's a narrow planting window just after the last frost, by which time you need to have all your seedlings ready to transplant. In southern climates, you can grow many vegetables year-round. This may render the planting information on the back of seed packets irrelevant. Here in Los Angeles, we start seeds when northern gardeners are closing their operations for the winter. This is why we like to say, *all gardening advice is local*. Get to know other gardeners in your area and consult gardening books written for your region.

The seedlings are ready to transplant when their first true leaves have emerged. These are their second set of leaves, the ones that look like miniature versions of their adult leaves. You can leave the seedlings in the flats a little longer, but don't let them get too old or they'll run out of room for their roots.

STEP 4: HARDENING OFF

Seedlings started indoors or in a cold frame need to be acclimated to the great outdoors. This is called hardening off. For a few days before planting the seedlings in the garden, take them out for a few hours to show them the world, then bring them back inside to recover. It's a big change for them to move outside. The temperatures, humidity, and brightness are all different. If you move them directly from their cloistered life indoors to the garden, they'll likely go into shock. So start slow, lengthening the time spent outside, until you can leave them overnight. After that, they're ready to plant. If you're using a cold frame, open the top for longer periods each day.

While hardening off, watch for signs of distress, like wilting. Seedlings are delicate. An unexpectedly hot day, a violent rainstorm, or an overnight cold snap can kill them. Once they're in the ground and a little bigger, they'll be much more sturdy.

Fit hardening off into your workweek by doing the first, crucial introductions over the weekend, leaving the seedlings outside in a sheltered place during the day and taking them in at night. By midweek, they'll probably be ready to stay out all night, and they'll be ready to plant the next weekend.

STEP 5: TRANSPLANTING

Before transplanting, be sure to read the next project on preparing your garden bed.

When planting time comes, gently scoop the plants out of the flat, taking a clump of soil with the plant. For this purpose, we like to use discarded plastic spoons, often the same utensils we use to label the plants. Handle seedlings gently, cradling the rootball in your palm or, if necessary, picking them up by the leaves. Never grasp a seedling by the stem. Open up a little hole in your garden bed and gently set the seedling down in it. Tap the soil down around the roots, firmly enough that there are no air pockets but not so hard that you compact the soil. Transplant the seedlings one by one. Don't expose their roots to sun and air longer than necessary. Water when you're done with all your transplants.

The spacing of the plants in the bed will depend on your gardening methodology. The one style we recommend against is planting in rows. Unless you plan to drive a tractor between your rows, it's a waste of space. Plants like to cozy up to one another. They don't want to be crowded to the point of choking, but they do like to be close. Ideally, their leaves will just touch when they are full grown. Close planting shades the soil, protecting it from drying out and keeping the temperature of the roots more consistent. This leads to happy plants and larger yields.

We arrange our beds using what's called a French intensive layout (see the illustration on page 178), a hexagonal pattern popularized by gardening expert John Jeavons. Planting this way ensures that the plants will grow close to one another, but not too close, and it's an efficient use of space. To lay out this shape evenly, we use cutout wooden triangles of various sizes ranging from 3 to 18 inches. The size of the triangle we use is determined by the spacing needs of the plant. Consult the seed package for recommendations on seed spacing, though we often plant a little more tightly than those recommendations. Jeavons's book also offers spacing suggestions for specific vegetables.

This is not the only way to plant, however. Some gardeners prefer to plant in grids, especially folks following another useful method detailed in Mel Bartholomew's book *Square Foot Gardening*. Others follow their own path, intuitively developing spacing and plant combinations that work for them.

Direct Sowing

In this project we've focused on starting seeds in trays, but of course you can plant them straight in your garden bed. Indeed, some vegetables, like lettuce and radishes, don't like to be transplanted. Seed packages will note this, saying "sow directly." To plant straight in the ground, you must wait until the temperatures are in the correct range outdoors—again, as noted by the seed packet. Follow the same basic instructions for planting in flats, except you will want to space the seeds at wider intervals, to account for the mature size of the plants. See the instructions on transplanting seedlings for hints on layout and spacing.

However, if the packet does not specify direct sowing, starting seeds in flats has some material advantages. Seeds and tiny seedlings are prey to many creatures and vulnerable to the weather, so your rate of loss with direct sowing will be higher than with transplanted seedlings. In addition, starting seeds indoors allows you to get a jump on the growing season.

On the other hand, direct sown plants don't suffer from transplant shock, so they grow fast and strong—if they survive their early days. We plant both ways, and most likely you will want to as well. The trick is to become familiar with the growth habits of different types of vegetables and the conditions in your own garden.

How to Prepare a Bed for Planting

IT'S ALL ABOUT THE SOIL. *Repeat this mantra over and over and you'll grow amazing vegetables. Topsoil is a living thing. Pop some under a microscope: You'll see a whole world of microbes, fungi, and countless other critters too numerous to name. Your job as a vegetable gardener is to help that life flourish. Here's another mantra:* YOU DON'T GROW PLANTS, YOU GROW SOIL. *Garden vegetables are some of the fussiest, most inbred plants nature has ever seen, and you'll need very rich, loose soil to grow them successfully. Here's how we prep our soil for our vegetable garden.*

YOU'LL NEED

* A soil test
* Quality compost (amount varies by the size of the bed being prepared)
* Soil amendments (as recommended by the soil test report)
* Sharp shovel or long-handled spade
* Pitchfork

PUTTING IT TOGETHER

STEP 1: TEST YOUR SOIL

A soil test tells you what amendments you need to add to make vegetables happy and also lets you know if your soil contains anything bad, such as lead or other heavy metals. All you have to do is send soil samples to a testing center. Just follow their directions. Many county extension offices offer free or low-cost soil testing services. The University of Massachusetts, Amherst (umass.edu/plsoils/soiltest) has an inexpensive soil test available to anyone regardless of your location. Timberleaf Soil Testing (timberleafsoiltesting.com) offers extensive testing services with easy-to-interpret results and specific recommendations. Tests for heavy metals, soil pH, micronutrients, and level of organic matter may cost more. Some companies charge for phone consultations, which can be useful if you're not familiar with soil science terminology. After the soil report, you'll know what kind of soil you have and what you can do to improve it. We test the soil when we're gardening a piece of land for the first time or if a crop fails mysteriously.

KELLY: I'd just like to point out that the soil test is not completely necessary. We gardened more or less successfully for years before we ever got one. Erik is just really enchanted with soil testing of late.

ERIK: In many places a soil test is free (ask your local county extension service), so why not use it? It can also save you money, since you won't be using fertilizer you don't need. And if those ain't enough reasons, you should know that too much fertilizer can be bad for the environment when it runs off your veggie patch and into the stormwater system.

KELLY: But I don't think anyone should get held up on starting a garden for lack of a soil test. You've got to admit that double-digging and adding good compost go a long way toward building healthy soil.

ERIK: Sure, but if you're having a problem and you can't figure out what's wrong, a soil test can give you a clue. It's especially important to test if you suspect your soil might be contaminated with lead or chromium.

If it turns out you've got lead or other contaminants in your soil, we recommend building raised beds and filling them with imported soil or growing in containers. Removing and replacing soil is expensive, and phytoremediation, the process of growing cover crops to remove toxins, is a science in its infancy and not practical for amateurs. Most likely, though, the report will not come back with bad news. Instead, it will give you a snapshot of your soil and tell you what you need to add to make it better. We'll get back to the topic of soil improvement soon.

STEP 2: LOCATE YOUR BED

Determine the perimeter of the bed and establish pathways around it. Once the soil in a garden bed is prepared, it should never be stepped on. Design the bed so you can reach the center of the bed from both sides. If you can access it only from one side, make it narrow enough that you can reach across the whole thing. For two-sided access, 4 feet wide is about right. Generally, it's best to orient the garden north–south. That orientation provides the most sun, and you can plant tall things on the north side where they won't shade the rest of the garden. However you position your bed, remember that vegetable gardens need as much sun as possible, at least 6 hours of good light a day, so take into account trees and buildings that might shade the location during the course of the day.

STEP 3: DOUBLE-DIG

Vegetables need at least 2 feet of rich, fluffy soil for best growth. They will not grow in hard, compressed soil. You should be able to plunge your hand into the soil without much resistance. If this is not the case (and it usually is not), you'll have to "double-dig."

Double-digging is a method for loosening the soil and working in compost. The addition of compost is essential. Compost not only provides nutrients that plants need, it also helps keep the soil loose and improves its ability to retain water. Double-digging is not the same as tilling. Tilling turns the soil upside down, sending the most biologically active part underground and bringing less-rich soil to the top. That's not what you want. Double-digging is about loosening the texture of the soil while disturbing it as little as possible.

Mark the boundaries of your bed and clear any weeds with a hoe. Once clear, distribute a 1-inch layer of compost evenly over the area of the bed. (See Projects 58 and 59 to learn how to make your own compost.) Starting at one end of the bed, dig out a trench a foot wide and a foot deep that stretches the width of the bed.^ Make the trench as neat as possible. Put the soil you remove

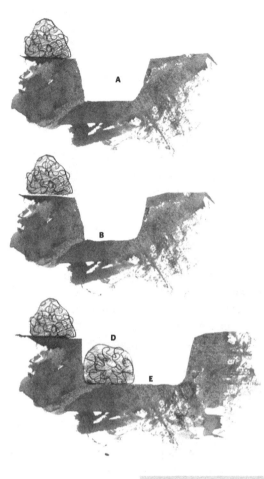

aside, away from the bed. You won't use this section of soil in this bed again. Next, take a pitchfork and plunge it into the bottom of the trench, using your foot to press it down.[B] Wiggle the prongs to loosen the soil at the bottom of the trench. Push the fork as deep as it will go, so that you're loosening as much soil as you can. Do this over and over, all along the length of the trench.

Now step onto the bed (the rule about never stepping on the bed commences once double-digging is complete) and position yourself a couple of feet away from the trench, facing the trench. Plunge the spade straight through the compost, 1 foot away from the trench. Push the spade as deep as it will go. Shove that 1 foot of soil forward into the open trench.[C] Don't scoop it up or mix it, just push it forward and let it fall into the trench.[D] This way you disturb the soil as little as possible. Work your way along the length of the trench, pushing one spade's depth worth of soil after another into the trench. When you've traveled the length of the bed, the original trench should be filled in, and a new 1-foot-wide, 1-foot-deep trench created. Loosen the soil at the bottom of this new trench with the prongs of the fork,[E] as you did the last time. Then step backward another pace and do it all over again.[F] Proceed like this until you reach the end of the bed. When it's done, the entire bed will be composed of loose soil.

Keep your shovel or spade clean and sharp! A good-quality shovel, which has been sharpened with a file, will make double-digging go a lot faster and easier.

STEP 4: AMEND

When you've finished double-digging, sprinkle any amendments as recommended by the soil test over the bed in the amounts specified by the test. Work amendments lightly into the top 3 inches of the soil with your pitchfork. Our most recent test said we were short on nitrogen, which we added in the form of alfalfa meal. Nitrogen depletion is one of the most common soil problems. Whatever your soil's diagnosis, we strongly encourage you to amend it with organic ingredients only. Artificial soil boosters are like crack cocaine in the garden.

STEP 5: WATER

Water the bed thoroughly and, ideally, wait 2 weeks before planting. This will germinate weed seeds, which you can pull out before you plant.

STEP 6: PLANT AND MAINTAIN

Plant your seedlings in this newly rich, fluffy soil. With the soil in such good shape, planting is a breeze and the seedlings should thrive. If you refrain from stepping on the bed, you'll never have to double-dig again. And this is a good thing for both you and the soil. Double-digging is the most gentle way of loosening soil, but any disturbance compromises the rich microbial and fungal networks within it. If your soil is in balance and full of compost, earthworms will do all future digging for you. But each time you plant, make sure to work in more compost. Work it gently into the top 3 inches of soil, just as you did the amendments. If you've added enough compost and the right amendments, you should not have to fertilize your vegetables. Veggies have a short life and the initial preparation—adding compost and amendments—should be enough to grow them to harvest without additional fertilizer. Note that double-digging is for vegetables and flowers only—you don't need to do it if you plan to grow sturdy native plants.

STEP 7: KEEP A HEALTHY PERSPECTIVE

If you experience any failures and frustrations in the garden, don't worry so much about the individual vegetable or the pest that's eating it. Instead, remember the mantra: It's all about the soil. Nothing is more important.

Healthy soil creates healthy plants that resist disease and insect infestations. Sure, you have to plant the right thing at the right time, and you can take steps to control pests, but if you have good soil, your problems should be few. In the end, it all comes down to composting, amending, and testing that soil. In the words of organic farming pioneer Sir Albert Howard, "Fertile soil is the foundation of healthy crops, healthy livestock, and, last but not least, healthy human beings."

DOUBLE-DIGGING AND RAISED BEDS

If you start with a raised bed and imported soil, you won't have to double-dig initially, but if the soil in a raised bed ends up compressed or your plants just aren't thriving, a soil test and a double-dig may be in order.

48›

PREPARATION: 1 hour

Grow Lights on the Cheap

To start seeds or grow microgreens indoors, you'll need light. If you've got a big south-facing window, you're in business. No sunlight? All you need is a set of cheap fluorescent shop lights.

A caveat here: This project is for starting seedlings, not growing full-size plants. There's a whole industry devoted to growing certain, shall we say, "cash crops" indoors. To grow full-size plants, like tomatoes or those cash crops, under artificial light requires a lot of powerful lights, fans, and other gadgets. It's not worth it. But starting seedlings indoors with fluorescent shop lights is easy.

YOU'LL NEED

- 2 (4-foot) florescent shop light fixtures
- 2 (40-watt) cool white tubes
- 2 (40-watt) warm white tubes
- Chain (to suspend the fixtures)
- Timer for the lights (optional, but recommended)
- Adjustable shelving—utility shelves or kitchen shelves (optional)
- Screw hooks (if suspending the lights from a ceiling or wooden bookshelf)

PUTTING IT TOGETHER

At your local hardware store, pick up two 4-foot florescent shop light fixtures, two cool white tubes, and two warm white tubes. Combining the cool and warm tubes gives your plants a full spectrum of light without having to buy expensive "plant and aquarium" tubes. Buy enough chain to suspend the lights in your chosen location. Florescent bulbs don't put out nearly as much light as indoor grow lights, so you'll need to suspend the two light fixtures side by side and as close as possible to your baby plants, no more than 3 inches away. The seedling trays could sit on a shelf with the lights mounted directly above them. This is the most compact solution. If you have more space, the trays could sit on a table and the lights could hang from the ceiling.

Load each fixture with one cool bulb and one warm bulb.

You'll see that the fixtures have hooks in them for attaching chain. Use the screw hooks or other suitable hardware to connect the chain to the ceiling or shelf. You're going to have to improvise here, depending on your situation. Leave a little extra chain for adjustments.

You don't need to turn on the lights until your seeds sprout. Once they've sprouted, keep the lights on for 14 to 16 hours a day. This is where an automatic timer comes in handy. As the plants grow, raise the lights. Keep the lights close to the plants but not touching the leaves.

The light quality of fluorescent tubes degrades, so consider replacing the tubes every 2 years, especially if you notice your seedlings getting leggy. When seedlings are tall and rangy, it indicates that they're not getting enough light. At current average energy rates in the United States, it should cost around 25 cents a day to run four 40-watt fluorescent tubes.

49.

**PREPARATION: 5 min
WAITING: 1 week**

Free Fertilizer from Weeds

*Elsewhere in this book, we've sung the praises of stinging nettle (*Urtica dioica*). It's a nutritious edible green and an excellent tonic in tea form. One reason for this is that nettles pull up minerals from the soil in heroic quantities and store them in their leaves. These minerals are as good for plants as they are for people.*

Studies have shown that liquid fertilizer made with nettles increases a plant's ability to take up nitrogen, and nitrogen depletion is a common source of plant woes. Nettle fertilizer also contains magnesium, sulfur, and iron—all excellent soil amendments. Making this potent fertilizer is easy as pie and free as can be.

YOU'LL NEED

* 5-gallon bucket with a lid
* Pruning shears
* Rubber gloves
* Spray bottle or spray pump (optional)

PUTTING IT TOGETHER

Go out and find a big patch of stinging nettles. See Project 34, Foraging Feral Greens, for tips on finding them in the wild. They're best young, so do this in the early spring. Nettles don't joke around with their hairs and spines—you should wear long sleeves and pants as well as gloves so you don't come home with battle wounds. Cut the stinging nettles rather than rip them up. You don't need their roots, and if you leave them in the ground, along with a few inches of plant, the nettles will probably spring back for future harvests. Stuff the bucket full of cut nettles.

Take your bucket of nettles home and fill it with water. Put the lid on the bucket, because this is an anaerobic fermentation—you don't want any air circulation. Like all anaerobic fermentation processes, it gets really stinky. Let the bucket sit outside for 2 weeks. During that time, give it a stir whenever you think about it.

When the 2 weeks are up, drain the liquid off the nettles into some sort of lidded storage container. The spent nettles can go on the compost pile.

Dilute the nettle tea before you use it: The right proportion is 1 part nettle tea to 10 parts water.

Use the fertilizer to water container plants and young seedlings prior to transplanting. When using it on plants already established in the ground, it's best to apply nettle tea as a foliar spray. This means misting the leaves of the plant with the fertilizer. The plants will absorb the nutrients through the leaves. Some research indicates that nettle liquid fertilizer applied as a spray repels insects, including aphids. It's fine to use an ordinary spray bottle for small jobs. For big jobs, use a gallon spray pump with a wand (sold in nurseries). Be sure to mist the whole plant, including the underside of the leaves. It's best to spray early in the morning, when temperatures are cool and the leaves have all day to dry.

Use the tea to water in-ground plants on a special needs basis only, rather than as a regular supplement. It's better in the long run to build balanced, healthy soil with lots of compost, rather than rely on frequent applications of high-octane supplements. See Project 47 for details about how to build soil.

VARIATION

Instead of nettles, use another weed, comfrey (*Symphytum officinale*). Make the tea the same way but don't dilute it. High in potash but relatively low in nitrogen, comfrey fertilizer is particularly good for fruiting plants—and that doesn't mean just fruit itself but vegetables that *make* fruits, like squash, eggplant, tomatoes, cucumbers, etc. You can mix comfrey and nettle teas to make an organic liquid fertilizer cocktail. Don't apply comfrey to plants that need acid soils, like hydrangeas and azaleas, because comfrey tea is somewhat alkaline. That's not a big concern for a vegetable gardener, because vegetables don't need acid soil. Be careful around berries, though. Many of them are acid lovers. They're just decadent that way, we guess.

50 ›

Saving Seed

Saving seed from your garden and replanting it the next year is an admirable practice. If you save seed from the best performers in your garden, you'll be selectively breeding plants adapted to the unique soil and microclimate of your garden. Saving seeds from rare heirloom varieties also ensures biodiversity and preserves our agricultural, culinary, and cultural heritage for future generations.

However—and this is a big however—to save seeds you need to do some homework. You have to read up on the sex life of each plant you're interested in reproducing. The mechanics of pollination vary, and if you don't know what you're doing, you'll end up collecting seeds from cross-bred vegetables that will yield unpredictable offspring, like bizarre squash-melon crosses or tomatoes that taste nothing like the fruit of the parent plant. The best resource we know on this topic is *Seed to Seed: Seed Saving and Growing Techniques for Vegetable Gardeners* by Suzanne Ashworth, which we recommend you read if you want to become an expert seed saver. In the meanwhile, we'll give you instructions for saving seed from a few popular vegetables that lend themselves well to this practice.

The three most common devices used by seed savers to ensure the purity of the seed they collect are distance, timing, and barriers.

ABOUT ROW COVERS

Row cover can be purchased online from organic gardening suppliers. It's a superlight nonwoven polyester fabric designed to keep bugs off plants but let sun in. Heavier weights of row cover (sometimes called garden blankets) protect plants from frost. Row covers are a staple of commercial organic gardening, but we actually use them in our little garden to protect our veggies from flying insects. We erect wire hoops over our garden beds and drape light row cover material over them. It's an easy way to manage pests without chemical intervention.

DISTANCE refers to the distance between the plant you'd like to save seeds from and all other plants in the same family that might cross-pollinate it. Different plants have different distance requirements.

TIMING refers to the window between the blossoming of your intended seed-producing plant and the blossoming of other plants in the same family that might cross-pollinate it. If you grow two varieties of the same plant in your garden, for instance, and one is blooming and forming fruit while the other is still a seedling, you don't have to worry about the two varieties crossing.

BARRIERS can be used to ensure that pollinating insects don't visit a blooming plant, thereby protecting it from accidental cross-pollination. Enthusiastic seed savers will lock up entire plants in mesh cages. On a small scale, you can save seed by "bagging blossoms"—that is, by enveloping a few blossoms of the plant with either a nylon stocking or a piece of row cover fabric, like Reemay or Agribon.

SAVING TOMATO SEEDS

Tomato plants aren't particularly promiscuous. Often you can get away with doing nothing but collect seeds from the fruit, but we've had tomatoes cross-pollinate. To be absolutely sure that the seed you're collecting will produce plants identical to the parent, you can bag a few blossoms. Tomatoes often have several blossoms on a single stem. Choose a stem with a grouping of flowers that have *not yet opened*. Envelop them in the toe of a nylon stocking or a square of row cover material, then use twine or a twist tie to secure the material to the stem. It's not necessary to cover more than two or three flowers at a time, because each tomato holds many seeds. Once the fruit begins to form, remove the barrier and mark the stem with a piece of colored ribbon so that you remember which tomatoes to save the seeds from.

To collect the seeds, wait until the tomatoes are fully ripe. Then squeeze out the juicy inner core that contains the seeds into a jar and cover it with a few inches of water. Tie a piece of cheesecloth over the mouth of the jar to keep insects out but let air in, store the jar at room temperature, and stir once a day. After about 3 days, a layer of fungus will form on the surface and the viable seeds will sink to the bottom of the jar. Pour off the excess water and any floating seeds. Using a colander, strain the remaining seeds and rinse them well. Spread the seeds on a sheet of newspaper, a paper towel, or a piece of screening and let them dry indoors. Store in a labeled paper envelope.

SAVING PEPPER SEEDS

Bees can easily cross-pollinate peppers, so you can't leave them unprotected if you want to save seed. Bag a few blossoms, exactly as described above for tomatoes, and removed the bag as soon as fruit sets. Be sure to mark the stems so that you know which peppers to save seeds from. Scrape the seeds out of the mature fruit and let them air-dry, then store in a labeled paper envelope.

SAVING EGGPLANT SEEDS

If you're growing only one variety of eggplant, and none of your neighbors within 50 feet are growing eggplant, you're safe to save the seeds without making any interventions. If there is a chance of cross-pollination, bag a few blossoms as described under tomatoes.

Let the eggplants designated for seed mature well past the point you would normally pick them—to the point that they begin to rot, in fact. The bottom of the eggplant is where you will find most of the seeds. Using a hand grater, grate the bottom half into a bowl of water. Squeeze the gratings to separate the seeds from the flesh. Dry the seeds and store in a paper envelope.

SAVING LETTUCE SEEDS

Let the plant bolt, which means let it grow until it throws up a central stalk and starts to form flowers. Bag several of those flowers before they open, as described for tomatoes. Once the flowers finish blooming and wilt, remove the barrier and mark the stems. In 12 to 24 days, depending on variety, the seed heads will be dry, which means they're ready to harvest. Shake the seed heads into a paper bag to collect the dried seed. Store in a labeled paper envelope. Lettuce seeds don't keep long, so be sure to plant them the next season.

SAVING PEAS

Cross-pollination is rare in peas, but sometimes a bumblebee makes its way into a bloom. More than likely, you can get away without making any interventions. If you want to be extra careful, keep different varieties of peas separated by at least 50 feet or simply grow one variety. If you've got several varieties of peas going at once and want to be absolutely sure about seed purity, bag the flowers before they open. Remove the bags once the fruit sets and mark the stems that have been bagged. Let the peas mature on the vine, until the pods dry out. Then open them and gather the seeds (peas). Make sure the pods don't pop open on their own before you get to them! Store the seeds in labeled paper envelopes.

SAVING BEANS

Some experts say you need to have a minimum of 150 feet between varieties to prevent cross-pollination, though this claim is under debate. We've never encountered crossed beans ourselves. Like peas, you simply let the bean pods dry on the plant, then gather the dry beans. To be extra certain, you could opt to bag the blossoms.

STORING SEEDS

The magic words for seed storage are *dry, dark, cool,* and *airtight,* with the emphasis on *dry.* Envelopes keep seeds in the dark but are not airtight. This is a good thing in one way. If your seeds aren't quite dry when you store them, they'll continue to dry in the envelopes. Canning jars sealed tightly make great seed storage containers, but they do let in light, and because they're airtight, improperly dried seeds will turn moldy. Get the best of both worlds by storing your seeds in envelopes (little manila envelopes from an office supply store work well) for a month or so to be sure they're absolutely dry, then tuck the envelopes in a canning jar for the winter. Seeds stored in airtight containers in the freezer will last considerably longer than those stored at room temperature. As seeds get older, their germination rates decline, but that doesn't mean they're not usable—you just have to plant more seeds. Most vegetable seeds last 2 to 6 years, depending on storage conditions.

51 ›

🕐
WAITING: 4–7 years

How to Espalier

Our gardening goal is to grow as many edibles as possible on our property. Fruit and nut trees are a big part of that plan. They're the backbone of an edible landscape. What other plant gives you so much food in return for so little effort on your part? If you're short on space for fruit trees yet high on ambition, an espalier may be the answer for you.

Espaliering is the art of training trees to grow flat against a trellis as a living fence or up against a wall. It's a charming old art, and a practical one as well. An espaliered tree doesn't take up much space, yet because it is rigorously pruned and all of the flowers and branches receive full light (and, in the case of those trained to a wall, extra warmth), it often bears more fruit than its three-dimensional counterparts, and that fruit is much easier to harvest.

Any fruit tree represents an investment in time. It takes years for a sapling to mature enough to bear a significant amount of fruit. In the case of an espaliered tree, you should expect to wait 4 to 7 years for your first harvest. But the reward—a beautiful living sculpture that gives you pounds and pounds of delicious organic fruit every year—is well worth the effort.

CHOOSING A LOCATION

When planning to put in an espalier, figure that each tree needs a space measuring about 6 x 6 feet. An espaliered tree can be grown against any fence or wall or can be staked on freestanding trellises. South-facing walls absorb and reflect the most heat for the tree. This is useful in northern climates and in those with short growing seasons. The extra heat coddles the tree and extends the harvest. In southern climates, a wall facing due south may be a little *too* hot. Put your hand on a wall on a sunny summer day to judge whether or not it will cook the tree. Does the wall burn your hand? Does anything else grow near the wall, or is it a parched dead zone? Eastern or western exposure may be better if that's the case. Either is generally acceptable in all climates. North-facing walls do not get enough light, at least not enough to grow fruit trees. Make sure the spot you choose, whether a wall or a freestanding trellis, gets at least 6 hours of sunlight a day during the growing season.

CHOOSING THE TREES

The most popular subjects for espalier are fruit trees, though nonfruiting trees are sometimes grown this way. Every tree has a unique growth pattern and pruning requirements that must be factored into the choice. Apples and pears have an orderly pattern of growth that makes them particularly suited to espaliers, and they bear a tremendous amount of fruit in this form. For this reason, they're the most commonly espaliered trees. Since we can't cover every type of tree in these pages, we're going to focus this project on apple trees.

Fruit trees come in different sizes: standard size (referred to as seedling rootstock) and those grafted on dwarfing rootstock (labeled "dwarf" or "semidwarf"). Because we live in an urban area where space is often limited, we generally prefer to plant dwarf or semidwarf trees because of their compact growth habit. However, it is worth noting that there are varieties of standard size apples that bear their fruit on short spurs as opposed to on the tips of their branches. These are called spur bearing apples. They'll be identified as spur bearing on their tags. If you can find a spur bearing apple suitable for your climate, it would be the ideal apple for espalier. However, spur bearing apples are somewhat harder to find than tip bearing. If you can't find one, don't worry. Choose any dwarf or semidwarf tree suited to your climate. These will be easy to find, and because they're smaller, they're easier to manage. Either way, you're good.

Espaliering is best begun on a very young tree, preferably on what is called a whip. This is a short, branchless sapling, which does, in fact, resemble a whip. It's much easier to espalier a whip than a sapling with branches. If you purchase trees by mail order, they will most likely be shipped in this state. We're going to focus on the training of whips, because reshaping the existing branches of an older sapling is a more complex undertaking.

READY-MADE ESPALIER

It's possible to buy a sapling that is already being trained into espalier form. They come in pots, with their branches preshaped on a piece of trellis. This will save you initial work and waiting, but the trained sapling will cost a lot more than a whip.

DO YOU NEED A POLLINATOR?

Many fruit trees need another fruit tree nearby for pollination. Trees that do not need a pollinator are labeled as self-fruitful. Many heirloom and rare varieties of fruits require cross-pollination, and some self-fruitful trees will bear heavier crops if they are cross-pollinated. Most apple trees require cross-pollination. The pollinator tree is always a different variety of the same tree. For example, we would choose two different kinds of apples for the garden, say a Gala and a Fuji, just to name two well-known varieties. If you only have room for one apple tree, make sure it is a self-fruitful variety.

PREPARING THE SITE

First, spend some time loosening and amending the soil in the area you intend to plant your trees. A modified double-dig method would work well for an area that has compacted soil. (See Project 47 for details.) Double-digging is usually performed on garden beds, but for an espaliered tree, apply this method to a 3-square-foot area, amend the soil with compost, and remove any rocks or loose masonry chunks from the planting area.

Next, string up wire to form the framework for training the tree. There are many forms of espaliers: Trees can be trained into grids, fans, or candelabra forms or allowed to grow in a natural branching pattern. For this project, we're

EXPERT HELP

Seek out a reliable fruit tree vendor in your region. Even if you have to travel a long way to find the vendor, or pay more for the trees, it will be time and money well spent. Many growers ship trees if you don't have local options. A reliable nursery, whether local or mail order, is a treasure trove of information. The staff will be able to tell you which trees do best in your climate and recommend correct companion trees. They also will be more likely to provide you with whips or preespaliered trees than chain nurseries.

going to focus on a classic cordon pattern (a modified T) in which the tree is shaped into a central trunk with three straight sets of branches growing parallel to the ground. This is a classic form for apple espaliers.

Attach three 6-foot lengths of wire to the wall at regular intervals. The first will be stretched horizontally 18 inches off the ground, the second 18 inches above the first, and the third 18 inches above the second. This spacing can be changed to accommodate the form of the sapling or the height of the wall, but the space between wires should be equal.

The wire must be firmly attached to the wall. For a wooden wall or fence, drill in eye screws or eyebolts. For a masonry wall, you'll need to drill holes and set plastic plugs into the masonry joints using a carbide drill. Then drive the screws in the plastic plugs. You could also mount a wooden trellis about 6 inches from a wall and train the tree to that. This is a good technique if you wish to grow the trees against the walls of your house. For a freestanding espalier, sink rot-resistant 4 x 4-inch posts into the ground 6 feet apart and string wire between them at the same 18-inch intervals. To ensure the posts don't fall inward, sink the posts into concrete. Look up basic fence-building techniques to learn how to do this.

The wire used should be galvanized and heavy gauge (12 to 15 gauge). It is sometimes called berry wire. It must be stretched tight and be sturdy enough to support the branches. Turnbuckles are useful for tightening and retightening the wire as needed.

PLANTING THE TREE

Center the location of the tree on the wire. That is to say, for a 6-foot stretch of wire, plant the tree at the 3-foot mark. Plant it 8 to 12 inches away from the supporting structure. Dig a hole a little bigger than the pot that holds the sapling and carefully lower the rootball into the soil. The top of the rootball should be even with the ground. Pat down the soil around it gently, then water. Place a wood chip mulch around the base of the tree. Always keep mulch a couple of inches from the actual tree trunk. Mulch holds moisture, which is great for the soil but can damage the tree trunk if it stays wet for too long.

FIRST PRUNING

Whenever you interfere with a branching plant's projected growth by pruning it, it responds by creating a flush of growth at the pruning site. People who keep houseplants know that if a plant is getting rangy, pinching it back will force it to put off side shoots, making it fuller. To espalier, you're going to use this same principle.

Examine the whip and find a bud that is about level with the first wire. A little higher or lower is fine. Trim the whip just above this bud with sharp pruning shears. Make sure there are at least three buds left below the cut. (If there are not, you'll have to let it grow a little more.) The whip will put out a cluster of new growth at the cut site, which can be trained onto the horizontal wires in the next step.

Let the whip grow for the rest of the year and put out new growth from your cutting point. Allow it to grow as much as it wants, however it wants.

Trim the whip to the height of the first horizontal support, leaving at least 3 buds beneath the cut.

Prune with sharp shears, making your cuts at a 45° angle.

Allow free growth.

Trim away all the new growth
except 3 little branches: 2 to
form the horizontal arms and
1 central leader to be the trunk.
Start training them into shape.

When the central leader
shoots past the second tier of
horizontal supports, cut it back
to the bud nearest the level
of the support, as you did in
step one.

Allow free growth at the
top. Meanwhile continue to
encourage the "arms" on the
first tier to grow straight.

Prune the flush of new growth at
the level of the second tier into
3 branches, 2 to grow sideways
and one to straight up, as before.
Repeat these steps until the tree
reaches the height you prefer.

SECOND PRUNING

In general, major pruning of trees is best done in the winter or early spring while the plant is dormant. In contrast, bending branches should be done in the spring, when growth is new and flexible. After a year's growth, the whip should sport several new small branches.

Train the whip into the cordon pattern by choosing two branches from the new growth, one on either side of the trunk, to be attached to the lowest wire. Designate one of the central branches to be the trunk, which will continue growing upward. Any other branches should be pruned away. Tie the small side branches to the wire with twine or rubber tubing. Let the central branch—the trunk—continue to shoot upward unimpeded.

REPEAT

When the tree reaches the level of the second wire, prune it to the bud closest to the wire, just as you did in the first pruning. A burst of branching growth will emerge from the cut point. Prune and train that growth, again, just as you did the first year, by choosing two new branches to train on the second level of wire and leaving a central shoot to grow upward, toward the third wire.

Meanwhile, the branches on the lower tiers will be lengthening. As they grow, cut off any big side shoots that look like they want to be branches. Leaf clusters and short shoots not more than 3 or 4 inches long can remain. You want the tree to have greenery for photosynthesis, but you also want it to focus most of its growing energy outward along the wires. As the branches lengthen, tie them down to the wire at 8-inch intervals. You can use a bamboo cane as a brace to achieve a straighter branch. Monitor the ties as the tree grows to make sure they are not squeezing or scarring the branches.

Similarly, buds will appear along the length of the central branch or trunk—pinch those off. All of its growth should be directed straight up. Basically, during these first years all of your focus should be on forcing the tree to grow in a clean cordon shape.

When the whip reaches the third wire, once again cut it to the bud nearest the wire and allow it to put out branching growth from that point. Train two branches to the wire, and cut everything else back. This is where upward growth stops (unless you want a four-tier espalier). From now on, it won't grown upward, only outward. Continue to diligently pinch off any new growth that doesn't conform to shape.

As tempting as it is, don't let the tree flower or fruit until the basic framework is established over all three tiers. Pinch off the flowers when they form. Fruiting takes a lot of energy that needs to be directed toward branch formation. The tree will not reach the third tier in less than 3 years. You should anticipate not having a fruit harvest for at least 4 years, perhaps as many as 7. This seems like a long time, but young fruit trees don't bear much fruit in the first few years anyway, so espaliering doesn't put you far behind.

The Magic of Fermentation

Vinegar, beer, and mead are all made by long-term fermentation processes, where friendly yeasts and bacteria turn one substance into another, as if by magic. Leftover wine or apple juice becomes vinegar, honey becomes mead, and barley becomes beer.

52›

PREPARATION: 10 min
WAITING: 2–3 months

Making Vinegar

Put broadly, vinegar is the natural end point of wine and fruit juice. When you make vinegar, you're just stepping in to harness the bounty. If you're wondering why you should bother making vinegar, you should know that homemade vinegar is better tasting than its store-bought counterparts, almost tasty enough to eat by the spoonful. Making vinegar is also a means of preserving excess, preventing waste, and eating well while saving money, all of which makes this one of our favorite kitchen projects.

HOW IT WORKS

Acetobacter is a genus of acetic acid bacteria that convert alcohol into vinegar in the presence of oxygen. If you leave a bottle of wine, juice, or cider sitting open for a long time, it will likely turn to vinegar on its own. The bacteria eat the alcohol and produce acetic acid, which is the active component in vinegar. The acetobacter form colonies that appear first as clouding, then as floating cobwebs. You may have seen them floating in old bottles of vinegar. Eventually, a colony solidifies into a rubbery pancake that covers the surface of the liquid. This is what vinegar makers call the "mother."

The mother is harmless and a sign that something good is happening in your bottle. She's not something we're used to seeing in our cupboards, though not so long ago every kitchen would have had a crock of vinegar topped with a vinegar mother.

The mother is what allows us to jump-start our own vinegar projects. The "leave it open and see what happens" school of vinegar making is a little haphazard and takes a long time. So to make vinegar, we're going to add a mother, or a quantity of living vinegar containing acetobacter, to wine or apple juice or hard cider. But that's about all we're going to do, because you don't have to *do* anything to make vinegar—you just have to be patient.

YOU'LL NEED

* The vinegar mother (see page 200)
* Organic, preservative-free apple juice or hard cider; or red wine (one varietal or a mix of leftovers)
* Clean, dry, widemouthed container

FINDING YOUR MOTHER

The best place to start would be with another vinegar maker who could give you a piece of a mother or a cupful of homemade, bacteria-rich vinegar. If you don't know anyone who makes vinegar, the easiest thing to do is go to the health food market and buy an all-natural, unpasteurized, unprocessed bottle of vinegar. Bragg's sells a cider vinegar that fits the bill. The vinegar you buy should be murky looking. That murk is a future mother. Understand this: The difference between a cup of murky all-natural vinegar and a slab of slimy mother is just time. If left alone, natural vinegar will form a mother. So one mother is not better than the other.

CONVERTING A MOTHER

If you want to make apple cider vinegar, it's best to start with an apple cider mother. If you want a red wine vinegar, it's best to get a red wine mother. It's certainly possible to force a cider mother on red wine and vice versa, but sometimes they don't take. The best way to convert a mother is to add a very little juice or wine to the mother—something like a 1:1 ratio. Let that develop for a couple of weeks, following the instructions in this project, then check to see if it looks like it's doing anything. Good signs are an increase in the size of the mother or an increase in the cloudiness of the liquid if you're using natural vinegar as a starter. As long as it's not covered in mold, it's probably okay. Add a little more liquid and let it sit some more. In this way, you'll slowly convert the mother.

It's harder to find, but if you want red wine vinegar, look for a bottle of unpasteurized red wine vinegar at health food stores, gourmet shops, or wineries. You can also buy wine vinegar starters at shops that sell wine- and beer-making supplies. Check your cabinets for old, forgotten bottles of red wine vinegar. They might be forming mothers—hold them up to the light and see if you see any clouding or string forms inside.

SELECTING A CONTAINER

The traditional container would be either a ceramic crock or little wooden barrel fitted with a spout at the bottom. We don't have one of those. We make do with glass jars. One of those iced-tea dispensers with a spout on it would be a good option, too. Widemouthed vessels are best. Not only does vinegar need surface space for good fermentation, but a wide opening makes it easier to fish out the mother later. Vinegar doesn't like light; that's why it's traditionally made in crocks. If you make it in a glass jar, keep the jar in a dark place. The size of the crock doesn't matter much. It really depends on how much vinegar you need. If you're just curious, a quart jar will do to start. Never use aluminum or plastic containers for making vinegar. Both of them react with vinegar.

Vinegar needs air, so you'll need some cheesecloth or similar fine material and a rubber band to go over the mouth of your jar to keep out fruit flies. Don't put a lid on it.

PUTTING IT TOGETHER

If you have a liquid mother (living vinegar), mix 1 part mother to 10 parts wine, cider, or juice. If you have a slime patty, just put the whole thing in your jar and add wine or juice to fill. Cover the jar with cheesecloth or some other fine, thin cloth and secure it with string or a rubber band. Put the jar aside to ferment at room temperature for 1 to 3 months.

The fermentation time will depend on many variables, so just watch and wait. The warmer the ambient temperatures, the faster the vinegar develops. If you began with a liquid mother, you'll see scum forming on the surface, which will thicken and solidify. Don't mistake it for mold! Be brave and patient. If you began with a solid mother, you should start to see her expand. Taste and sniff to chart progress. Half-finished vinegar won't hurt you. Young apple cider vinegar is fruity and appealing, while young red wine vinegar tastes like bad wine. Finished vinegar is not at all sweet and has a distinct, eye-watering punch when you sniff it.

When you decide it's done, strain the vinegar to remove any chunky bits. The vinegar mother will have formed several pancake layers. The one floating on top is the freshest. Save that one to make your next batch and compost the rest. You could also save a cup of finished vinegar for the next batch.

Transfer the finished vinegar to very clean, lidded bottles. You want to deprive the vinegar of oxygen so the acetobacter will stop working. The best bottles for this purpose are narrow-necked bottles (less surface area for oxygen exchange). All bottles should be filled to the very top. Filled like this, they can be stored in a cool, dark place for years.

Once you open a bottle, store it in the fridge if you're not going to use it quickly. Refrigeration will keep the acetobacter quiet—they won't make rubbery colonies in the bottle that may dismay your dinner guests, and they won't be able to overdevelop the vinegar, either.

SOME HINTS REGARDING FINISHED VINEGAR

If your finished vinegar takes on the distinct odor of nail polish remover, don't despair. Aerate it by passing it back and forth between two containers, let it rest a couple of days, and sniff it again. It should improve.

All new vinegar has a sharp bite. Vinegar will mellow and improve over time, like wine.

Don't forget about your vinegar and let it sit abandoned for months and months, far past its finishing point. Eventually the acetobacter will run out of alcohol to make vinegar with. Then it will begin to entertain itself by turning the finished vinegar into carbon dioxide and water. You'll be able to see and taste that it's not vinegar anymore.

53›

PREPARATION: 1 hour
WAITING: 1 year

Making Mead

The gathering of honey long predates the cultivation of wheat and grapes, and honey sometimes ferments on its own, even in the comb. Once HOMO SAPIENS *discovered funny honey, it couldn't have been long before we figured out how to ferment it on purpose. Thus was born the first happy hour.*

Mead is made of honey, water, and yeast. Sometimes it's carbonated, sometimes fruits or spices are added to it, but the most important determining factor for flavor is the yeast. Of course, the honey is important, too, as its flavor nuances will influence the mead, but the yeast is the major player. Colonize the same type of honey with two different yeasts, and you end up with two entirely different meads. Depending on the yeast, mead can run from sweet to dry and from mild to strong. We've made mead that tastes like cheap Chablis, and we've made mead that is honey-flavored rocket fuel.

The recipe calls for some specialized ingredients and equipment, all of which can be found in a brewer's supply shop. Some of it can be used to brew beer, too, which is the next project. Honey mead is the easiest alcoholic beverage to make, a good entrée into the world of homemade hooch. All you have to do is stir up honey, water, and yeast—and wait.

YOU'LL NEED

* 3 pints filtered or bottled water
* 2 pounds honey
* 1 teaspoon yeast nutrient (such as Fermax)
* Ice cubes, enough to chill a sink (or a bin) full of water
* 4 pints filtered or bottled water, chilled in the refrigerator
* 1 packet wine yeast (such as Lalvin 71B-1122)
* Couple of spoonfuls of cheap vodka
* 5 teaspoons honey (for carbonation; optional)

EQUIPMENT:
* Food-grade plastic bucket
* Iodine-based sanitizer (such as iodophor)
* 6–8 quart stockpot
* Kitchen thermometer
* 2 (1-gallon) glass bottles, such as a cider jugs
* Funnel (any size)
* Fermentation lock and stopper to fit one of the jugs

* Auto siphon
* Swing-top capped bottles or ordinary beer bottles, a set of caps, and an inexpensive bottle capper

PUTTING IT TOGETHER

STEP 1: SANITIZE YOUR EQUIPMENT

You're not working in a lab here, but a few precautions will keep you from making honey vinegar instead of honey wine. The easiest thing to do is to fill a food-grade plastic bucket full of water mixed with an iodine-based sanitizer. Refer to the sanitizer label for the dilution amounts. Submerge any utensils that will touch the mead in the sanitizer solution for a minute or so before using. There's no need to rinse. You can sanitize the jugs by simply swishing around a bit of sanitizer solution inside them—you don't need to fill them completely.

STEP 2: PREPARE AND PASTEURIZE THE "MUST"

Bring 3 pints of water to a boil in the stockpot and boil for 5 minutes. Turn off the heat. Add the honey to the water in the stockpot. Scoop up some of the boiling water and swirl it around in the honey jars to dissolve the leftover honey and add that to the pot, too. Stir well.

Add the yeast nutrient and stir again. Honey is low in nitrogen, which yeasts need to thrive. The yeast nutrient adds nitrogen to make fermentation go faster.

Check the temperature. The goal is to hold the "must" (the honey and yeast mixture) just above 150°F for 10 minutes to pasteurize it. If you need to bring the temperature up a little, turn the stove back on and stir over low heat. Watch the temperature carefully. Never boil the must, as this will degrade the flavor of the honey.

During the pasteurization period, take a moment to fill your kitchen sink or a big tub with ice.

When the 10-minute pasteurization period is over, it's time to bring the temperature down. You want the cooling period as short as possible to minimize the chance that wild yeasts and bacteria will get into the must. Add the 4 pints of reserved, chilled water to the must and stir to combine. Next, speed cooling further by putting the pot in the ice-filled sink or bin.

While the must is cooling, mix half the package of wine yeast in 2 tablespoons of 100°F water in a sanitized bowl. Let it sit for 15 minutes.

Once the temperature of the must falls beneath 80°F, transfer it to a sanitized jug using a funnel.

STEP 3: PITCHING THE YEAST AND FIRST FERMENTATION

Now that the must is in the jug, you're ready to add the wine yeast. This is called "pitching the yeast." Lalvin 71B-1122 is a wine yeast that comes in a pouch and looks just like bread yeast. The kind of yeast you use will affect the flavor of the mead. If the yeast is too dry, the flavor of the honey is lost and mead tastes like a boring white wine. If the yeast is too sweet, the mead will be cloying. We like

the Lalvin 71B-1122 because it splits the difference between sweet and dry. Using the funnel, pour the bowl of water mixed with yeast into the jug.

Fit the opening of the jug with a stopper and a fermentation lock. A fermentation lock is a small, inexpensive device that lets carbon dioxide out of the jug but doesn't let air in. Fill the reservoir of the fermentation lock with cheap vodka instead of water. That way, if some of it spills into the bottle, you won't contaminate your mead. Put the jug in a cool, dark place. An ambient temperature of 60° to 75°F is ideal for fermentation. The mead will start to bubble vigorously in a day or two. Eventually, the bubbling will subside and debris will settle to the bottom. This will take about a month. This process is called the first fermentation.

STEP 4: RACKING

After a month, liberate your mead from the debris that has settled to the bottom of the jug. The process of siphoning the liquid from one vessel to another, leaving debris behind, is called racking. The easiest way to rack the mead is with an auto siphon. To start siphoning, position the jug to be filled lower than the one holding the mead. For example, the mead can sit on the counter and the empty jug in the sink. Put the plunger of the auto siphon in the mead and the hose end in the empty bottle. Raise the plunger on the auto siphon and bring it back down slowly. The mead will start to flow into the empty bottle. The second jug will soon fill with clean mead.

Transfer the stopper and fermentation lock to the new bottle.

Transferring the mead to the second jug often starts the fermentation process going again, so you'll probably notice a little more bubbling activity in the first days after the transfer. When the mead is quiet for at least 2 weeks and the liquid has cleared, you're ready to bottle the mead.

STEP 5: CARBONATING THE MEAD (OPTIONAL)

If you wish to carbonate the mead, do it just before you bottle. Simmer the 5 teaspoons honey in ½ cup water, stirring to dissolve. Let cool and then stir into the jug of mead.

This small amount of sugar will reawaken the yeast and cause another fermentation to take place in the closed confines of the bottle, thus creating carbonation. Be careful not to add too much honey—this might lead to exploding bottles.

STEP 6: BOTTLING THE MEAD

We bottle mead with the same equipment we use for beer: used beer bottles, new bottle caps, and a bottle capper. You can also use bottles with resealable stoppers, like Grolsch bottles. Wine bottles could be used as well, but a wine bottle corker is more expensive than a bottle capper, and less mead is lost in testing from smaller bottles.

Before bottling, scrub the bottles with a bottle brush, then soak them in a big bucket filled with the iodine solution, or run them through the dishwasher, without soap, on a sanitizing setting. Then fill the bottles with the mead and cap them.

How long it takes for the mead to finish varies. Like wine, mead gets better over time. It takes a minimum of 6 to 8 months for something drinkable to ferment. Test it at that point. If it tastes like cleaning fluid, don't despair. Let the rest of the bottles sit for a few months longer. It should be better at about 1 year in, but it may take several years for your mead to reach peak flavor. Reserve a few bottles from every batch for long-term testing. Take good notes. Like making wine, making mead is an art, and the flavors of each batch unfold over time.

STORAGE SAFETY

For safety reasons, and to preserve your furnishings from flying mead, store carbonating bottles somewhere bombproof, such as in a lidded plastic tub or in the basement or garage.

54▸

Making Home Brew

Don't let the equipment list and the length of the instructions here fool you. If you can make soup, you can make beer. Darn good beer. And the equipment is not that expensive, especially if you build some of it yourself.

We'd like to see home brewing liberated from the hands of obsessive middle-aged men. (If you visit the typical brewer's supply shop, you'll see what we mean.) It's been all but forgotten that beer making was part of a housewife's domain for centuries. What we mean to say is that brewing beer isn't a gender-specific activity, but it is an important activity, so *someone* has to be the brewmeister in your house. Sharing home brew with your friends and family is one of the best parts of DIY living.

Let's begin with a quick overview of how beer is made. First, grain is allowed to sprout slightly—this is called malting—and then it's roasted. The roasted malt is soaked in hot water and drained slowly, a process that extracts the fermentable sugars from the grain. This sugary water, called the wort, is boiled with hops, cooled down, spiked with yeast, and allowed to ferment. In the fermentation process, the yeast converts the sugars to alcohol. Once the fermentation is complete, a little bit of sugar is added and the beer is bottled. This second sugar boost gets the yeast going again and causes a second fermentation to take place in the bottle, thus carbonating the beer.

There are two ways to make beer at home. The simplest way is to use ready-made malt extract, which comes in the form of a syrup or dehydrated powder. Malt extract is a concentrated form of the malty sugars extracted from the grain. All you do is mix malt extract with water and hops and boil, cool it down, and then add yeast. You can make great beers with extracts and do it on a regular kitchen stove. Some home brewers only use extract, and there's nothing wrong with that.

But we like to take it a step back and extract our own wort in a process called all-grain brewing. You need a few extra items of equipment to do this, and it takes a little more time, but the advantage is that you have more control over the types of grain you use and so more options for brewing. It also gives you bragging rights.

Most beer recipes are delivered in a format similar to the one on page 221, which might be a little confusing at first glance. They assume you know how to make beer already and that you just need a list of ingredients and some notes on timing. To teach you how to read a standard beer recipe, we're notating this recipe to make it a little more transparent, then we'll break down the process step by step in the instructions. You can find the ingredients in this recipe in any brewer's supply shop.

Brewer's Vocabulary

GRIST: Ground malt.

HOPS: The hop plant (*Humulus lupulus*) is an attractive flowering vine. Its fragrant, cone-shaped flowers are called hops. Hops are a bitter herb that gives beer its distinctive flavor. Different varieties of hops add specific characteristics to the flavor profile of the beer. Hops are divided into two basic categories: bittering hops and flavoring hops. Some types of hops serve both purposes.

MALT: Malt is grain (usually wheat or barley) that has been sprouted ("malted") and roasted for brewing. Malt is crushed before mashing and brewing. After it's crushed, it is called grist.

MASH: Mash is the combination of hot water and grist (ground malt). Grist is steeped in water ("mashed") to release its sugars. The product of mashing is wort.

MASH TUN: A lidded, insulated container in which the grist and water are mixed and soaked off heat. We use a converted 10-gallon drink cooler.

WORT: The malt sugar solution that is drained from the mash tun and boiled with the hops, the precursor to beer.

PREPARATION: 5 hours
WAITING: 6 weeks

Makin' It California Pale Ale

Beer recipes are strange beasts, written in obscure beer-geek shorthand which can only be intended to scare off the uninitiated. Instead of breaking our recipe down into a more readable form, we've presented it as you would likely find it if you came across it in a typical brewing book, but we've footnoted it to unlock the code. Once you understand the code, you'll be able to crack any beer recipe you come across. Don't worry if you don't understand the recipe at first, the instructions following the recipe will make all clear.

MALT

* 8 pounds American two-row pale malt
* ½ pound American crystal malt 60L [1]
* ½ pound American crystal malt 20L
* ½ pound Munich malt 10L
* ½ pound Victory malt

HOPS SCHEDULE [2]

* 60 mins ¾ ounce Columbus hops (also called Tomahawk)
* 30 mins ½ ounce Cascade hops
* 15 mins ½ ounce Cascade hops
* Dry hop ½ ounce whole Cascade hops for 2 weeks in secondary fermenter [3]

YEAST

California Ale White Labs WLP009 [4]

GRAVITY

Original gravity: 1.053 – Final gravity: 1.013 [5]

---

1 L notations after malt ingredients refer to a Lovibond measuring unit and denote the darkness of the grain after roasting. Grain is sold labeled like this.

2 The hops schedule tells you not only what type of hops you have to buy, but when to add them to the beer. For example, "60 mins" denotes the portion added 60 minutes before the brew period ends, and "15 mins" refers to the portion added 15 minutes before the brew period ends.

3 Hops are sold in several different forms, including pellets, plugs, and whole hops. In this case, you need ½ ounce of whole dried Cascade hops. If the hop is not designated as whole, you can use hops in any form you can get them in. Your shopping list from this recipe should read: ¾ ounce of Columbus hops total, 1½ ounces total of Cascade hops, at least ½ ounce of which must be whole.

4 This is a specific brand and type of yeast, one that should be easy to find. All brew shops sell a wide variety of yeasts. If they don't carry this yeast, they can recommend a close substitute.

5 Original gravity is a measurement of the concentration of sugars in the wort; final gravity indicates the alcohol content of the beer. These measurements are taken with a simple device called a hydrometer. You don't need to own a hydrometer, but testing helps you make sure that your recipe is on track. Think of these numbers as a quality assurance device.

YOU'LL NEED

EQUIPMENT AND MATERIALS TO MAKE, SCAVENGE, OR BUY:

* 8 ½ gallons filtered or bottled water
* 24-quart and 32-quart aluminum pots (You don't need expensive stainless steel for beer making.)
* Outdoor burner and propane tank (Find one in a restaurant supply store or a big Asian market.)
* Oven mitts
* Mash tun (Project 62)
* 2-quart pitcher
* Wire mesh skimmer/strainer with a handle
* Wort chiller (Project 63)
* Couple of spoonfuls of cheap vodka
* 45–50 used beer bottles, or new bottles from a brew shop

EQUIPMENT AND MATERIALS YOU'LL FIND IN A HOME BREW SHOP:

* Iodine-based sanitizer (such as iodophor)
* Thermometer
* 6-gallon food-grade bucket with a lid (The lid should have a hole for a fermentation lock.)
* Fermentation lock and matching stopper
* 5-gallon glass carboy (jug)
* Auto siphon
* ⅔ cup corn sugar (for carbonation)
* Bottling wand with spring/pressure-flow tip
* Bottle capper
* 50 bottle caps (approximately)

PUTTING IT TOGETHER

BEFORE YOU START

At the home brew shop, pick up your malted grains, hops, yeast, and corn sugar. Malted grains are sold whole. At the store, you'll weigh out all the malted grains you need and then put them through a grinder, which will roughly crack them. It's fine to grind them together, all at once, and bring home the grain combined in one bag. It's best to brew the beer within a few days of grinding.

Brewing yeast comes in may different forms. The yeast we recommend comes as a liquid. If you use a different kind of yeast, follow the directions on the label.

WHEN YOU'RE READY TO BREW

Remove the yeast from the refrigerator so that it can come to room temperature. Clean and set up your equipment. Sanitize the plastic fermenting bucket, stopper, funnel, fermentation lock, and anything else that will come into contact with the cooled wort. The easiest way to do this is to fill a big bucket with water and add iodine-based sanitizing solution, like iodophor, to the water. Follow dilution instructions on the bottle. Submerge all of the equipment to be sanitized in the water for 1 minute. Don't rinse afterward. You don't need to sanitize the brew pots or the mash tun, since they will be holding hot liquids, but they should be clean.

Gather some friends. Beer making is a long process but doesn't take a lot of attention. It's a great thing to do on a nice day while hanging out on the back porch and maybe grilling some food. Friends can help you lift the heavy pots and are generally enthusiastic about sampling and rating previous batches of brew.

MAKING THE MASH

1. Heat 5 gallons of water to 160°F in the 24-quart pot. It's hard to heat that much water on a stovetop. This is why you need the propane burner. That and the fact it's better to make this mess outside.

2. Preheat your mash tun by tossing ½ to 1 gallon of the heated water into the barrel and swishing it around. Return this water to the 24-quart pot to quickly reheat it to 160°F.

3. Pour all the cracked grain (grist) into the mash tun. Slowly stir in the 5 gallons of 160°F water. Add the water bit by bit and stir to make sure the grain is moistened evenly. Never throw grain into a pot of water—always add water to the grain. This grain-and-water mixture is called the mash.

4. Measure the temperature of the mash using the thermometer. The target temperature is 152°F. Stir in a little hot or cold water to get it there. The temperature is critical here. There is a narrow range at which enzymes break down the grains in the mash into fermentable sugars.

5. Once the temperature of the mash is at or very near 152°F, put on the lid of the mash tun and let the mash steep for 1 hour. Check the temperature every 15 minutes and add cold or hot water, as needed, to keep the mash at or very near 152°F.

6. Toward the end of the steeping period, heat an additional 3½ gallons water to 165° to 175°F on the propane burner, using the 24-quart pot again.

DRAINING THE WORT

7. The mash tun is equipped with a valve and a drainage tube. Stick the end of the tube into the pitcher and open the valve just a bit to let the wort slowly trickle out. The slower, the better. Open the valve too much and you risk clogging the valve with chunks of grain. Slow draining also extracts more of the fermentable sugars. Drain out about 2 quarts into the pitcher and pour this straight back into the mash tun. Repeat this three or four times, until the wort you're pulling out drains reasonably clear and no bits of mash are present.

8. At this point, drain all of the wort out of the mash tun, draining it into the 32-quart pot. Be sure to drain the wort off slowly, just as in step 7. Don't rush it.

9. Now you're going to add more water to the grain for a second round of extraction. Add the 3½ gallons of 165° to 175°F water to the mash tun. This is called the sparge water. Let the grain steep with the sparge water for 15 minutes to extract the last of the sugars. Repeat step 7, draining off a little sparge water at a time, checking the clarity, and pouring it back in the mash tun.

HEATING THE WORT

10. When the sparge water is showing reasonably clear, drain it slowly into the brew pot, the same one that is now holding the wort. Combined, the two extractions should mostly fill the pot. Put the wort onto the burner and bring it to a boil. As it heats, foam will appear. Skim this off with the handled strainer. Once the wort is at a full, rolling boil, start your timer. The total boiling period will be 60 minutes.

HOPPING THE WORT

11. During the boiling period, you'll follow the hopping schedule shown in the recipe on page 209, which is notated in the form of a countdown. This is standard form for beer recipes. Adding hops to the wort at varying points in the boil results in subtle changes of flavor in the finished beer. The hops added at the beginning of the boil are known as the bittering hops. The hops added toward the middle and end of the boil are the flavoring hops. Hops varieties are grouped into these two categories, with bittering hops having more of the alpha acids that make beer bitter and flavoring hops having more subtle tastes and aromas. In this case, the Columbus hops are bittering and the Cascade flavoring.

Premeasure the hops so they are ready to go, and stir them into the wort at the prescribed time intervals:

* Add ¾ ounce Columbus hops at the very beginning of the boil, at the 60-minute mark.

* Thirty minutes into the boil, add ½ ounce Cascade hops.

* Forty-five minutes into the boil, add another ½ ounce Cascade hops. This is noted as "15 minutes" on the schedule, because they are added 15 minutes prior to completion.

12. Fifteen minutes before the end of the 60-minute boil, just after you add the second ½ ounce of Cascade hops, submerge the entire wort chiller into the pot with the wort. Doing so will assure that the chiller is sterilized by the boiling wort. It will remain in the pot for the next step.

CHILLING THE WORT

13. Once the boil is complete, remove the pot from the burner and hook up the wort chiller to a faucet or a garden hose. Once the wort starts to cool down, it becomes vulnerable to contamination. The wort chiller is a heat exchanger that cools the wort rapidly, minimizing the likelihood of contamination. Cool water goes into one end of the copper pipe and passes through the beer, chilling it. The heated water spills out the other end, outside the pot. We use the water draining from the wort chiller to water the yard, so it doesn't go to waste. A wort chiller can cool 5 gallons of beer in about a half hour.

14. As soon as the wort is chilled below 80°F, pour it into the 6-gallon plastic fermenting bucket, pouring it through a strainer to catch the hops. Hold the strainer high. Making as big a splash as possible is a good thing. Splashing introduces oxygen into the wort, which the yeast will appreciate. Be sure to sanitize the bucket with iodophor prior to this step.

PITCHING THE YEAST AND STARTING THE FERMENT

15. Toss the liquid yeast into the bucket. It should be room temperature at this stage. You don't need to stir it in.

16. Put the lid on the fermenting bucket and plug the hole in the lid with a stopper fitted with a fermentation lock. Put some cheap vodka in the fermentation lock. For ale, the ideal temperature for fermentation is between 65° and 75°F, so keep the bucket in a temperature-controlled part of your home, if possible. Also keep it out of direct sun.

17. In about a day, you should see the fermentation lock thumping. Let the beer ferment for a week. During this period, the beer will produce a gunky, foamy head that leaves a residue on the side of the bucket. You'll see the remnants of this when you transfer the beer to the carboy.

RACKING THE BEER

18. After a week, rack (siphon) the beer into the 5-gallon glass carboy using the sanitized auto siphon. The goal of racking is to transfer clean beer into the carboy and leave behind all the debris on the bottom. Put the plastic bucket in a higher position than the glass carboy to facilitate siphoning. Put the plunger end of the auto siphon in the plastic bucket and put the hose end into the glass carboy. Raise the plunger and lower it slowly, and suction will begin. The beer will flow from one container to the other. Keep the end of the hose at the bottom of the carboy to minimize splashing the beer around.

19. Add ½ ounce Cascade hops to the freshly racked beer. No need to stir it in, just let it float on the surface. When you add hops at this point, it's called dry hopping. Once it's in, transfer the stopper and fermentation lock from the plastic bucket to the mouth of the carboy. Allow the beer to ferment for 2 more weeks in the carboy.

BOTTLING THE BEER

20. After 2 weeks, it's time to bottle. Clean and sanitize the beer bottles with iodine solution, as you did the beer-making equipment, or run them through a dishwasher set on the sanitize setting with *no detergent*. Fill a small saucepan with water and heat until it's just below a boil. Do not let it reach a boil. While at this temperature, drop the bottle caps in the water to sanitize them. Turn off the heat. It's okay to leave the caps in the water while you do the other steps.

21. Stir the ⅔ cup corn sugar into 2 cups of water and boil for 5 minutes. Allow to cool back down to room temperature. The sugar will provide the carbonation in the beer.

22. Drag out the 5-gallon plastic bucket you used for the first fermentation. Sterilize it by swishing iodine solution inside of it, then draining. Toss the sugar water into the bottom of the bucket. Now, rack the beer from the carboy back into the bucket using the auto siphon again. This ensures that the sugar will be thoroughly mixed with the beer.

23. Line up your beer bottles somewhere you don't mind beer spilling. For us, it works to use the inside lid of the dishwasher as a table to hold the bottles while they are filled. That way any spillage goes into the dishwasher drain. Fill each bottle from the bucket using the auto siphon and a bottle filler wand. If you fill the bottle all the way to the rim with the bottle filler wand inside, when you withdraw the wand the beer will be at the correct height in the bottle. About 1½ inches of headroom is necessary between the beer and lid to ensure the right amount of carbonation. Put the caps on the bottles and use the capper to seal them down.

24. Wait. It takes about a month for optimal carbonation and for the flavor of the hops to mellow. Resist the urge to pop open the beer prematurely. If you open it prematurely and don't like what you taste, wait a little longer and try again. You'll be surprised by how much it can change over even a couple of weeks. Enjoy it within a year.

GROWING YOUR OWN HOPS

If you've got some space, consider growing hops that you can use for flavoring beer. The hop plant (*Humulus lupulus*) is a huge, fast-growing perennial vine, very beautiful and fragrant. Let it run up the sunny side of your house or travel along a fence. Hops are grown from rhizomes that you plant in the spring. Harvesting the flowers takes place in mid- to late summer. In the fall, cut the vines to the ground. Choose a variety that grows well in your climate. Try to grow both a flavoring hop and a bittering hop so that you can be self-sufficient—at least hop-wise.

Section Five
Infrastructure

The final section in this book focuses on permanent systems, tools, and structures, from setting up a compost pile to installing drip irrigation to building a chicken coop. These are lasting projects, the type you tackle one time only or, at the most, once every few years.

55›

Drip Irrigation for Vegetables

⏱ **PREPARATION: 3 hours**

There's a pleasant debate among our gardening friends about whether it's better to water by hand or to use drip irrigation. We think it depends on your personality. We're forgetful, so we're in the drip camp. Hand-watering partisans think the time they spend watering puts them in touch with their garden. The problem with hand-watering is that it's easy to underwater the plants.

For those who prefer hand-watering, the best method we've heard of to ensure deep irrigation is "beer watering." You turn on the hose, crack open a bottle of beer, and start drinking. When you've finished drinking your beer, you can stop watering.

We like the efficiency and certainty that comes with a drip system on a timer. The work you put in on the front end planning and laying out the system saves loads of time in the long run. (And it means you can drink your beer sitting down.) Drip irrigation consists of plastic tubes with small in-line emitters that let out a slow dribble of water. The parts you need will vary depending on the idiosyncrasies of your garden. Good online drip-irrigation suppliers and nurseries can help you design a drip system. For this project, we'll use the example of setting up a system for a 4 x 8-foot vegetable bed.

YOU'LL NEED

DRIP-IRRIGATION PARTS:

* **Hose bib vacuum breaker**[A]
  (They come in brass and plastic; get brass, if you can.)
* **Hose Y connector**[B]
* **Battery-operated timer**[C]
* **Filter**[D]
* **Pressure regulator (25 psi or below)**[E]
* **Female hose beginning**[F]
* **½-inch mainline tubing**[G] **(Purchase enough length to reach from your water source to your vegetable garden.)**
* **½-inch elbow fittings (The number depends on installation—one for each 90-degree turn in the mainline tubing. See instructions on page 221.)**
* **Figure-8 end fitting**

* **¼-inch emitter tubing** [H] **(Get the kind that has emitters spaced every 6 inches. It comes in a roll. For a 4 x 8-foot bed you'll need 48 feet.)**
* **6 (¼-inch) hose barbs (one for each run of ¼-inch emitter tubing)**
* **6 (¼-inch) goof plugs (Get a few extras in case you make a mistake.)**
* **Hole punch (a specific tool for making drip-irrigation connections)**

  TOOLS:
* **Teflon pipe tape**
* **Thermos**
* **Scissors or knife**
* **Sturdy scrap wire, any sort, cut into approximately 12-inch lengths and bent into a U shape (These will be used to pin down the irrigation tubing. You'll need at least 20 for this project.)**

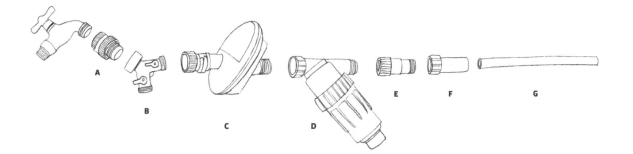

PUTTING IT TOGETHER

A drip-irrigation system comes in two parts: the parts near the hose (which we'll call the "headworks") and the drip lines that run through the garden bed (which we'll call the "drippy parts"). You can get a drip-irrigation kit that will simplify things, but make sure that it contains the parts listed above.

ASSEMBLING THE HEADWORKS

Assemble the headworks in the following order, starting at the faucet: hose bib vacuum breaker, hose Y connector, timer, filter, pressure regulator, female hose beginning, and ½-inch mainline tubing. As you connect the threaded parts, wrap Teflon tape on the threads to ensure a watertight seal. Hand-tighten— don't use a wrench.

Here's what these parts do:

HOSE BIB VACUUM BREAKER: This is a backflow preventer, a one-way valve that keeps soil from getting siphoned back into your water supply.

HOSE Y CONNECTOR: This allows you to run a hose from the same spigot as your drip system, so that you can still hand-water when needed.

TIMER: A battery-operated timer ensures that the garden is always watered, even if you're out of town. We've also used manual timers, which are kind of like a kitchen timer—you dial in a time and it runs for a set amount of time and then turns off. A manual timer is more durable but depends on your setting it daily. In a way, this is a good thing, because it makes you evaluate the water needs of your garden each day. The kind of timer you choose depends on your preference and lifestyle.

FILTER: The filter removes particulates from the water supply that could clog tiny drip emitters. A filter isn't optional.

PRESSURE REGULATOR: Ordinary household water pressure is so high that it would burst the connections in the drip system. The pressure regulator reduces the pressure so that this does not happen.

FEMALE HOSE BEGINNING: This connects the headworks to the ½-inch mainline tubing that runs out to your vegetable bed.

HALF-INCH MAINLINE TUBING: Made of high-density polyethylene (HDPE) plastic, this tubing is flexible and easy to work with. You can bury it or leave it on top of the soil. In cold climates, you will need to bring in the whole drip system for the winter so that the parts don't burst.

QUARTER-INCH EMITTER TUBING:" This is tubing with little drip emitters built in. We use the kind that comes with emitters spaced every 6 inches. Note that we are not talking about a soaker hose, which leaks water along the entire length of the hose. Emitter tubing is more durable, lasts longer, and is more efficient. Quarter-inch emitter tubing is connected to mainline tubing with the barbed connectors. You use a "goof plug" to plug up the ends.

When working with ½-inch main-line tubing and ¼-inch emitter tubing, keep a thermos of boiling water at hand. To make it easier to slide the tubing into fittings, dip the tubing into the hot water for a few seconds. This will heat the tubing and make it more pliable.

ASSEMBLING THE "DRIPPY PARTS"

Run the ½-inch mainline tubing from the water source to the vegetable bed and lay 4 feet of it across one of the short ends of the bed. If on the run out to the bed the tubing needs to make any tight turns, say around a building corner or up the side of a raised bed, you'll need to cut the tubing and install elbow fittings to facilitate each turn. You don't want to crimp the hose by bending it. Seal off the end of the mainline tubing with a figure-8 end, and secure the mainline down along its length with U hooks.

Once the mainline tubing is staked in the bed, you're ready to run the emitter tubing off the mainline. Space the emitter tubing every 8 to 10 inches along the length of the mainline. In this example, you'd need six tubes spaced 8 inches apart. Each tube will be cut to 8 feet in length. Note that when using ¼-inch emitter tubing (the kind with emitters spaced every 6 inches), you should not run any length of tube for more than 20 feet or you'll lose water pressure.

To connect the emitter tubing to the mainline, use a hole punch especially made for drip tubing. Punch a hole every 8 to 10 inches into the ½-inch mainline tubing. Stick a barb connector into the ¼-inch emitter tubing, then stick the other end of the barb into the hole in the mainline tubing. Close the far end of the emitter tubing with a goof plug. Use U pins to hold the emitter tubing flush with the soil. Test the system and check carefully for leaks. If you accidentally punch a hole where you don't want one, you can repair it with a goof plug.

H

RUNNING THE SYSTEM

Imagine the distribution of water beneath the soil as a teardrop shape extending down from each emitter. The surface may look dry, but beneath the soil, there's a wide wet zone around each emitter, wide enough that the combined emitters will saturate the underground soil evenly. Once a plant is established, its roots will be long enough to reach this wet zone. You need not plant right up against the emitters; in fact, it's best if plants are positioned at least a couple of inches away. Basically, don't think much about the position of tubing or the emitters when planting. Underground, where it counts, the soil will be evenly moist. Do be sure, however, to hand-water seedlings or sown seeds until they are established. Drip emitters do a poor job of watering the *surface* of the soil—and newly planted seedlings are shallow rooted.

How much and how often you should water varies greatly by climate, the time of year, the type of plants you're growing, and whether you're growing them in the ground or in a raised bed. When you first set up your system, keep a close eye on the plants, and stick your hand deep into the soil to check it. It should feel moist, not soggy. Reevaluate water needs as plants mature and the summer heats up—and be sure to turn off the system when rain is forecasted.

KELLY SAYS... If this project's parts list makes your head spin, there is an alternative to installing a drip system: You can use a soaker hose. This is a thick, black, porous hose sold in home improvement centers. It hooks to your outdoor tap like a regular hose. You snake it though your garden bed in an S pattern, staking it down every so often to keep it flat. To use, you turn on the tap no more than a quarter turn, and the hose slowly leaks along its length, soaking the bed after an hour or so of running. It's not nearly as efficient as a drip system, and it breaks down faster. Still, it does the job well enough and takes only minutes to install.

56›

Seedling Flats

Over the years, we've started seeds in everything from egg cartons to plastic flats to expensive peat pots. Usually the seeds sprouted, but sometimes they'd be sickly and slow to grow, or we'd lose an entire flat to some mysterious malaise. This no longer happens now that we start our seeds in wooden boxes, as recommended by John Jeavons in HOW TO GROW MORE VEGETABLES.

Wood provides the seedlings with the perfect balance of insulation, drainage, and ventilation. Fill one of these with seeds and soil and water gently, and your seedlings will grow like gangbusters.

YOU'LL NEED

* **Side pieces:** Use scrap pieces of 2x4 or 2x6 lumber. Any kind of wood is fine, as long as it's not chemically treated or painted. Ballpark measurements for a flat made with 2x4 lumber would be 16 x 24 inches, and one made of 2x6 lumber would be 12 x 12 inches.
* **Bottom boards:** Use bender board (landscape edging), paneling, or slats liberated from a shipping pallet. Thinner wood on the bottom reduces the weight of the boxes and looks nicer.
* **Saw**
* **Electric drill or hammer**
* **3½-inch-long wood screws or nails, marked as suitable for outdoor use**
* **Chicken wire (optional)**

PUTTING IT TOGETHER

Cut the side pieces of the box to length and use two nails or screws to secure each corner. Then measure the dimensions of the assembled frame. Cut the bottom boards to match the bottom of the box. The bottom slats can run lengthwise or crosswise, whichever you prefer. Place them as close to one another as you can and attach them to the frame using one nail or screw at both ends of each slat. Predrill your lumber to prevent splitting, especially when working with thinner wood.

For general purposes, a box constructed from 2x4s is plenty deep for seedlings. Sometimes, though, gardeners like to let seedlings mature a bit more in their flats prior to transplanting. A box constructed out of 2x6s allows for the additional root room plants need if they stay in the flat for more than 4 weeks. Once filled with wet soil, these boxes get heavy, so don't make the standard

flats larger than 18 x 24 inches and limit the ones made with 2x6 lumber to about a foot square.

Don't paint, stain, or seal your finished boxes. They're best left as raw wood so that the wood can breathe and the seedlings aren't exposed to any chemicals.

Tip: Curl a piece of chicken wire over your finished box once it is planted to keep birds and squirrels out of your seedlings. Tack down the wire if the critters seem ambitious.

How to Compost

Compost is the life force of your vegetable garden. When you compost, you assist nature in an alchemical transformation by taking "dead" things such as kitchen scraps, yard waste, and manure and magically turning them back into living matter. A compost pile teems with life: fungi, nematodes, microbes, and worms, just to name a few. These critters form mutually beneficial relationships with the roots of plants. As a vegetable gardener, you foster these beneficial relationships and thus the life of the soil. Active soil grows healthy vegetables. In fact, you could say that your primary duty is to the soil, and the vegetables are the fruit of this labor.

The compost pile is the beginning of a chain of life that stretches from what you add to the pile, to the soil you enliven with it, to the plants that thrive in that soil, to the moment those veggies nourish you. Healthy, pest-free vegetables come from a compost pile built with care and love. Need more reasons to compost? There are almost too many to list. Compost raises soil fertility, increases water retention, corrects soil imbalances, and reduces toxic heavy metals, to name just a few.

The different composting methods depend on such factors as how much green waste you generate, your climate, and the types of plants you're growing. In our own yard, we maintain two different piles. One is a slow pile that heats up only slightly and takes a year to be ready for use. The slow pile is where the majority of our kitchen scraps and some of our yard waste goes. We also build "fast" piles from time to time, when we need a lot of compost. Fast compost piles are built all at once, rather than accumulated, and they are ready to use in just a couple of months. The kind you build will depend on your situation, so we provide instructions for both (Project 58 and Project 59), though they are similar in principle.

THE ART OF COMPOSTING

When it comes to building a compost pile, the process is more art than science. We like to use alchemical metaphors for composting, describing a healthy pile as a balanced combination of earth, air, fire, and water. Strike the right balance between these elements and a magical transformation begins.

EARTH. The "earth" part of the pile is the carbon-rich material—usually brown in color—like dried leaves, straw, wood chips, etc. Carbon provides the food that the critters in the pile will break down.

AIR. Since a compost pile is a living thing, it needs air. This is why a compost bin needs to have holes. It's also important to include bulking materials, like straw and dead leaves that, in addition to supplying carbon, will help air get into the center of the pile.

FIRE. The metabolic activity generated by microorganisms heats the pile up. To start this process, you need materials containing nitrogen. Microorganisms use nitrogen to generate enzymes that break down the carbon. Some common sources of nitrogen-rich material are kitchen scraps, lawn clippings, and manure. Using insufficient nitrogen materials is one of the most common novice composting mistakes. No nitrogen, no fire.

WATER. The life forms in your compost pile need water to survive. Aim to keep the pile as moist as a wrung-out sponge.

FIRE (NITROGEN)

Alfalfa meal
Blood meal
→ Grain free! Brewery wastes (hops, spent grains)
Coffee grounds and tea leaves
Fresh grass clippings
Fruit
Hair
Hay
Leaves and trimmings (fresh)
Manure — chemical free
Potato tubers
Seaweed (dried and fresh)
Urine (human)
Weeds (green) — caution

EARTH (CARBON)

Corncobs (ground) only organic
Dry leaves
Dry grass clippings
Garden waste (dried)
Sawdust (use sparingly—very, very
   high in carbon)
Straw
Wood chips (finely ground)
Wood shavings

SOME OTHER CONSIDERATIONS

VARIETY: The greater variety of items you put in the pile, the higher quality the compost will be in the end. It's kind of like eating—you wouldn't want to just subsist on mac and cheese alone, would you? Organic materials all contain differ-ent nutrients. Make your compost pile a smorgasbord, and your garden will reap the benefits of that diversity.

CHOPPING: The more finely chopped your materials, the faster their decomposi-tion. We use a machete and shovels to chop incoming items; you can also run a lawn mower over materials, such as dry leaves, to chop them finely.

WEEDS contain many valuable nutrients and can make a great addition to a com-post pile. A hot pile will kill weed seeds, but if you want to be conservative, add weed materials before they go to seed. The exception here is any pernicious weed (like Bermuda grass) that spreads via rhizomes. If one little piece of rhizome ends up in your compost, you've got more Bermuda grass.

MANURE speeds up any compost pile. The most accessible source in most urban and suburban areas is horse manure. Make friends with horse folks. They'll be more than happy to have you haul off their waste. Just be sure their horses are well cared for and not full of drugs. Most of the time, you'll be getting horse bed-ding, a combination of manure and wood shavings that line the stables. The wood shavings bring carbon along with the nitrogen-rich manure, so balance the rest of your pile accordingly, adding a little more nitrogen in the form of green plant materials. Chicken manure mixed with coop bedding works much the same way. Since animal manure can contain pathogens, like *E. coli*, it's important to get the pile hot, let it fully mature before use, and, for extra safety, wash root vegetables grown with it. Alternatively, you can use alfalfa meal as a nitrogen source instead of manure.

COMPOSTING IS A BALANCING ACT between earth, air, fire, and water. Get the bal-ance right, and the pile will heat up and turn into rich, dark, garden gold. Don't worry about screwing it up. You can't fail. Eventually *everything* breaks down, it's just a matter of how fast that happens. If you always cover green matter (fire) with carbon matter (earth), you'll balance them. If you keep the pile moist but not soggy, it won't smell, and everything in it will break down more quickly than if it were dry. If your pile has enough air to breathe, but not so much that it's dried out by wind and sun, all the tiny creatures in it will flourish and work to your benefit. Know your pile. Trust your intuition. If you look at the pile and your first reaction is that it's a little dry, it probably is. If it looks soggy, maybe you should turn in something dry and airy, like dead leaves. Or maybe you should take off the cover and let it dry out for a day. Both would work. There are many paths to good compost.

CHOOSING A CONTAINER: MASS MATTERS

Compost organisms do best when the pile reaches the mass of 1 cubic yard. While composting can be done in an open pile, in most situations it's best to keep the pile in some sort of container, such as an extralarge garbage can, a store-bought compost container, or a cube made from old shipping pallets. (See the next project for pallet instructions.) Stay away from gimmicky, expensive compost containers. Most are too small to give you the volume you need, and anyway, composting should be cheap.

WHAT DOESN'T GO IN COMPOST?

This is a more complicated question than most compost pundits would have you believe. The truth is that you can compost almost any organic material, but a pile of rotten fish, for instance, smells really bad and attracts rats. But thanks to the miracle of nature, compost piles can break down just about anything, including a lot of bad pesticides, herbicides, and diseased plant materials. If the compost is intended for an edible garden, though, be careful about what goes in the pile. Use your judgment and think about the chain of life that stretches from what you add to the pile to the plants you grow with the compost to the moment those veggies end up on your dinner plate.

57

A Compost Bin Made of Shipping Pallets

Composting is the ultimate form of recycling, so shouldn't the container used for composting also be made from reclaimed materials? One of the most ubiquitous castoffs in our cities is the humble wooden pallet. It takes just a few minutes to hook together a few pallets to make a phenomenal compost bin.

PREPARATION: 1–2 hours

YOU'LL NEED

* 3 wooden shipping pallets^, all the same size (Find them behind stores.)
* Attachment hardware: your choice of screws, nails, bolts, twist-ties, or wire
* Scavenged boards to act as slats for the front of the composter^B (2x6s, 2x8s, etc.), at least 3 feet in length
* 12 to 16 total feet of 2x4 lumber^C (You can piece together scraps, if necessary.)
* Chicken wire, hardware cloth, and/or flattened cardboard boxes (optional)

PUTTING IT TOGETHER

Choose a level site, preferably on soil and in the shade. Orient the back pallet of the compost bin with the slats running vertically and on the inside of the bin. Attach the side pallets of the compost bin to the back pallet with the slats running horizontally and also facing in. Alternating the orientation of the slats makes the bin stronger and gives you a nailing surface on the front. Connect all three pallets at their corners with screws, bolts, nails, twist-ties, or wire. Predrill the holes if you are using screws or bolts, as pallet wood splits easily.

The front of the bin can be left open, but it's neater to place slats across the front. The slats also allow you to build a taller pile. By using stacking slats, you can add or remove slats to access the pile at different heights. Most pallets measure 3 feet across, but some don't, so measure the width of the front of your bin. Cut three or four lengths of sturdy 2x6 (or wider) lumber to the width of the bin to serve as slats. How many lengths you cut depends on how wide the individual slats happen to be, but most likely four slats will do to close the front of the bin.

Make guides for the front slats by cutting four pieces of 2x4 lumber to 48 inches (or whatever the height of your shipping pallet happens to be). Using nails or screws, attach two 2x4s to the inside of the bin and two more to the outside of the bin. See the illustration on the opposite page for their orientation. Slide the slats horizontally between the guides.

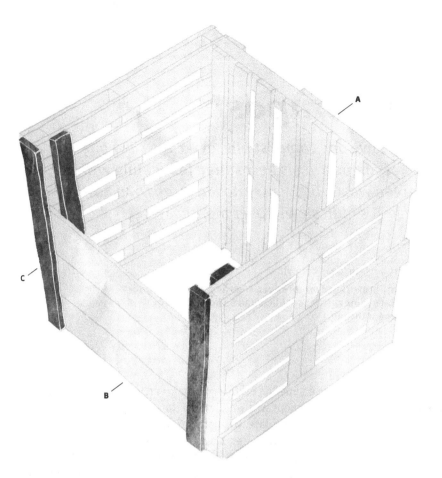

Line the walls of the bin with the chicken wire or hardware cloth to critter-proof it and hold in loose materials. To help retain moisture in dry climates, line the bin with cardboard: Flatten cardboard boxes around the inside walls as you fill the bin. Depending on your climate, you may want to improvise a cover for the bin. We've used both cardboard and plastic tarps as covers to keep out rain and retain moisture.

VARIATIONS

Add two more pallets to one side of this bin to form a two-bin system. Add two more pallets to the opposite side to form a three-bin system. Having multiple bins makes it easier to turn the pile.

With a two-bin system, you just need one set of front slats. To turn the pile, you transfer the front slats to the next bin as you fill it. You can then turn the pile back and forth between the two bins as often as you like, transferring the slats as you shovel.

With a three-bin system, you start out building compost in one end, turn into the next, and then let it finish in the third and last bin. After you turn your initial pile into the middle bin, you can add new compost to the end to start a compost assembly line.

58

Slow Compost

If you only have one compost pile, make it a slow pile. This sort of composting is best suited for dealing with day-to-day green waste, like your kitchen scraps and garden trimmings. It's built slowly, over months.

PREPARATION: 15 min
WAITING: 1 year

YOU'LL NEED

* A compost bin (see ideas below).
* A source of "brown" matter for cover, such as straw, dead leaves, or dried grass clippings. These things can be kept in a bag or container near the bin.

PUTTING IT TOGETHER

CHOOSE A BIN

What kind of bin you choose depends on how much green waste you expect to generate. A slow pile can be kept in a smaller bin than a fast pile, though in general, the more mass you accumulate, the better. You don't need any fancy gizmos to compost, just a sturdy container. Many cities give away compost bins or sell them at reduced rates, so you may want to start your search by checking with your city's recycling program or waste management agency. You could also use a large garbage can. Just cut the bottom out or put many holes in the bottom, so that worms can come and go, and punch the sides full of airholes. The more holes, the better. Or build a bin from discarded shipping pallets, as described in Project 57. If your bin doesn't have a lid, you will want to improvise one with a tarp or a board. While it is possible to keep a lidless bin, lids help retain even moisture levels in the pile, and discourage visits from critters.

FILL THE BIN

Place your bin on soil, not concrete. Always start a new bin by putting down a 4- to 6-inch layer of straw or twigs in the bottom to help with airflow. Then all you have to do is add kitchen scraps and yard trimmings as they appear. Almost anything from your kitchen can go into the pile. Some people compost nearly everything. We avoid foods that are greasy, salty, or milky, and we never compost fish or meat so the pile doesn't attract vermin or develop odd smells. Everything coming out of your kitchen is guaranteed to be nitrogen rich, whether it be coffee grounds or carrot tops. This nitrogen-rich matter must be balanced with carbon materials. So when you put down kitchen scraps, bury them under a layer of dry, carbon-rich matter, like dead leaves or dried grass clippings or straw. This not only balances the nitrogen but it prevents bad smells and insect infestations.

Always cover fresh material with dry material (balancing fire with earth), and your compost pile will be well on its way.

Don't forget the other two elements, though: air and water. Compost must be moist but not soggy. Depending on your climate, your bin, and the types of materials you're composting, you may have to water the pile now and then to keep it from drying out. Air is provided both by the addition of dry matter, which breaks up the density of wet, decomposing materials, and by ventilation in the bin itself. If your compost pile is perennially soggy, add more dry matter and poke more holes in your bin.

Once in a while, add a thin layer of garden soil to the top of the pile to inoculate it with beneficial organisms.

WAIT UNTIL IT'S FINISHED

Keep building until you reach the top of your container. If you're only adding kitchen scraps and trimmings from a small garden, this will take a long time, because the pile shrinks as the material decomposes. Once it's completely full, stop adding materials and let it sit for about a year to cure. In the meanwhile, start a new pile. During that waiting period, you don't have to do much. You don't have to turn it, but doing so will accelerate the composting process slightly and allow you to adjust moisture levels in the pile. Add water if it looks like it's drying out. When it looks like soil, it's ready to use.

As you can see, this is a slow system—thus the name. Yet it's a simple, effortless way to recycle kitchen waste and garden trimmings. If you produce very little green waste, you may wish to use a worm bin instead (Project 61), which will make castings of your scraps in just a couple of months. If you want lots of compost in a hurry, you should build a fast pile, as described in the next project.

SIFTING COMPOST

All compost benefits from sifting. When your compost is finished, meaning you can't recognize most of the source material anymore, run it though a sifter to remove twigs and random pieces of matter that haven't broken down yet, like stubborn orange peels. Small quantities of compost can be sifted through a kitchen strainer. For larger amounts, use a piece of ½-inch hardware cloth or chicken wire. Have someone hold it and shake while you shovel the compost on top of it. If you feel ambitious, you can staple the wire to a wooden frame or the bottom of a shallow box. For instance, you could take out the bottom of an old desk drawer and staple screening material to it. Save all the chunks that don't make it through the screen and put them back in the bin.

59

PREPARATION: 30+ min
WAITING: 2+ months

Fast Compost

Use this method when you want a lot of compost in a short period of time. A fast pile is built all at once with preassembled materials. The mass of the pile in combination with the aeration provided by regular turning breaks down organic matter quickly.

YOU'LL NEED

* Compost bin at least 1 cubic yard in size. We recommend our shipping pallet bin (Project 57).
* Big pile of green matter. This could be cuttings from your garden, green plants of any sort, green lawn trimmings, weeds, anything that doesn't have a woody stem. When we don't have much green matter at hand, we go to the farmers' market at closing time and collect boxes of vegetable trimmings and discards.
* Big pile of dry, carbon-rich material, like dead leaves, straw, or dried grass clippings
* About a gallon of good soil from your garden
* Water source—hose or bucket
* Shovel and/or pitchfork
* Compost thermometer. You'll probably have to order one by mail. It's a thermometer with an extralong probe. In hot composting, it's critical to monitor the interior temperature of the pile.

PUTTING IT TOGETHER

1. Set up your bin over soil, not concrete, so that earthworms and beneficial microbes can migrate up from the ground.

2. Gather all the materials for your pile. At a minimum, you will need enough material to build a pile 1 cubic yard in size, larger in cold climates. Mass is important for the bacteria to build up heat. Once the pile is assembled, you won't add anything else unless you need to correct for an imbalance.

3. Chop the green materials as finely as you can. We do this with a machete and shovel. The more finely chopped this material, the faster the composting process will happen.

4. Begin assembling the pile by putting down a 3- to 4-inch layer of dry bulky material such as straw or chopped-up branches. This loose layer will help oxygen (your "air" element) reach up into the pile.

5. Add a 6-inch layer of green plant material.

6. Top with a light covering of soil from your garden. The soil layer will act as a compost "inoculant" to jump-start the pile with microorganisms. Carefully moisten each layer in the pile with water as you go—not too much. If you squeeze some of the material and water comes out, you've added too much.

7. Next, add a 4- to 6-inch layer of brown, carbon-rich materials. Top with a light covering of soil. Add water to moisten the dry materials.

8. Keep building, repeating steps 5 through 7, until you have a pile that is at least 3 feet high. When you're done, top with a thin layer of soil. Keep the pile covered. The contents should be moist at all times, but not soggy. If your bin doesn't have a lid, put a tarp over it.

9. Within 1 to 2 days, the pile should start to heat up. Check the temperature with your compost thermometer. You want the pile to get into the thermophilic range—between 113° and 158°F. If, after a few days, the pile fails to heat up, the odds are it needs more nitrogen-containing materials. Turn the pile and add more "fire"—that is, shovel the contents out and replace them in the bin, mixing in more green matter, or manure.

A pile that gets over 160°F needs to be cooled down. To do this, you turn it and add more carbon or "earth." If at any time the pile smells rotten or like pickles, the odds are it has gone anaerobic because it either contains too much green stuff or too much water. Mix in bulking materials like straw to aerate the pile.

10. Commence regular turning. If you turned the pile every day, you could, theoretically, have usable compost within 2 weeks. We think you get better compost by letting nature work her magic more slowly. Monitor the temperature. If it dips below 110°F, definitely turn the pile. When you turn, try to move the materials on the outside of the pile into the center. We've found that weekly turning yields finished compost within a couple months. It's also okay not to turn at all, but the pile will need to sit for at least 6 months.

When is compost ready? When it has cooled to ambient temperatures and the materials you put in are no longer recognizable. It should be as dark as coffee grounds and have a nice earthy smell. If your compost is not moving in this direction after a couple of months, evaluate the pile's condition. Is it too dry? Too wet? Is there enough green material to heat it up? You may have to adjust the ingredients, as in Step 9, and wait a little longer. Remember, no matter what, it will decompose eventually. Do be patient and let it finish. You never want to add unfinished compost to the garden, because soil microbes will use nitrogen to digest the unfinished compost. In so doing, they will steal that nitrogen from your plants.

Finally, sift your finished compost. Once it is sifted, rake a few inches worth into the top of a depleted raised bed or use it to improve compact soil—see Project 47. Topdress around established plants or trees. Or use it to make your own planting mix by combining it in equal parts with good soil from your garden.

60

PREPARATION: 1 hour
WAITING: 1–2 years

Building a Dry Toilet

Flush toilets take two valuable resources, clean water and nitrogen-rich human waste, and combine them to create a problem: sewage. Dry or "humanure" toilets combine sawdust and human waste, which is then composted to make soil. It's a simple, elegant system that follows nature's dictate that there is no such thing as waste.

A dry toilet uses no water, power, or chemicals, and it doesn't require plumbing lines or septic tanks. This makes it perfect for off-grid living as well as situations where plumbing is not available. It's a convenient way to add an extra toilet to any house.

We'd be lying if we said it does not seem strange at first to use a toilet with no water, but you do get used to it quickly. If you've been raised with flush toilets, your most basic impulse is to make your waste vanish. *Pronto.* However, once you grasp the indisputable logic of the system, know firsthand that it does not smell, and have seen the contents transformed into sweet-smelling, clean soil through the power of composting, you'll never look at flush toilets the same way again.

YOU'LL NEED

* Sturdy plastic milk crate^A
* 5-gallon bucket^B
* Toilet seat, complete with seat bolts^C
* Felt-tip pen or china marker (optional)
* Jigsaw or keyhole saw
* Utility knife
* 4 wood scraps or table legs^D
* 8 plastic cable ties^E
* Several gallons of sawdust and a bucket to store it in, and a scoop

PUTTING IT TOGETHER

SCAVENGE

Find a milk crate and a 5-gallon bucket. Make sure that the crate is large enough to accommodate the width of the bucket. When you scavenge the crate, ask permission or be discreet. We know of someone arrested for scavenging milk crates behind a strip club, of all places. When the police finished booking the milk crate scavenger, the officer placed the paperwork in … you guessed it, a scavenged milk crate doubling as an in-box.

C

A

E

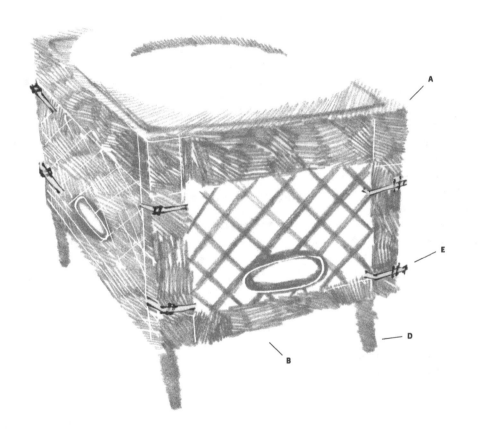

B

D

ATTACH THE TOILET SEAT TO THE CRATE

Forage a toilet seat or pick one up at your local hardware store. Turn the crate upside down and attach the seat to one of the short ends. Be sure to center the seat. Slide the plastic bolts that come with the toilet seat through two holes in the grating on the bottom of the crate. Slip the nuts over the bolts on the inside of the crate, then tighten. Don't overtighten.

CUT A HOLE IN THE CRATE

Lower the toilet seat so it sits on the crate. Lightly mark the position of the seat hole by making a few a lines on the crate using a marker or china pencil, or scoring with a knife, using the inner rim of the seat as a guide. Now you know where the bucket will sit. Lift the seat and position the bucket upside down over the markings. Trace the outline of the top of the bucket onto the crate. Cut out the circle with a jigsaw or keyhole saw.

CUT THE LEGS

The legs of the toilet support the crate so it sits flush with the top edge of the bucket. To figure out how long the legs should be cut, measure both the height of the bucket and the thickness of the crate's bottom. Subtract that fraction of an inch representing the crate's bottom thickness from the height of the bucket. The resulting number will be the length of the legs. The legs on our toilet are 13 ½ inches long, but your measurements may vary, depending on the height of your bucket and the thickness of your crate.

ATTACH THE LEGS

The legs are positioned at the four corners of the crate, their ends braced against the floor of the crate. Attach them to the crate by threading cable ties through the plastic mesh of crate corners and tightening. Two ties, one high and one low, should hold the legs securely. If cable ties don't appeal to you, you could bolt or screw the legs to the crate.

READY-MADE COMPOSTING TOILETS

You can buy 5-gallon buckets with small toilet seats attached. Look for them at outdoor supply stores. Using one of these on a daily basis is not the most comfortable proposition—they're tippy—but it's a good alternative if you won't be using the bucket for long and don't want to make a housing for it. You could fill one of these ready-mades with sawdust and store it away for emergencies.

OPERATING INSTRUCTIONS

You'll need a constant supply of sawdust to use as cover material. Ask around at wood shops and lumberyards for sawdust. Don't use sawdust from chemically treated lumber, fiberboard, or plywood. This will be soil one day, and you don't want those toxins in the soil. Sawdust works best in terms of coverage and odor control, though you can experiment with other carbon-rich cover materials, like chopped straw or hay. Whatever you use should be fine textured for proper coverage. Don't use wood chips or wood shavings. They're too "airy" and won't control odor well. Wood chips don't compost easily, either.

Keep a covered container of sawdust next to the dry toilet. You'll need a scoop for the sawdust. We splurged on a nice metal scoop. Kelly insisted that if we were going to poop in a bucket, we needed that touch of class. You could make a scoop by cutting the end off a plastic jug: Keep the jug handle intact and make the cut at an angle, to form a scoop shape.

Before the first use of the toilet, put a deep layer of sawdust in the bottom of the bucket, about 3 to 4 inches. Do your business. The toilet handles both solid and liquid waste. When you're finished, cover the deposit with a layer of sawdust. Try not to use too much sawdust—just enough to cover is plenty. Toilet paper can go in the bucket, but nothing else. Always keep the lid down when not in use. If odors arise, you're probably not using enough sawdust. All you should smell is wet sawdust.

When the bucket is full, take it outside to the compost pile. Read on.

HOW TO COMPOST HUMANURE

Compost is compost. All of the principles of composting that we described in the previous two projects apply to humanure composting. Like horse manure or chicken droppings, human waste is a nitrogen source. And like any other compostable manure, it can carry pathogens, but those pathogens are killed by both heat and time. Don't confuse humanure composting with the practice of using raw human waste as fertilizer, which would be dangerous. Remember, composting is a cleansing process—and a transformative one, as well. Composting turns everything to soil.

Expert humanure composters use their compost to grow food. They trust the power of composting, and they're experienced enough to know how to manage the pile to ensure its safety. We'd recommend that as a beginner, you only spread your finished humanure compost around nonedible plants and fruit trees.

For this reason, keep your humanure compost in its own, separate bin. The bin should be a closed-sided and lidded container to reduce the ick factor. A 50-gallon drum, metal or plastic, could be used, as could a big garbage can or a commercial compost bin. Unless you plan to move the bin, the bottom of the bin should be cut out or perforated with holes for drainage and to allow worms to get in. Worms will help purify the soil. If you're using a drum or garbage can, provide extra aeration by drilling two rings of small (¼-inch) holes all around the top edge.

Because the pile is built up over time rather than all at once, humanure composting is a form of slow composting, with a little extra attention paid to temperature and aging. We'll talk about these two factors as we go along. First, though, we need to talk about sawdust. Sawdust is an extremely carbon-rich material, much more so than dried leaves or straw. Over the last couple of projects, we talked about how composting is the art of balancing the earth, air, fire, and water elements. Sawdust is an earth element. It's very "cool." If it's not balanced with plenty of nitrogen-rich material, it will make your compost pile cold and inert. Human waste is rich in nitrogen but isn't quite "fiery" enough to balance all that carbon-rich sawdust on its own. This is particularly true if your household is heavy-handed with the sawdust when using the dry toilet. To provide the correct balance between earth and fire, you will need to add additional green stuff to your pile each time you empty the toilet bucket onto it.

This is the basic procedure for humanure composting:

* When you start a new pile, put a layer of something absorbent at the bottom of the bin, like straw or a bunch of dead leaves, to help aerate it and soak up extra liquid.

* When the toilet bucket is full, dump the contents on the pile. It's not as gross as you'd imagine. The sawdust leaves a lot to the imagination.

* Rinse the bucket and pour the water into the pile. It helps to have a hose near the bin, as well as a dedicated swabbing brush. You can wash the bucket outside, using a small amount of biodegradable soap, and pour the wash water on the pile.

* Add an extra layer of "green" stuff to the pile. This includes kitchen scraps and coffee grounds and green trimmings from your yard, as well as other types of manure like horse, chicken, or rabbit droppings. A convenient concentrated source of nitrogen is alfalfa meal, which can be purchased inexpensively in large bags. Sprinkle a cup of it over the surface. That small amount carries as much nitrogen as an armload of greenery.

* After adding this layer, top the pile with a thin layer of dry carbon material, like dead leaves, dry grass, more sawdust, or even a layer of dirt, to control odor and discourage insects. Cover the bin.

* Repeat this process each time you empty a bucket.

You don't have to turn this pile. Good news, huh? If you balance the four elements of earth, air, fire, and water, the pile will decompose on its own. By adding extra nitrogen, you've balanced earth and fire. The water element is moisture. Much of that comes naturally from urine and rinse water, but if the compost pile ever looks dry, add water. Air comes from the ventilation holes in the bin and airy materials like leaves and straw. If any one of these elements seems out of balance, take steps to correct it. For instance, if the pile seems soggy, add dry, fluffy material like straw or dead leaves to soak up some moisture. If it smells bad, you might have too much nitrogen, or the pile is insufficiently covered. The solution is the same—top with lots of dry stuff.

The fresh nitrogen from the toilet bucket and the greens will heat up as it decomposes. If you take the temperature of the top layer of the pile with a compost thermometer a day or two after a new addition, you should see temperatures of 130°F or higher. This will cool over time, and the lower portions of the bin will also be cool. But if the new additions hit 130°F, you can be sure that any potential pathogens (like parasites or E. coli) in the compost are being destroyed.

Time is also a great cleanser. Whether your pile is regularly hitting 130°F or not, it must be aged. When the bin is full to the top, put a lid on it and let it sit undisturbed for at least a year. Insects and smaller life forms will move in and finish the decomposition process. In the meanwhile, set up a new bin right next to it and carry on.

After a year, the contents of the bin should resemble soil. If they do not, take remedial action. Empty the bin. If the material still looks like it did when it went in, you probably didn't add enough nitrogen. The sawdust kept it too cool. Shovel the compost back into the bin, adding a layer of fresh green material every 6 inches or so. The combination of fresh nitrogen and the mass of the pile should start the composting process again and generate enough heat to finish the pile.

PATHOGENS IN THE PILE

The subject of pathogens in humanure is complex. In general, if no one in your household is carrying parasites or suffering from bacteria-borne intestinal diseases, your compost pile will not carry these things either—unless they are introduced to it via animal manure. Even so, hot temperatures and long aging will kill most everything. For a detailed discussion of these issues, read Joseph Jenkins's *Humanure Handbook*. You can buy it in paper form, and he also offers it as a free pdf file at humanurehandbook.com. Also, remember these concerns are most pertinent if you're planning to use the compost on food crops. If you plan to spread it around decorative landscaping or fruit trees, there's little chance at all of any bad beasties coming back to you.

Worm Farming

Worms eat kitchen scraps and create worm castings, which are a valuable soil amendment and plant tonic. Though castings are often called fertilizer, they're actually not very high in nitrogen, but they are full of plant-supporting nutrients.

Sprinkle castings on potted plants and over garden beds. A little goes a long way. A handful can go into the bottom of a planting hole to get a plant off to a good start. Unlike nitrogen-rich fertilizers, worm castings won't burn the plant's roots. They can also be mixed with potting soil, in concentrations of up to 20 percent castings, to make an extra rich growing medium.

Here's what you should know before you start: A worm bin is a supplement to a compost pile, not a replacement for one. Worms don't consume indiscriminately, the way a compost pile does, and they can only eat so much at a time. But as we said above, castings are a fantastic resource, so it's well worth keeping both a worm bin and a compost bin. That said, a worm bin makes a fine green-waste disposal system for an apartment dweller. If you don't have yard trimmings to worry about, worms can handle a good deal of your day-to-day food waste—like coffee grounds, wilted lettuce, stale bread, and so on—and give you castings in return that you can apply to container plants.

Worm bins are best kept indoors. Worms thrive in temperatures between 50° and 75°F, and those conditions are usually found in the cool parts of a house, rather than outdoors. During hot summers, worms dig down deep to keep cool. They can't do that in a worm bin, which will heat up to ambient summer temperatures. In the winter, freezing cold will kill them, too. Of course, it all depends on your climate and situation. If you have cold winters and mild summers, the worms could spend the summer outdoors and the winter indoors. Or in the opposite situation, they could come in for hot summers and stay out for mild winters. You can also take steps to keep the bin's temperatures reasonable, like insulating it. Just remember that when temperatures are extreme, worms are unhappy.

SOURCING WORMS

While you can buy worms from online suppliers, it's more fun to get them from a friend who keeps worms or to hunt them in your own garden. Worms from a friend are truly local and already well adapted to life in a worm bin. In addition, they've not undergone travel stress. Mail-order worms are understandably freaked out on arrival (as freaked out as worms can be) and will often try to escape from the bin their first few nights until they calm down.

It's most satisfying to hunt worms in your garden. The worms you want aren't the big fat night crawlers, they're the smaller red or purplish worms that live close to the surface of the soil, usually in leaf litter or in cool compost. They are most populous in the spring and the fall and can be hard to find in the summer and winter. Make a trap for them by burying something tasty in your garden beds or in an area rich with leaf litter. Worms adore squash. It draws them like a magnet. You could also use leftover oatmeal or wet bread. Bury these offerings about an inch under the soil or leaf litter and come back in about 3 days. More than likely, you'll find some worms bellied up to the bar. Scoop them up and take them to their new home.

WHICH WORM IS WHICH?

Red worms (*Lubricous rubellas*) are the worms you most often find in leaf litter and garden beds, but they also hang out in compost piles. Compost worms (*Eugenia fetid*) are about the same size and can be red, too, but they also come in purple and tiger-striped varieties. These are true compost worms whose preferred habitats are compost and manure piles. *Eugenia fetid* are the type sold for worm bins, but *Lubricous rubellas* adapt to life in the bin very well.

Worms are hermaphrodites, so they're not picky about mates. They breed at a rate that puts rabbits to shame. If you're willing to be patient, you only need to hunt up about a cup of them to get started. If you buy them, you'll buy a full pound—that's usually the minimum amount on offer. Whichever way you go, it all works. More worms eat more scraps and make more castings. If you start with lots of worms, the bin will be productive faster. If you start with only a handful of worms, they'll start breeding as soon as they settle into their new home, and you'll be up to speed in a couple of months.

Making a Worm Bin

Although you can buy or build elaborate multilevel worm composting systems, we've come to believe less is more when it comes to worms. A simple container is all you really need.

YOU'LL NEED

* **Power drill or a sharp nail and a hammer**
* **Rectangular plastic storage bin with a lid, any size**
* **Newspaper and cardboard**
* **2 cups ordinary soil, any type**
* **Red worms (*Lubricous rubellas*) or compost worms (*Eugenia fetid*)**

PUTTING IT TOGETHER

Using the drill or the sharp nail and a hammer (the latter is much more difficult—use a drill if you can), create two rows of ventilation holes around the top edge of the bin, starting beneath the lid. Space the holes about 3 or 4 inches apart. The exact size of the holes doesn't matter much, but they should be ¼ inch or less in diameter. To make sure that the bin doesn't leak and can be kept anywhere, don't put any holes in the bottom of the container. Lack of bottom drainage means you will have to be vigilant to make sure the contents don't get too soggy, because there's nowhere for water to go.

Shred newspaper into fine strips. Use plain newspaper, not shiny inserts, which might contain harmful dyes, and not office paper, which has been bleached. If you have a paper shredder, run the newspaper through that, because the finer the paper shreds, the better. Otherwise, rip the paper into strips. While you're at it, rip up some plain corrugated cardboard, too, if you have it. It must be bare cardboard, not paper coated, because again, that paper might contain bleaches or inks. It's easier to rip up cardboard that has been soaked in water first. Worms really like corrugated cardboard—they snuggle up in the channels, so tear it into worm-size chunks roughly 4 inches square.

Wet the newspaper strips by placing them in a bowl or bucket and drizzling water over them and stirring until they're all equally damp. Add the shreds to the worm bin by the handful, squeezing them first to make sure they're damp, not sodden. The ideal consistency is that of a wrung-out sponge. You don't ever want to have standing water in the worm bin.

When you've added about 4 to 6 inches of newspaper to the bin, add the cardboard pieces and about 2 cups soil. The soil adds grit to the mix, which helps with the worm's digestion. Toss it all together to mix it. Add the worms. Put a little paper over them right away because they don't like the light.

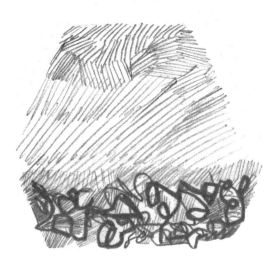

START FEEDING

Theoretically, worms can eat their weight in food scraps each day, but in practice, the amount they eat is highly variable. One factor is newness. A new bin doesn't eat nearly as much as an established bin, no matter how many worms you start with. It may take a few months for a bin to hit its stride and become an eating machine. In the meanwhile, don't overfeed. If you add more food than the worms can handle, it will lead to bad smells and possible invasions by undesirable insects.

Start off with just a cup of scraps on the first day. See table below for suggestions. Bury the scraps in one corner of the bin and cover it with about an inch of newspaper. The worms will find the food. After a couple of days, add another cup of scraps in another corner. Proceed cautiously, even if you have lots of worms,

WORMS REALLY LIKE:
Coffee grounds and tea leaves
Crushed eggshells
Dry cornmeal, just a sprinkle, as a treat
Fruit of all sorts, except citrus
Lettuce
Oatmeal and other cooked grains
Squash
Wet bread and bready things like cooked pasta

WORMS WILL EAT:
Just about any chopped vegetable matter, fresh
    or cooked
Newspaper and uncoated cardboard
Rabbit droppings

DON'T FEED WORMS:
Citrus of any sort (It's antimicrobial.)
Dairy (Traces are okay.)
Meat
Oil
Salty or processed food
Sugar (Traces are okay.)
Vinegar

because they might not want to eat much at first. Develop an intuition for what is enough and what is too much. While it's important to feed them plenty if you want them to breed, don't worry much about their going hungry. If they get hungry between feedings, they'll eat the newspaper. Eventually, they'll eat everything in the bin. All of the newspaper, cardboard, and food scraps will be reduced to black gold: worm castings.

WHAT TO FEED THEM

Worms aren't hamsters. They don't rush to nibble your fresh offerings. Instead, they work in concert with fungi and bacteria to break down rotten food. If it's not rotting, they're not interested. That's why it usually takes a couple days before they approach new food. Overall, they prefer soft food, like oatmeal and squash, to hard food, like carrots. Of course, even carrots will rot eventually, and the worms will get to them then. Don't put large chunks of food in a worm bin. Take a moment to rip or cut food scraps into small pieces to speed decomposition.

Worms don't eat vegetable seeds. Nature designed seeds so that they don't break down easily. More often than not, the seeds will end up mixed in with the castings and thus could sprout wherever you spread the castings. If this concerns you, separate out seeds before you give food to the worms. Send seeds to the compost pile instead.

MAINTAINING THE BIN

Put the bin in a safe, quiet place out of direct sunlight. Otherwise the sun will shine through the plastic walls and irritate the worms. Wherever you stow the bin, be sure the temperatures are moderate. Keep the lid on tight if you have dogs in the house—canines don't have discriminating palates. Our dog once nosed off the lid on our worm bin and ate half the contents before we stopped him. We don't know if he was more interested in the worms or the rotten food, but he swallowed it all. If your bin is outside, lock down the lid with a bungee cord to keep raccoons and skunks and other insectivores out at night. And heaven help you if a wandering chicken ever came across your open worm bin!

Aim to keep the contents of the bin always at that magic consistency: *moist as a wrung-out sponge.* In the first few weeks, you might have to use a spray bottle to mist the paper to keep it from drying out. Worm castings hold water, so once they appear, the bin will stay wet on its own. Then your challenge will become keeping it dry enough. It's important that it stay a damp, airy environment. If it seems to be getting soggy and dense, mix in a few handfuls of dry shredded newspaper to dry it out and fluff it up. If lots of worms are hanging out on the sides or lid of the bin—or trying to wiggle out the airholes—it's definitely too wet.

Note: Keeping the lid on the bin keeps out the light and also keeps out flies. However, it holds in a lot of moisture. If you're having trouble keeping the bin dry enough, you could cut a window out of the lid. Then use duct tape to secure a piece of window screen over the hole. That way, you have both air and protection. If you do this, keep the bin in a dim place for the worms' sake.

The deeper the contents of the bin, the greater the danger of the bottom portion of the bin turning swampy and anaerobic. To prevent that, don't let the contents of the bin get too deep. Keep the depth of the contents between 6 and 8 inches and you should be fine. If you have a ton of worms and 6 to 8 inches doesn't seem enough room, it's time to start a second bin, give your extra worms to friends who want to start their own bins, or feed some spares to your chickens. You could also distribute a few handfuls in a cool compost pile.

Don't be afraid to dig around in the bin every so often to make sure all is well. Check regularly to be sure there's never any standing water in the bottom of the bin. Bad smells will ensue, and worms will die. If all is well, eventually you should see tiny baby worms in the mix, as well as the little lemon-shaped beads that are worm cocoons. These are good signs. Your worms are happy and breeding. As your bin matures, you might find that other critters, decomposers such as mites, pot worms and tiny black beetles, will make it their home as well. This is nothing to worry about. They're all doing the same work, and the worms don't mind the company.

Before you go on vacation, feed the worms well and add fresh bedding. They'll be fine for a couple of weeks.

HARVESTING THE CASTINGS

When the contents of the bin start looking more black than anything else, it's time to harvest some castings. This will probably happen about 2 months after you start the bin. The simplest way is to stop adding fresh food for a while and let the worms finish up the little scraps and bits dotting the bin. When there's not much recognizable food in the bin, put a big portion of something delicious, a proven favorite like squash, at one end of the bin. The worms will migrate that direction. Wait a few days, then scoop out the material on the opposite side of the bin and pile it on the bin lid. Do this during the day or under bright lights. Form the pile into a pyramid or cone shape. There will still be worms in the mix, and they'll dive down to the bottom center of the mound to hide from the light. Then you can harvest the castings from the top and sides of the mound and transfer them to a bucket or bowl. Return the worms hiding at the bottom of the pile to the bin.

Add fresh wet newspaper and soil to the bin, just as you did at the beginning, to rebuild after harvest. Mix this material with the remaining material and start feeding normally again.

Freshly harvested worm castings are very wet. Spread them out on a tray and let them air-dry for a few days, then sift them through a screen or colander. This will catch any remaining food scraps and give the castings a nice granular texture that's easy to spread. Store them in a bag or covered container.

WORM TEA

One excellent use of castings is in a liquid plant tonic. Put 1 pint of castings in a bucket. Add a gallon of warm water and a spoonful of molasses. Stir this well, and stir it frequently over the course of 24 to 48 hours. Dilute the resulting liquid at the ratio of 1 part tea to 4 parts water and use it to water container plants and fruit trees. You can use it in your vegetable beds, but they should already be well nourished by compost and thus don't need it as much. It's best to use all of your worm tea in a week or so.

PREPARATION: 2 hours

A Mash Tun

To make beer from scratch, you need a mash tun. "Mashing" is the process of converting starches in malted grain to sugar that you'll ferment to make beer. A mash tun is the vessel you'll "mash" in. You can buy one ready-made, or you can make one.

Our mash tun is nothing more than a repurposed 10-gallon cooler with an improvised valve instead of a spigot and a filter made out of the braiding from a dishwasher water supply hose. Take a trip to the hardware store, spend a few minutes assembling the pieces, and you'll be ready to brew. To use, you mix hot water and grain in the cooler, let steep for an hour, and then, using the valve, let the fermentable sugars slowly drain through the braided hose and out the valve into your brew pot. The braided hose at the bottom acts just like a tea strainer, keeping the grain in the cooler and letting the "tea" drain out into your brew pot. (See Project 54 to learn how to make beer with a mash tun.)

YOU'LL NEED

* **Round 10-gallon cooler**
* **9 inches vinyl tubing**[A]
* **24 inches (⅜-inch) copper pipe**[B]

FOR THE BULKHEAD FITTING:

* **⅜-inch braided stainless steel hose**[C] **(most commonly sold as part of a dishwasher installation kit)**
* **2 (½-inch) brass barb to MIP adapters**[D]
* **⅜-inch brass T #12**[E]
* **4 (½-inch) hose clamps**[F]
* **3 (⅝-inch) stainless steel washers**[G]
* **Washer that came with the cooler**[H]
* **⅜ x 1 ½-inch brass nipple**[I]
* **O-ring (⅝-inch I.D.)**[J]
* **⅜-inch ball valve**[K]
* **⅜-inch brass barb to MIP adapter**[L]
* **Teflon tape**

TOOLS:

* **Tin snips**
* **Needle-nose pliers**

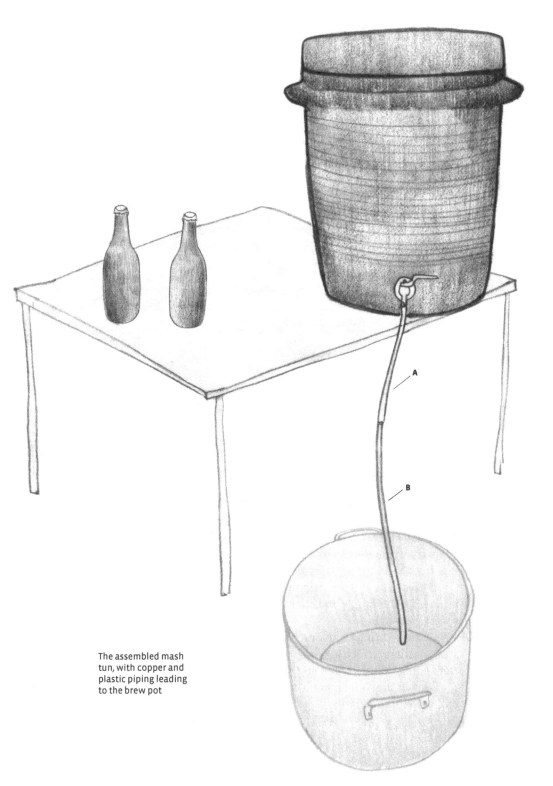

A

B

The assembled mash
tun, with copper and
plastic piping leading
to the brew pot

Note: Instead of the braided dishwasher hose, you can buy a short length of stainless steel screened tubing called a "bazooka screen" at a home brew shop. If you are using a bazooka screen, substitute the brass T and two ½-inch brass barb to MIP adapters with a single ¼-inch brass barb to FIP adaptor. The rest is the same as above.

PUTTING IT TOGETHER

PREP THE COOLER

The cooler's insulation makes mashing easy, since it retains heat throughout the mashing period. You'll want a 10-gallon circular beverage cooler for this project. Look for a cooler on sale at big-box stores, where we've found them discounted as much as 50 percent. Remove the spigot that came with the cooler and hold on to the washer, which you'll be using later. (Keep the spigot so that you can put it back on whenever you want to use the cooler for serving drinks.)

ADAPT THE STAINLESS STEEL HOSE

Remove the plastic lining from the braided stainless steel hose, since you just want to use the braided part for this project. The braided hose will sit at the bottom of the cooler and act as a kind of strainer, preventing bits of grain from draining into your brew pot. To remove the plastic liner the hose comes with, cut off the threaded adaptors on both sides of the hose with tin snips. You'll need 28 inches of hose, so trim accordingly. Now, grip one end of the plastic liner with a pair of needle-nose pliers and *push* the liner out of the braiding. This takes some patience—take it slow and don't try to pull it off as this will stretch it. Dispose of the liner.

ASSEMBLE THE BULKHEAD FITTING

Reinsert the washer from the cooler if it isn't still in place. Put a few winds of Teflon tape on all the threaded fittings. Attach the two ½-inch brass barb to MIP adapters to the ⅜-inch brass T. Using two ½-inch hose clamps, attach the stainless steel braid to the barbs to form a circle as shown in the illustration.

Thread the ⅜ x 1½-inch brass nipple into the T. Put one stainless steel washer on the nipple and stick the nipple through the rubber washer where the spigot used to be.

Put the O-ring on the nipple on the outside of the cooler. Put two stainless steel washers (which act as spacers) on the nipple on the outside of the cooler. Depending on the cooler, you might need to add more washers.

Attach the ⅜-inch brass barb to MIP adapter to the ball valve and attach the ball valve to the nipple.

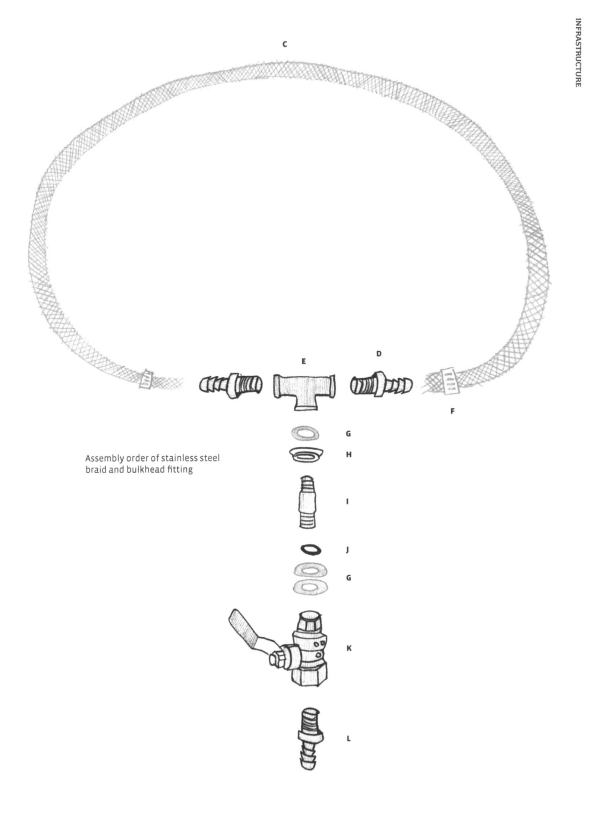

C

E   D

F

G

Assembly order of stainless steel
braid and bulkhead fitting

H

I

J

G

K

L

ADD THE DRAINAGE PIPE

On the end of the brass barb that sticks out of the ball valve, attach 9 or so inches of food-grade vinyl tubing and connect to a 24-inch piece of ³⁄₈-inch copper pipe. The copper pipe will extend down to the bottom of the brew pot. Use ½-inch hose clamps to make the connections. This arrangement lets you drain off the wort from the cooler directly into your brew pot without splashing it around—it's important not to aerate wort before you boil it.

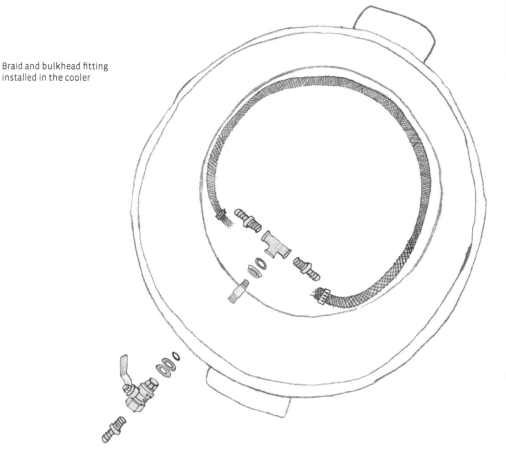

Braid and bulkhead fitting installed in the cooler

63 › A Wort Chiller

An immersion wort chiller is another critical piece of equipment for home brewing that can be made easily at home. A wort chiller is a copper coil that you stick into your hot beer or mead at the end of the boil. Cold water passes through the copper coil to cool the liquid rapidly.

PREPARATION: 1 hour

When you minimize the time that elapses between the end of the boil and the point when the wort is cool enough to throw in the yeast, you reduce the chance that wild yeast will take up residence in your brew or, worse, that contamination will cause the brew to turn to vinegar. A wort chiller is basically a simple heat exchanger. All you need are a few brass fittings and a length of copper pipe to put it together.

All the parts listed can be found in the plumbing supply aisle. Some of the names of the parts are exotic, but trust us—they're common, and the store staff can help you find them.

YOU'LL NEED

* ⅜-inch tube bending spring
* 25–50 feet ⅜-inch copper pipe[A] (Copper is expensive, but the longer the coil, the more efficient it will be—let your pocketbook be the deciding factor.)
* 2 (⅜-inch) compression x ½-inch FIP [B]
* Wrench
* 2 (¾-inch) male hose x ½-inch MIP adapter [C]
* Teflon tape
* 2 garden hoses, length variable (see instructions)

PUTTING IT TOGETHER

Find a cylindrical object to use as a form to coil the pipe. We used an 8-quart pot that fit inside our larger 32-quart brew pot. The wort chiller needs to fit in the brew pot without hitting the sides, and you'll need to leave a straight length of pipe leading from both ends of the coil, as seen in the illustration on page 254, both long enough to reach over the top of the brew pot.

Tube bending springs are available in the plumbing tool isle and are used to bend copper pipe without causing a crimp in the pipe. To use, slip the spring over the copper pipe and bend only the part of the pipe covered by the spring. Carefully coil the pipe, wrapping it in a tight coil around the cylindrical form you've chosen, leaving only the aforementioned straight sections to reach over the top of the pot. Make a 90-degree bend at both ends of the pipe, as shown in the illustration below.

Attach the compression fittings using the wrench. Wrap the threads of the two ¾-inch male hose x ½-inch MIP adapters with the Teflon tape and attach to the compression fittings.

With a permanent marker, mark the fitting that extends down to the bottom of the wort chiller as "out" and the topmost one as "in."

TO USE THE WORT CHILLER

The wort chiller comes into play at the end of the brewing process. The wort or mead has been boiling and will need to be cooled rapidly so that yeast can be added. When there is only 15 minutes left of cooking time for the brew, drop the wort chiller in the brewing pot. The hot brew will sterilize it.

When the boil is done, take the brew pot (with the chiller immersed in it) to the water hose, or bring the hose to it. Hook the water hose to the "in" fitting of the chiller and hook a second hose to the "out" fitting. We use a long hose for the out fitting so that we can run the water anywhere in the garden. (We like to use the water to irrigate trees.) If you're brewing indoors, you can buy two short hoses normally sold as water supply hoses for washing machines. You will need to find an adapter to hook the in hose to your particular kitchen or bathroom faucet. Direct the out hose to the bathtub or sink. Turn on the tap and let water run through the coils until the temperature of your brew drops to the range specified by your recipe.

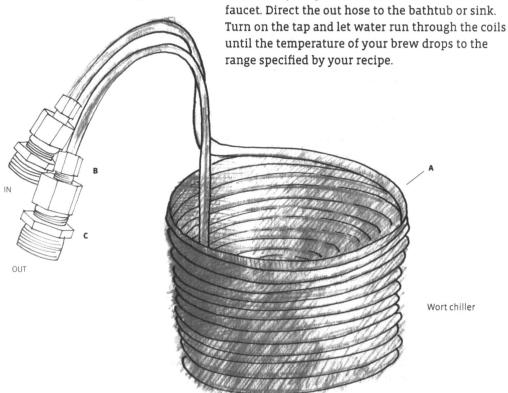

IN

B

OUT

C

A

Wort chiller

64 ›

PREPARATION: 2 hours

A Solar Cooker

What's a solar cooker? It's a slow cooker powered by the sun and a fun way to cook during the summer when the sun is high and the kitchen is hot. We use ours to make staples, like rice and polenta. All you have to do is mix up the ingredients early in the morning and set the pot out to cook. Most foods will be ready as soon as lunchtime, but if you're not around, they'll keep until dinner. Due to the low operating temperatures, it's almost impossible to burn or overcook food in a solar cooker.

We used this design to make our own solar cooker, so we can vouch for its effectiveness. It's a panel-style cooker constructed out of foil and cardboard. Anyone can make one with a little patience and a utility knife. We like it a lot because it's designed to collapse flat. This means it can be easily stowed away in the winter, and it also travels well for picnics or camping. It's called the CooKit.

The CooKit was designed by Roger Bernard and a team of engineers associated with Solar Cookers International, a nonprofit organization that disseminates solar cooker plans worldwide to help decrease reliance on cooking fuels. It's simply the best panel cooker we've seen anywhere, and we're happy and grateful that Solar Cookers International has given us permission to reproduce their plans here. Visit solarcookers.org for more designs and solar cooking advice.

YOU'LL NEED

TO ASSEMBLE THE COOKER:

* 36 x 48-inch (or larger) sheet of cardboard (Look for discarded furniture and appliance boxes.)
* Roll of heavy aluminum foil
* Spray mount, craft glue, or flour paste glue
* Paintbrush or foam brush
* Sharp utility knife
* Ruler

FOR COOKING:

* Black, lidded pot or casserole (It must be black. Look for black speckleware or enamelware. Cast iron is too thick. The cooker will accommodate a range of pot sizes.)
* Oven roasting bag (These heat-resistant plastic bags are sold by the box in supermarkets.)
* 1-inch (or larger) binder clip

HOW TO MAKE FLOUR PASTE

Mix 3 tablespoons white flour with just enough water to make it liquid. Meanwhile, heat 1 cup water on the stove. When the water is hot, add the flour-water mixture and bring to a boil. Stir constantly to prevent burning. Let cool just a bit, then it's ready to use like any other glue. The unused portion can be stored in a bottle in the fridge for a few days.

PUTTING IT TOGETHER

TO ASSEMBLE THE COOKER

Transfer the diagram to the right onto a large sheet of cardboard using a pencil to mark out the external measurements. Start with broad measurements, like overall length and width, then make the smaller internal measurements, then connect the lines. If the measurements are correct, all the shapes and angles should take care of themselves. The only place you have to work freehand is on the outer curves, but the curves do not have to be perfect or symmetrical for the cooker to work. If you're nervous about laying it out this way, you could draw a grid of 1-inch squares on the cardboard and transfer the design over, matching square to square.

Once you have the pattern transferred, cut where the diagram indicates a solid line. Before you start cutting, make sure you have a fresh, sharp blade in your utility knife. It will save you a world of frustration. To make the folds, which are marked by dotted lines, score the cardboard by slicing through the paper on one side, being careful not to push the knife blade all the way through.

After you cut out the shape and score the fold lines, cover the interior of the cooker with foil. Spray or brush on the glue in sections that match the width of your foil, and lay down a sheet at a time, shiny side up. It helps to have pieces of foil already cut and ready to go, because you have to work quickly. Overlap each sheet a little. It doesn't have to be pretty. Once the glue dries, bend the cooker into shape.

WHEN TO USE THE COOKER

Unless you live in the tropics, panel cookers are best used when the sun rides high in the sky—the summer months. Stand outside and look down at your shadow. As a rule of thumb, when your shadow is shorter than you are, it's solar cooking season. Ambient temperature is not as important as having a good, clear sunny day. If it's cold, but sunny, you can still cook.

SETTING UP THE COOKER

Use a black pot, because black attracts the most solar heat. Other types of pots won't work nearly as well. The roasting bag helps seal in the heat. Fill your pot with whatever you're cooking (see the recipes on page 259 for a start), put the pot in the roasting bag, twist the top of the bag closed, and secure the bag with a binder clip or similar object. Set the pot in the CooKit and point the cooker toward the sun. You might have to move the cooker periodically to follow the sun, but the wings of the panel cooker have a broad reach, so you should not have to reposition often. Dishes that cook over the course of 2 or 3 hours will need no

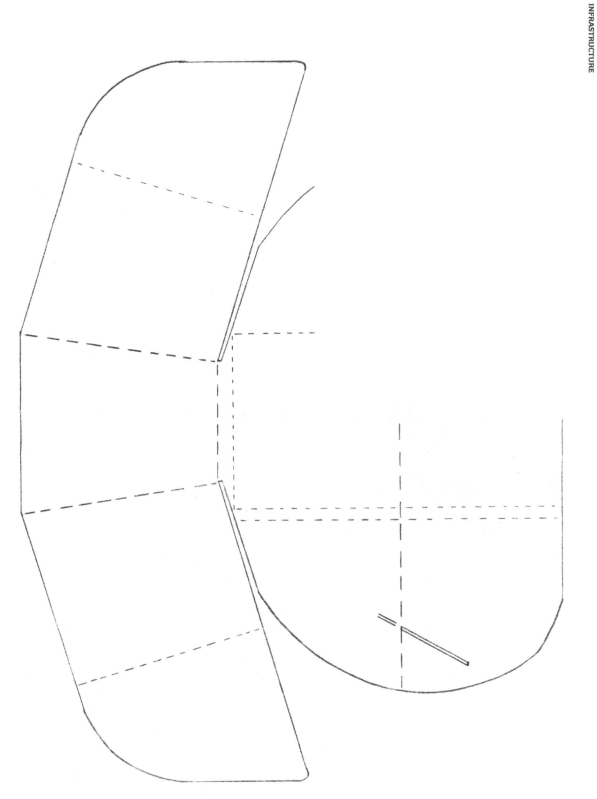

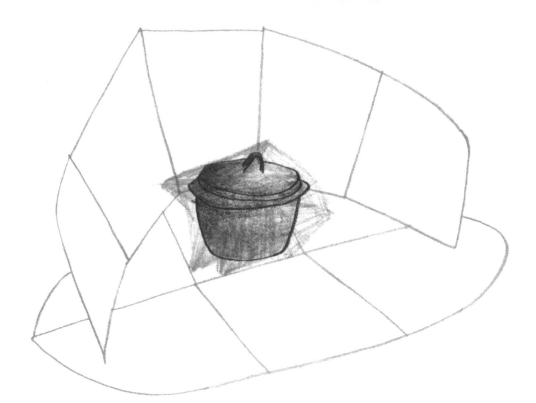

SAFETY NOTE

Make sure you wear oven mitts
if you need to move the pot. It
gets very hot. And be prepared
for a rush of hot steam if you
peek inside.

repositioning, while longer-cooking dishes will require more cooker adjustment to track the sun. You can weight the corners of the CooKit to keep it from blowing over in the wind.

Anything that can be slow cooked at low temperatures will work in your CooKit. The sun is strongest between 10:00 a.m. and 2:00 p.m. That's when most solar cooking is accomplished. Put the food out by 9:00 a.m. to take advantage of the sun at its zenith. It's difficult to dry out or burn food in a solar cooker, so you can collect the food anytime after it's done. The sun will keep it warm. The food will cool as soon as the sun's rays are no longer on the pot; if you want hot food, you have to collect it while the cooker is still in the sun.

While the sun is on the pot, the temperature inside will be high enough to pasteurize food (150°F), meaning there's no need to worry about spoilage during long cooking. However, if the solar cooker ends up in shadow, or the sun goes down and the food is forgotten for a few hours, then it's subject to the same risk of spoilage as any food left sitting out. If you suspect your food has been sitting at temperatures less than 125°F for 4 hours or more, you should heat the food thoroughly before serving or consider discarding it for perfect safety.

Basic Solar Cooker Recipes

COOKING RICE

You can cook brown and white rice in the solar cooker using the same method. White rice cooks faster and is the best choice when time is short or the conditions substandard. Use 2 parts rice to 3 parts water. There's little evaporation, so you use less water than you would on a stove. Combine the cold water and rice in the pot, add a pinch of salt, wrap the pot in the roasting bag, and stick in the CooKit. Cooking times vary quite a bit, depending on the weather and the time of day you're cooking. You'll probably have rice ready to eat in 2 or 3 hours. Go ahead and peek in the pot to check. If it's still a little crunchy, just tie up the bag again and wait a little longer. If you set it out in the morning, you should have hot rice for lunch. And since the temperature is low, you'll never have to worry about burning the rice.

COOKING POLENTA

Polenta in a solar panel cooker is truly miraculous. Imagine perfectly cooked polenta with no stirring, lumping, or burning. Combine 4 parts water with 1 part cornmeal in the cooking pot. Use cold water and stir in the dry cornmeal briskly, adding it to the water a little at a time, so that no lumps form. Add a pinch of salt. Put the pot in the bag and clip it shut, put it in your cooker, and a couple of hours later, Bob's your uncle. Perfect polenta. Top with some Parmesan cheese or other goodies.

WATER PASTEURIZATION

If you're camping, or an emergency situation makes you doubt the purity of your tap water, you can pasteurize water in your solar cooker. If you heat water to 150°F for a short period, all bad bugs will be killed. The majority of them are dead at 140°F. Average temperatures inside a solar cooker in full sun range from 180° to 275°F. A quart of water heated in a solar cooker in a black pot and bag should be pasteurized in about an hour.

ERIK SAYS... For that matter, you can also treat water, in emergency situations, by putting it in clear glass or plastic bottles (quart size) and laying the bottles on their side on a black surface in the sun. The combination of heat and ultraviolet rays will purify the water in as little as a couple of hours. Purify water this way and you can still use the solar cooker to make dinner!

65 › *Build a Chicken Coop*

If you're thinking about raising a few hens in your backyard, we encourage you to go for it. Once you taste your first homegrown egg, you'll never want to buy eggs at the store again. Chickens provide lots of good manure for your compost pile, and, if you direct their efforts, they'll clear your garden of weeds and bugs. Beyond these practical advantages, they bring life and color to the garden and draw you into it more often.

There's something hypnotic about the way chickens move and the soft sounds they make when content. Many a time, we step out in the yard on an errand and end up talking to the hens, or just standing there, watching them, caught in their spell.

However, we don't want to paint too rosy a picture of poultry keeping. It is a significant responsibility. Chickens require daily care and an initial investment in equipment and housing to keep them healthy and safe. The biggest investment you'll make is in the construction of their coop. Time spent planning and building a sturdy, well-designed coop pays off in the long run. The right coop for you is going to depend on a lot of factors, including the size of your flock, the climate you live in, and the specifics of your yard. There is no one-size-fits-all solution. We'll lay out some general guidelines and show you an idealized version of our coop, complete with all the additions we'd make if we had to do it over again. We hope this might become a template for your own design.

CHICKEN COOP GUIDELINES

CHICKENS NEED A PLACE TO ROOST AT NIGHT. The house they sleep in is called the henhouse. The word *coop* refers to the henhouse and outdoor run combined. The henhouse should be darkish, waterproof, and predator proof. The materials it's constructed of depend on your climate. In cold climates, insulate the walls of the house. Just make sure that the insulation isn't exposed to the chickens, because they will eat it. In milder climates, the walls of the house can be constructed out of plywood or sheet metal. All henhouses should be windproof, too. Chickens can keep themselves warm, but drafts and leaks interfere with their ability to do so. Most important, the house should be built sturdy enough that predatory critters cannot dig or pry their way in at night. Pay close attention to the doors and floors. Persistent predators can pull up weak siding or plywood and pull off poorly attached wire mesh. Raccoons can even manipulate latches.

It's a good idea to make the house human friendly, too, for easy cleaning. Large houses should be fitted with a proper door so you can walk in and out without banging your head. Small houses are most convenient if they're elevated to hip height and designed so that one wall swings open, allowing you to reach inside easily.

THE HENHOUSE DOES NOT HAVE TO BE LARGE. Chickens never hang out in their house during daylight hours. They use the house for two main purposes, sleeping and laying eggs. When they're awake, they want to be outside. This means the house doesn't have to be big. The dimensions of the coop depend on the size of the flock. They sleep (roost) off the ground, lined up on a pole. Each hen needs about 1 foot of roosting space. This measurement determines the dimensions of the house. A flock of four hens would therefore need a 4-foot pole to roost on. The roosting pole stretches from wall to wall inside the house, meaning that a house intended for four hens would be 4 feet wide at minimum.

THE ROOSTING POLE should be rounded, measure 2 inches in diameter to accommodate a full-grown chicken of standard size, and be made of wood for good traction. You could use a rod intended for a closet or a length of tree branch. If you're raising bantam hens, they need a 1-inch-diameter perch. It should be mounted approximately 1 to 2 feet off the floor of the house. They can flap up to higher perches, but we believe lower perches minimize the risk of foot injuries during the dismount. Our ladies are not exactly svelte, and they land with a thump. Position the bar 1½ to 2 feet away from the nearest wall so they have plenty of elbow room for landing and squabbling. If you're raising bantams, the bar can be closer to the wall.

A NESTING BOX gives hens somewhere safe to lay their eggs. If you don't provide one, they'll find their own spots, and you'll enjoy daily Easter egg hunts. They like to lay somewhere dark, snug, and out of sight of predators. Locating the nesting box inside the house gives them the security they crave, and making the box just large enough to fit a hen makes it extra appealing. A box measuring 12 x 12 x 12 inches is about the minimum size necessary for a regular hen. Allow one box for every four hens. They like to share, so if you build more than that, you'll find some going unused.

The nesting box could be as simple as a wooden crate backed into the corner of the house. Or, more ambitiously, it could be built into the wall so that it projects outside of the house. In this case it would be fitted with a hinged roof to allow easy access to the eggs. It's a good idea to include a raised lip on the open side of the box to help keep the nesting material inside. If the box is located inside the coop (rather than projecting out), fitting it with a steeply canted roof will dissuade the chickens from roosting on top of it and covering it with droppings Always fill the nesting box with bedding material to cushion the eggs and encourage the chickens to nest there. We prefer fluffy wood shaving to straw, and the hens seem to prefer it as well.

AN ATTACHED RUN allows the chickens to go in and out of the house at will. The run is a screened structure that either projects off the front of the house or envelopes the entire house. It keeps the chickens contained while outdoors, which protects them from predators and protects your garden from the chickens. They love to free range, but if your yard is small and your crops unprotected, they can make short work of your vegetable patch. The run should always be on dirt, not concrete, because they need to dust themselves in dirt for their health. They also entertain themselves by scratching and digging holes. A chicken raised on wire or concrete is an unhappy chicken. Put a thick layer of straw in the run to absorb their waste and give them more material to scratch around in. It's more hygienic, and it smells and looks better than bare soil.

The size of the run depends on how many birds you have and how they spend their days. If they are allowed to free range, the run can be smaller, just enough space to contain them safely when you're not around to let them out. If they're going to spend all of their time in the run, it should be bigger. Exactly how big is your call. In our opinion, the bigger the better. The more room the birds have, the less likely they are to pick on one another—or at least the picked-upon hens have somewhere to run. The coop will also be cleaner and healthier if they're not crowded. In cases where the hens never leave the run, we'd allow a minimum of 12 square feet per hen.

THE RUN SHOULD HAVE A ROOF to shelter the chickens from rain, shade them from intense sun, and protect them from hawks. The most minimal roof would be avian netting overlaid by a tarp for shade. The easiest roof to build would be a shed-style roof designed to direct rain away from the coop.

THE RUN SHOULD BE PREDATOR PROOF. Chicken predators include dogs, raccoons, possums, skunks, snakes, foxes, coyotes, weasels, rats, owls, and hawks. The run should be screened in with ½-inch hardware cloth, not chicken wire, to keep all these critters at bay. Hardware cloth is not cloth but galvanized metal material made up of ½-inch squares. Chicken wire doesn't protect chickens. Raccoons, the most persistent chicken predators of all, can reach through chicken wire, grab a chicken, and eat it by the mouthful right through the wire. Hardware cloth should be firmly attached to support posts with U-shaped galvanized poultry staples, which are nailed in. Don't use staples from a staple gun, because those rust and can be pried up. The hardware cloth should also be sunk beneath the soil by at least a foot, so nothing can dig its way into the run.

ADD STORAGE SPACE TO THE RUN. Allow a couple of extra feet behind the henhouse to stack hay bales and store bins of feed or tools. It looks tidy, and it's more convenient than storing these things elsewhere. If supplies are under the coop's roof, it saves you from scrambling around to cover everything with a tarp each time it rains.

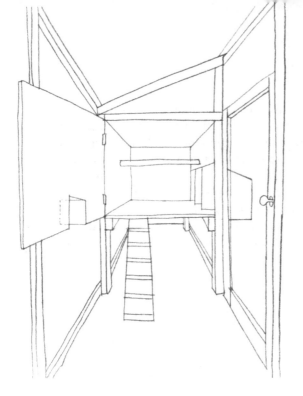

E

A Henhouse

B Nesting box with outside access, hinged and fitted with a lock

C Door fitted with a raccoon-proof lock

D Separate storage area, open to the outside or also fitted with a door. The wall between the coop and storage area can be solid or made of hardware cloth.

E Walls covered with ½-inch hardware cloth, not chicken wire

F Roof for shade and protection from the rain, tilted to shed water off the back

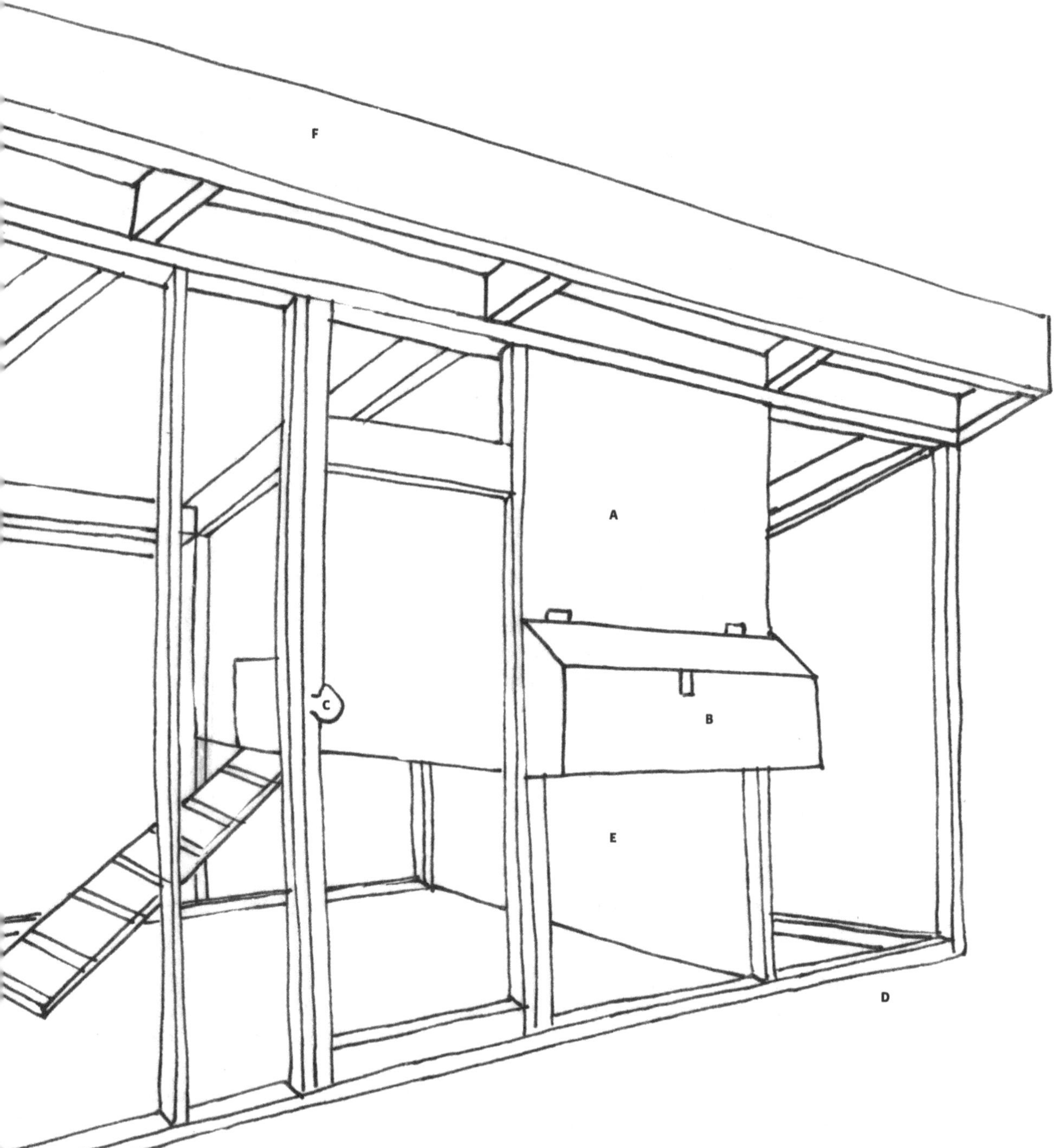
F
A
C
B
E
D

THE HOUSE DOESN'T HAVE TO BE HEATED. Hens are fairly cold hardy. They've got lots of feathers, and they cuddle together to keep warm at night. Roosting off the ground protects them from the cold, as well. Line the house with lots of straw during the winter months to provide extra insulation. In general, big chickens have more body mass to protect them from the cold than miniature and thin-bodied breeds. If you live somewhere with especially bitter winters, you should consider keeping breeds noted for their cold hardiness. One factor in cold heartiness is comb size. Chicken combs and wattles are vulnerable to frostbite. In cold places, the smaller the comb the better. No matter what kind of chickens you keep, one of the biggest concerns in cold weather is keeping their water from freezing. Chickens need constant access to clean water for good health. If you're not wild about the prospect of making regular trips to the coop to break the ice in their water dish, invest in a heated poultry waterer.

HEAT IS ACTUALLY MORE DANGEROUS THAN COLD. When chickens are hot, they stand around with their wings slightly spread, and they pant like dogs. This is one way they regulate their temperature. When the mercury hits 100°F (less if it's humid), chickens start expiring unless they have a cool retreat. During daytime hours, they must have access to shade and soil in the run. They'll find the shadiest spot they can and dig holes into the cool dirt. If the coop and run area aren't shaded naturally, stretch a tarp over a portion of it for summer months. Give them lots of extra water when it's hot—they drink copiously to keep themselves cool. If you live where sweltering heat is the rule rather than the exception, consider keeping bantams or thin-bodied breeds. They regulate heat better than "big girls." On the hottest days, we use a hose with a sprayer set to a fine sprinkle to dampen the run—and the chickens.

While shade is a necessity in the summer, it's not wise to site the chicken coop in a perennially shady area. It's unhealthy for the chickens to live in constantly dank conditions. Sunlight is a good thing. Sunshine dries out soggy litter and keeps the run more hygienic. The ladies enjoy basking in the sun, too. The ideal location for the coop would be a spot that received sun for part of the day but that was protected by some shade in the summer. Our coop is under a pair of deciduous trees. They shade the coop on summer afternoons, but in the winter, their bare branches allow sunlight all day.

INSIDE THE HENHOUSE, GOOD VENTILATION IS CRITICAL, no matter what the climate or season. Henhouses are usually small, the sleeping quarters tight. The combination of bedding and dander makes the air dusty, and their droppings release ammonia as they dry. Good ventilation is necessary to make sure chickens don't develop respiratory infections from sleeping in bad air. The henhouse should have adjustable vents in the wall to allow for healthy airflow and to let heat escape. You can also drill a row of ½-inch holes near the roofline to improve ventilation. If you put one set of holes on the north side of the house and another on the south side, you'd set up a cross breeze. In the winter, you could screw a board over the north-facing holes to keep the house warmer. Staple ½-inch mesh over the holes to keep rats out.

GENERAL TIPS FOR CHICKEN KEEPING

YOU CAN BUY CHICKS, BUT PULLETS ARE EASIER. Most people get chicks from feed stores or via mail order. If you buy chicks, you have to keep them indoors in a heated cardboard box (a brooder) until they grow their adult feathers, because they're sensitive to cold. While it can be fun to play chick nanny for several weeks, they do require a lot of attention. If you don't have the time or inclination, buy pullets (young hens) at a poultry show. Keep an eye out for shows in your area and go early in the day for the best selection. The great thing about buying from professional breeders is that they really care about the health of their stock. You'll go home with high-quality chickens that are "coop ready" and just about old enough to start laying eggs.

NEVER KEEP JUST ONE HEN. Chickens need to be part of a flock for their psychological well-being. Three or four hens is a good number for a small backyard coop. Roosters are illegal in most urban and suburban settings and unnecessary unless you want to breed chicks. Hens lay eggs whether or not a rooster is present.

CHICKENS ARE RACISTS. Or rather, shape-ists. While we know people who keep mixed flocks successfully, our own experience and that of others tells us that if any chicken is shaped different from the others, the dominant chickens in the flock may decided to harass it ruthlessly. This doesn't mean they all have to be the same breed—many breeds have the same general shape. For instance, our Rhode Island Red and Plymouth Rocks are the same shape and get along well, but they all pick on our Americauna, which has (*had!*) long tail feathers. The others—all of which have stubby tails—rip her tail feathers out as fast as they can grow.

FEED THEM CHICKEN FEED. Our DIY ethos does not extend so far that we make our own chicken feed. Laying hens have intense nutritional needs, because they've been engineered to lay eggs at an astonishing rate. While it is possible to make your own chicken feed, if you fail to meet their nutritional needs, the results can range from reduced laying to laying soft-shelled eggs, which is dangerous for the hen. Just save yourself the trouble and buy high-quality organic feed formulated for laying hens. Supplement the feed with lots of fresh vegetables and whole grains.

Provide the feed in a poultry feeder, not on the floor. You don't want the birds gobbling up their own poop along with the feed. Poultry feed attracts rodents, so consider putting the feeder away at night. The chickens usually make sure there isn't any feed left on the ground, but a full feeder is an all-night buffet for mice. After noticing mice around our henhouse, we started taking our feeder out of the coop at night when we lock up the chickens. We place it in a small, lidded trash can until the next morning.

GIVE THEM LOTS OF FRESH WATER. Constant access to fresh water is critical to good health. Don't place the water in a dish. Invest in a poultry fountain, a device that dispenses clean water a little at a time. Keep it off the ground, so the water doesn't become clogged with dirt and straw. A fountain can either be set on a pile of bricks or suspended from the roof of the run.

KEEP THEM ENTERTAINED. To prevent chickens from causing mischief—like beating each other up—keep them busy. A chicken's motto is "I scratch, therefore I am." While their feed should be kept in an elevated feeder to keep it clean, we scatter handfuls of chicken scratch or whole grains in the run to give them something to hunt. Line the run with hay or dead leaves, any dry organic matter to provide them plenty of material to scratch through. Give them fresh greens whenever possible. We feed them weeds we've pulled, trimmings from the garden, bugs from the garden, and scraps from the kitchen. When we go to the farmers' market, we beg boxes of green trimmings from the vendors and toss those in the coop as a special treat. A whole apple can entertain chickens for a good while, as can a head of lettuce. If they don't have an area to free range, an hour or so of supervised play in the yard is thrilling to them and pretty fun for onlookers, too.

PRACTICE THE DEEP-BEDDING METHOD. While the inside of the henhouse should be cleaned out at least once a week, the run itself doesn't have to be cleaned if you follow the deep-bedding method. As suggested above, line the run with about a foot of straw (or other dry organic material, like dead leaves). Deep bedding not only gives the birds lots of material to search through, it also absorbs their waste. As they scratch, they break down their own manure, mixing it with the straw to make compost. Bits of green waste that they don't consume—like stalks and rinds—also get absorbed into the compost. The upshot is that the run does not smell or look unsightly, the chickens are happy, and you don't have to muck out the run. Just keep adding fresh material as the old stuff gets broken down. About once a year, we go in and harvest the coop compost and transfer it to one of our compost piles. After harvesting, we put down a thick layer of fresh straw and let the cycle begin again.

DEEP-CLEAN THE HENHOUSE IN THE SPRING AND THE FALL. Twice a year, give the henhouse a thorough cleaning. Keeping it clean will help prevent parasite infestations. Scrub down all surfaces and expose them to sun, if you can. Some people use bleach and water, but we use a vinegar water, about 2 cups white vinegar per bucket of hot water. Leave the house open to dry out. After it dries, we apply a thick coating of linseed oil to the wooden surfaces. All the wood in our henhouse is unfinished plywood, with the exception of the roost, which is a tree branch. When the house was first built, we saturated the wood inside the house with as much linseed oil as it could absorb. This is an old-fashioned method of preventing parasites, like mites, from taking refuge in the pores of the wood. Actually, the old-fashioned method calls for crank shaft oil, but we don't have

WARNING

Oil-soaked rags can spontaneously combust. Don't pile them up or leave them sitting on or near flammable items. Hang them out on a line to dry, or seal them in a metal can.

a lot of that around here. The oil treatments have worked for us so far. During the deep cleans, we apply a fresh coat of oil with a rag to all wood surfaces, including the roosting bar and the laying box, then use a dry cloth to wipe up any excess oil. We do this early in the morning, so the house can stand open and air out all day long.

IF A CHICKEN GETS SICK, isolate it from the others as soon as you notice something is wrong. A sick chicken will stand around idle while the others are busy, often with its feathers puffed up. Look for signs of disease, like discharge from the beak or a dirty bottom. Chickens don't have much defense against disease. Someone once told us, "Chickens have two settings: on and off." Meaning they're either well or they're dead, and they usually go fast. A sick hen might pull through if you isolate her, keep her warm, and give her TLC, but often there is nothing you can do. A trip to the vet is expensive, and city vets don't usually know much about chickens. For this reason prevention is the cure—and it's simple, too. Give them good food, lots of water, fresh air and sunshine, clean bedding, and room to exercise. Most health problems arise from poor management. If you get new chickens, keep them isolated from your existing flock for a couple of weeks to make sure they're not carrying any diseases.

IF A CHICKEN HAS AN OPEN WOUND, isolate the bird quickly from the other chickens. They will peck at the wound and make it worse. Wash the wound and put antibiotic cream on it. Keep her warm and safe indoors and protected from flies, which may lay eggs in the wound. To help her heal faster, feed the hen extra protein, like worms, tuna, or scraps of cooked meat.

IF YOU PLAN TO EAT THEM, DON'T NAME THEM. And raise a flock of the same breed of chickens, so they all look alike. It's much easier to consider them dinner if you don't consider them as individuals.

Backward Beekeeping

Bees are the new chickens. Over the past few years, backyard chicken keeping has enjoyed a renaissance among self-reliant urbanites and suburbanites. We predict beekeeping will be the next big thing. A beehive is a time-honored and useful addition to any working garden. Honeybees not only provide vital pollination services, they also provide a home with organic, raw honey for the table and beeswax for salves, lotion, and candles. Beyond that, a hive is a powerful and enigmatic force that adds what we can only describe as a spiritual presence to the garden. We don't really keep bees, we host them, honor them, and learn from them.

66 ›

Getting Started with Beekeeping

Honeybees are in trouble. You've probably heard the reports of colony collapse disorder (CCD), the malady that is destroying the commercial beekeeping industry. Their fate seems to weigh on our collective consciousness. And it should. The plight of honeybees is emblematic of the plight of the natural world as a whole. We believe human interference— including the widespread use of insecticides and the management techniques of professional beekeepers—is to blame for their decline. The reason we believe this is because feral bee populations are quite healthy. When left to their own devices, bees do okay. So how do you keep bees, yet not interfere with them? You become a "backward beekeeper."

Natural beekeeper Charles Martin Simon coined the phrase "beekeeping backwards." Simon sums up his approach by saying, "Work with Nature, not against Her." We learned about Simon and the backward methodology from our own beekeeping mentor, Kirk "Kirkobeeo" Anderson, leader of Los Angeles's pioneering beekeeping club, Backwards Beekeepers. Backward beekeeping is founded on principles that fly in the face of established beekeeping practice. The overriding principle is Kirk Anderson's watchwords: "Let the bees be bees."

Until you delve into the world of beekeeping, you'd never guess how heavy-handed normal beekeeping practice is toward the bees. Laying it all out would be a book in itself, but in broad strokes, humans have been trying to increase honey production by micromanaging the bees. We force them to build large comb to breed large bees. We control the ratio of male bees to female bees. We don't let the hive create its own queens, we import them, preseminated. We limit the queen's movements within the hive. The list goes on and on. The upshot is that kept bees are frail bees. They are particularly vulnerable to a parasite called the varroa mite. To "protect" bees against mites and other problems, beekeepers spray hives with all kinds of chemicals. Conventional beekeeping has become an endless treadmill of chemical treatments that, in the end, weaken the bees and strengthen their enemies.

Backward beekeepers manage bees as little as possible. All we ask of the bees is that they use our hive boxes as homes. We peek in the hive once in a while to make sure they have enough room—and, of course, we harvest

As far as we're concerned, fear of
"Africanized" wild bees is overblown.
Much of it is hype fostered by
government agencies and extermi-
nating businesses. Yes, an aggressive
strain of bees imported from Africa
was loosed in Brazil in the 1950s.
Yes, they've been working their way
north ever since. But all along the
way, they've been interbreeding
with gentle local bees. We live in
Los Angeles, far enough south that
our feral bee population is certainly
Africanized. To us, this just means
our bees are strong and productive,
because those are also traits of these
dreaded bees. We've not found them
to be particularly aggressive. They're
not pussycats— you do have to
wear protective gear when handling
them—but their evil reputation
is undeserved.

honey when they have some to spare. Other than that,
we don't interfere in their affairs. Healthy hives manage
mite infestations on their own. If they don't, they die, and
we go out and get new bees. This brings us to one of the
most important distinctions between backward beekeeping and normal beekeeping. We keep feral bees. Instead
of importing delicate European beestock, we capture
wild bees. Feral bees are smaller than their commercial
counterparts and much hardier. They're proven survivors,
well adapted to your local climate and conditions.

Another radical difference in this style of beekeeping is that we allow the bees to shape their own comb.
Man-made beehives are wooden boxes filled with frames
that sit in the boxes like hanging files. The bees build their
comb in these frames instead of in freeform shapes, as
they would in nature. This structure allows beekeepers to
pull out frames, inspect them, rearrange them, and harvest
honey. Backward beekeepers use frames, too, but the
frames are put into the hive empty, save for a narrow wax
strip at the top called a "starter strip." Standard beekeeping practice provides the bees with frames filled with a
preformed comb stamped out of wax or plastic. This is
called *foundation*. The theory behind this is that the less
time the bees spend building their home, the more time
they'll spend making honey. The foundation dictates how
large each cell of the honeycomb will be. The purpose of
this is twofold. First, it encourages the production of larger bees—jumbo bees that
make more honey—because the size of the cell an egg is laid in dictates the size
of the bee, and man-made cells are larger than bees would make on their own. The
second purpose is to limit the number of drones a hive makes.

Drones, male bees, are bred in larger cells than female bees. Preformed
foundation provides only so many drone-size cells, artificially limiting their
numbers. From a human perspective, drones are useless. They don't make honey.
They don't do anything at all except inseminate new queens. Therefore, in our
infinite wisdom, humans decided to cap the number of drones per hive. Backward
beekeepers let the bees decide their own gender ratios. It just makes sense—and
there's some evidence to prove that the bees know best. One thing we know is
that mites prefer to invade drone cells. If they're bothering drones, they are not
infesting the more critical worker bee cells.

All of this is to say that we believe that bees should be the size they want to
be, and they should manage their own gender ratios and build their own home.
For this reason we give them empty frames. They build comb in the frames

to their own specifications, but they do shape it within the frames, so we can manipulate the hive when we need to.

To recap, if you want to be a backward beekeeper, you do the following:

* Keep feral bees.
* Allow them to build their own comb in empty frames.
* Never spray them with anything to treat mites, not even "natural" remedies, like powdered sugar.
* Always let bees be bees.

Assembling Your Beekeeping Equipment

PREPARATION: 3 hours

Preparation is the first step. Have all of the following equipment collected, assembled, set up, and in place before you acquire your bees. The supplies listed below can be found at any beekeeping supply store or online retailer of beekeeping equipment.

YOU'LL NEED

* Hive tool (like a miniature crowbar)
* Cheapest smoker you can find. They all work the same.
* Protective gear: bee suits (full length) or bee jackets (half length) and long leather or heavy canvas gloves. A full suit or jacket with an integrated hat and veil is best, because there are no gaps at the neckline. But you could buy a separate hat/veil combo and wear it with ordinary heavy clothing, like a sturdy canvas jacket.
* Bee brush, which looks a little like a windshield brush (handy but optional)

HIVE PARTS:
* Cover (telescoping or migratory cover)
* Inner cover (optional, for added insulation)
* Bottom board
* 2 medium (16 x 20 inches) hive boxes—more boxes as the hive expands
* 20 empty hive frames (10 per box) sized to fit the boxes

MATERIALS FOR PREPARING THE FRAMES:
* 8–10 ounces organic or cosmetic-grade beeswax. The beeswax could be purchased at the beekeeping supply store.
* 30 12-inch wooden stir sticks, the sort used for paint
* Wood glue
* Cheap paintbrush
* Clean tin can

IS BACKYARD BEEKEEPING LEGAL?

The answer depends on what city you live in. Check your city code. There's an encouraging movement afoot to legalize beekeeping in cities where it's been forbidden. Denver, Cleveland, Minneapolis, and New York City have all legalized it recently, and we hope they're just the start of the wave. Get involved and support beekeeping in your own city. If beekeeping is illegal where you live, all we'd say is that beekeeping codes are seldom enforced, and when dealing with city agencies, it's generally better to ask for forgiveness than permission.

PUTTING IT TOGETHER

ASSEMBLE THE HIVE AND FRAMES

You can buy the hive boxes and frames preassembled or in pieces. If they're sold collapsed, assembly instructions will come with them. Don't buy "everything you need to get started" kits, because those will come with extra parts that you don't need for backward beekeeping. Buy the pieces separately, as listed on page 273. You can paint the assembled hive if you wish, but use latex paint and only paint the outer surfaces.

As a backward beekeeper, you'll have to fit the empty frames with starter strips, because starter stips are not standard equipment. As discussed above, we don't use frames filled with foundation. We let the bees build their own comb, but we give them some help by putting a narrow wax strip at the top of the empty frame. If you look at the top bar of an empty frame, you'll see a groove running along the underside of it. Glue a stir stick lengthwise into the groove of each frame to serve as a foundation for the wax. The sticks will be shorter than the length of the frames, so you will need to snap additional sticks into smaller pieces to fill the gaps. The fit does not have to be perfect.

Put the beeswax in a clean tin can, and put that can in a saucepan of gently simmering water. Once the wax is melted, paint both sides of the strips with a coat of beeswax. Be sure to dab some along the groove to help hold the strips securely. The beeswax will set up as soon as it cools. Hang the frames in the boxes, 10 per box.

SET UP THE HIVE

To ensure happy bees, position the hive so that it receives morning sun. The bees need that warmth to get going. Beyond that, the hive should be sited in a remote corner where there's not a lot of human traffic. A side yard is an ideal spot. Bees will be coming and going from the hive all day long. They usually approach from high and land at a steep angle, and they head straight up when they take off. As long as there's a clear space of about 5 feet in front of the hive, you won't often cross their flight path. But if you find that they've established a flight pattern that interferes with your routines (say they're flying right over your garden bed), don't be afraid to put up a standing trellis or screen near the hive to subtly reroute traffic. When they come across an obstacle like a screen or fence, they fly straight up the face of the obstacle, and then continue in whatever direction they wish to go.

The hive should not sit on the ground. Elevate it to coffee-table height to deter casual intrusions by skunks and other critters. But more important, bees need protection from ants. Ants love honey, and bees under attack from ants will often pack up and leave. For this reason, there needs to be an ant moat around the hive. The easiest way to do this is to put the hive on a footed table or stand. (Make sure the table is sturdy. As the hive grows, it will become heavy, perhaps as much as 200 pounds.) Sink each foot of the table in a can—a tuna can is enough, though you could use a deep can, like a tomato can—filled with oil of any kind: cheap cooking oil, motor oil, whatever you have. Make sure there are no other access routes available to ants. Trim away foliage that touches the hive, for instance. Even tall grass can become an ant bridge.

If necessary, fence off the hive area to protect pets or small children from their own curiosity. We've got low fencing set up about 3 feet away from the hive entrance to keep our dog from nosing around where he should not. Some dogs are bee wise, others are incorrigible.

CATCH YOUR BEES

There are three ways to catch feral bees. First, you can capture a swarm. Second, you can cut an established hive up and move it into your own box. This is called a cutout. Or third, you can rig up an established hive so that bees can exit the hive but can't return. Then you lure the homeless bees into a box. This is called a trap-out. We're not going to cover trap-outs, because you need brood comb from an existing hive. Brood comb is a bee nursery, a comb filled with infant bees. The presence of needy brood convinces the worker bees to move into the box. We assume that as a beginner, you won't have access to brood comb, so the next two projects focus on the other two techniques. Of the two, we'd recommend capturing a swarm as the easiest method for the novice bee handler.

67 ›

Bee Acquisition Method 1: Swarm Capture

You may have seen a swarm: clouds of bees flying past or congregating in piñata-like clusters in trees or on light poles or clinging to yard furniture. A bee swarm can cause a panic at a picnic, but the truth is that bees are never less dangerous than they are when swarming.

Swarms are the mechanism by which a bee colony reproduces itself. When conditions in the hive get crowded, the colony raises a new queen, and either the new queen or the old queen leaves the hive with a substantial number of the workers to search for new digs. They can't survive long without a hive, so a swarm is a temporary entity. They either find a place to live, or they all die. While they're homeless, they have nothing to protect—no honey, no brood, no hive. As a result, they're very mellow. They're really just trying to get by.

To capture a swarm you have to be ready, since they often just settle down for a few hours. If you're in the market for bees, it pays to have your swarm-capture gear ready at all times. In temperate climates, springtime is swarm time. In warmer climates, swarms can happen anytime, but spring is still the busiest swarm season.

YOU'LL NEED

BASIC PROTECTIVE GEAR: A veil and gloves at minimum, a bee suit for the most protection. Show-off beekeepers capture swarms with their bare hands, because they know they're unlikely to be stung.

A NUC BOX: This is a temporary beehive, a box about as big as a filing box. (*Nuc* is short for nucleus, but they're never called nucleus boxes.) They're sold by beekeeping suppliers. Get a cardboard rather than a wooden nuc box, because they're easier to heft around and they're cheaper. The nuc box has a circular hole on one side for the bees to come in and out of. The hole comes with a plug to block the entrance during transport. If it's very hot when you're hunting swarms, consider cutting out a window on the lid of the nuc box and duct-taping some screen over the opening so that the bees will have more air, minimizing the chance that they will overheat when you transport them. For a really big swarm, you may need more than one box. In a pinch, you could improvise a nuc box with any sturdy cardboard box.

Note: You don't have to use a nuc box. You can use an empty wooden hive box, if it's convenient. The advantage of the nuc box is its light weight and portability. If you can manage to capture the swarm in your wooden hive box, you'll have less to do later.

You'll also need:

* 5 empty frames fit with starter strips. A standard nuc box will hold 5 frames.
* Spray bottle filled with a dissolved 50/50 mix of sugar and water
* Ladder
* Coil of rope
* Roll of duct tape
* Pair of pruning shears and/or small saw
* Bee brush

BRIBERY HELPS

When you first bring home your bees, open the top of the nuc box and drizzle a couple of lines of honey over the tops of the frames. Use just enough to make lines, not so much that lots of excess honey drips into the depths of the box. This gives the bees a little food to sustain them. It might also make them more willing to stay. Check back in a few days and see if they've cleaned up the honey. If so, add a little more. Once you transfer the frames to the permanent hive box, you can continue to feed them using a spacer frame and bags of sugar water, as described in the next project on cutouts.

PUTTING IT TOGETHER

DON YOUR GEAR AND APPROACH THE SWARM TO ASSESS THE SITUATION. How big is the swarm? Will it fit in one box? How high is it? Will you need a ladder? Check to see if there is any comb visible. If there is, they're building a hive, they're not a swarm anymore. To move them, you'll have to do a cutout. See the next project.

MIST THE CLUSTER OF BEES WITH THE SUGAR WATER. This will keep the bees preoccupied cleaning themselves and they'll be less likely to fly off.

MAKE A PLAN. Basically, you have to move that cluster of bees into the box. That's not as hard as it might seem. Two basic rules of bee behavior will help you. This first rule is that where the queen goes, the rest follow. The queen is guaranteed to be somewhere in the heart of the swarm. The second rule is that bees prefer dark places and are naturally attracted to the confines of the nuc box (or a proper hive box, if that's what you're using) as well as the familiar scent of the wax on the frames. If you put the box beneath the swarm (if it's hanging) or on the ground in front of them (if they've clustered somewhere low) and step back to give them some room, they might move into it on their own. They often do, and it's an amazing sight. The entire swarm will flow into the entrance of the nuc box on its own accord. If the swarm is way up high, you can hoist the box beneath it on rope or balance the box on a ladder. Scouts will check out the box, and if they give the all-clear, they'll all move in.

If they don't move in on their own, you can be more aggressive in your approach. Do remember to spray them with sugar water before you do any of this! If they're hanging on foliage, cut the branch above the swarm and lower it into the box. If you can't do that, you might be able to give the branch (or table or whatever) a hard thump or shake, and the swarm will fall into the box. Or you can use a bee brush or your hands to gently brush them into the box. As long as the queen lands in the box, the rest will follow, even if they're disturbed and flying around. Just give them a chance.

In either case, there might be some stragglers hanging out on the front of the box. If they show no sign of moving in, and you need to go, just sweep them into a dustpan and dump them into the top of the box.

The worst thing that can happen is that you'll lose the swarm. If the queen doesn't make it into the box, they'll follow her elsewhere. Even if she lands in the box, she might decide she doesn't like the box, and they'll all flow out. There's nothing you can do to stop her from leaving. All you can do is try again another day.

ONCE THE SWARM IS IN THE BOX, tape down the lid to secure it during transport. Be sure to secure the plug in front, too, and tape up the corners of the box. You don't want a car full of bees! Make sure that the bees have plenty of ventilation— they need to breathe just like we do.

GET THEM TO THEIR NEW HOME AS FAST AS POSSIBLE. Set the nuc box *on top* of the hive you hope they'll inhabit one day. That hive should be all set up and ready to go. The legs should be set in oil cans so it's ant proof. You're putting the nuc box on top of it because it's a safe place, and because they'll orient to that particular location as "home." Unplug the central opening (wear your gear when you do this). The bees will come out and look around. It's possible they might all fly away in a huff, but it's more likely they'll opt to stay, at least overnight. There's no predicting if they'll stay or go over the next couple of days. They'll probably fly around the hive and hang out on the front of it while they make their decision. If they stay, you'll start to see more orderly bee behaviors, like workers flying busily in and out of the box. If they leave, don't take it personally. You'll find another swarm.

AFTER THEY'VE SETTLED IN FOR ABOUT 2 WEEKS, suit up and visit the box midday on a nice, sunny day, when most of the workers are out. Watch the bees coming and going. If you see any with pollen on their hind legs, that's a sign they're building comb and raising young. To confirm, suit up and lift out the frames and check for signs of comb building. Once you see comb, you know they mean to stay, and the bees should be transferred to the permanent hive. Move the frames from the cardboard nuc box to the permanent hive box. Work very gently and carefully, trying not to squish any bees in the process—you don't want to kill the queen. Tilt the nuc box over the open hive box and spill in any bees that remain after the frames are transferred. As before, if the queen is on one of those frames you just moved, everyone should move into the hive to be with her. Cross your fingers and hope they don't get mad and leave. If they stay, you've got bees!

Baiting with Swarm Lure

A more passive way to capture a swarm is to make the swarm come to you. This method only works in about one out of seven attempts, but it's worth trying, especially if you don't have time to chase swarms around.

During the swarm season (springtime, when the fruit trees are blossoming), bait a nuc box with a scented pheromone called swarm lure. Swarm lure contains something called Nasonov scent, the smell that says "home" to a bee. You can purchase swarm lure from beekeeping suppliers. It usually comes as a small vial in a paper envelope. Refrigerate the lure until you're ready to use it. Tape the envelope to the bottom of the lid inside of the nuc box. You don't need to open the envelope or the vial.

Bees usually congregate up high, so position the nuc box in a tree, about 10 feet up. Choose a tree that bees like. We know someone who captured a swam by wedging her box in a blooming peach tree. The lid should be on, but the hole in the front (the "door") should be open. Swarm lure is good for about 4 to 6 weeks, so leave the box out that long and hope for the best. If you're lucky, a scout from a swarm will fly by and catch the scent.

Once you see activity in the box—bees flying in and out—you'll know you have guests. Put on your bee gear and go to fetch the nuc box at dusk, when all the bees are sure to be inside. Tape the lid down, shut the front door, and take the box home.

Some people have had luck putting the Nasanov scent in an empty backyard hive as an invitation to passing swarms. The advantage of this is that you don't have to transfer the bees, but the chances of their taking the bait are fairly low. Still, there's not a lot to be lost by trying this, other than a few bucks for the lure.

68 ›

Bee Acquisition Method 2: Cutout

A cutout is a technique used to capture and relocate an established hive. Feral bees take up residence in the darndest places. They invade walls and roofs, dead logs and stumps, birdhouses and dollhouses, suitcases, barbecue grills, and even hot tubs. Our own bees had taken up residence in an abandoned shop vacuum. More often than not, a feral hive is under a death sentence. Homeowners and city agencies will send an exterminator after them. If you're there first, you can save them.

We're not going to say that a cutout is easy. We'd rate it up there with chicken slaughtering as one of the most intense projects in this book. It's hard work, and the bees will be angry. If you can capture a swarm instead, do that. But saving a feral hive from the exterminator is extremely satisfying, and unlike swarms, which are flighty, bees taken in a cutout are less likely to abandon the hive (*abscond*), because your hive box will be holding their food supplies and their young. They have a lot of incentive to settle down. This isn't to say they *won't* abscond—they might, but it is less likely.

Every cutout is different, depending on where the bees are living. The easiest cutouts are those where the bees are in something no one cares about—like a suitcase or broken shop vacuum. The most difficult are hives imbedded in architecture. Those involve sawing open walls. If you do this at someone else's house, make sure they know that there will be a mess afterward, and agree in advance who will make the repairs.

YOU'LL NEED

* Nuc box or hive box, complete with empty frames that have been fitted with wax starter strips (perhaps more than one box, depending on size of the hive)
* Box of short nails or flat-headed thumbtacks
* Hammer for the nails
* Ball of thin cotton twine, like kitchen twine or kite string
* Assembled spacer frame (see the instructions on page 282)
* Box of gallon or ½-gallon zipper-lock bags
* 2 pounds white sugar
* Smoker

* **Full protective gear: hat, veil, suit, and gloves**
* **Long, sharp knife, like a kitchen knife**
* **2 (5-gallon) buckets with lids, or 2 trash bags**
* **Spray bottle filled with a 50/50 mix of white sugar and water**
* **Bee brush and dustpan**
* **Crowbar, screwdrivers, saws, utility knives—anything needed to get at the hive**

PUTTING IT TOGETHER

Before you begin the actual cutout, there's some preparation to do, so that you have everything handy when you need it.

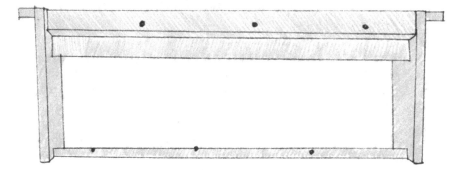

STRING THE FRAMES

During a cutout, the existing comb in the feral hive is cut out in chunks and secured in the frames with string. This way, the bees don't lose their comb—which contains their young and their food. Over time, they'll repair the broken pieces of comb to fill the frames. When they're done, they'll chew away the string and drag it out of the hive. All you've got to do is set up a temporary framework to hold the comb in place.

Weave string across one side of each frame by putting four or five nails or tacks across the top bar of the frame. Place another set of nails or tacks across the bottom. Offset the spacing of the two rows slightly. Don't push the nails or tacks all the way in. Weave the string in a zigzag pattern from upper nail to matching lower nail, up and down across the frame. At each nail or tack, wrap the string around once or twice to secure it, then push the nail or tack in.

Reverse the frame and install nails or tacks in the same way on the opposite side, pushing them only halfway in. On-site, after you cut out the comb and put it in the frames, you'll wind the string around this side, securing the comb in the frame.

How many frames you prepare really depends on the size of the hive you're targeting. A hive cut out of a birdhouse would be tiny, and you might only need three frames. A big one might take 10 or more. It doesn't hurt to prepare more than you need, just in case.

BUILD A SPACER FRAME

A spacer frame is a shallow, bottomless box that matches the dimensions of your hive. You'll need one for this project. It sits on the top of the hive, between the topmost box and the lid, to provide space for supplemental feeding when the hive needs the support after a cutout. In general, we don't feed the bees, because the food they find in nature is so much better than what we can provide. This is an exception.

To make the spacer box, take a 6-foot length of 1x3 lumber (any kind of wood is fine as long as it's untreated) and cut it into four pieces total: two pieces measuring 16 inches and two pieces measuring 20 inches. The size of a standard medium-size hive box is 16 x 20 inches. If your hive is not this size, adjust the size of your frame accordingly. Nail or screw the corners together, using two nails or screws in each corner. Don't sand it or paint it.

MIX UP A BAG OF SUGAR WATER

Fill a half-gallon or gallon zipper-lock bag halfway up with the white sugar, then fill it the rest of the way with water. Shake to dissolve. Put it aside until the end of the cutout. This will be used to feed the bees after their trauma. Use only white sugar. Less processed sugars, like unbleached or brown sugar, can make bees sick.

PRACTICE WITH THE SMOKER

If you've never used a bee smoker before, take it outside and give it a test run. Put some wads of newspaper in the bottom. Put a handful of small, dry twigs in, then more newspaper. Light the tinder, let it catch fire well, then close the lid of the smoker. When you pump the bellows of the smoker, smoke should come out the spout in big puffs. A smoker can be left to smolder for a bit, but you may have to refuel it or relight it if you're going to use it several times over the length of the cutout. Practicing ahead of time will give you a feel for using the smoker without the distraction of thousands of bees swarming around your head.

KIDNAP THE BEES, IF POSSIBLE

If the bees are in something portable, it's best to take the hive home and do this in your own backyard, near your hive boxes. Approach the feral hive at dusk, after the bees have come home for the night. They won't be sleeping. In fact, they're extra cranky when disturbed at night, but this way you won't lose all the worker bees who are out foraging during the day. Put your gear on and quickly and quietly block the entrances to the hive. Tape old window screening over the entrances with duct tape. Make sure you seal all the openings (but do use screening on the big openings, so the bees don't suffocate). Transport the hive to its final location, put it next to your empty hive—on top of it would be best, if it will fit—and take off the screen and tape. The next morning, they'll come out, reorient themselves, and start working. You don't have to do the cutout immediately. It's good to let them settle down a bit, actually, a day or two, or until the next weekend, when you have time to move them. Don't leave it too long, though, and be sure the hive is protected from ants and critters in the meanwhile.

MAKE THE CUTOUT

Choose a nice sunny day for the cutout, and work midday, when the workers are afield. That way you'll have fewer angry bees to deal with.

Whether you've brought the bees home or are working on-site because the bees are in something immovable, the basics of the cutout are the same. You should have the following things set up in your work area:

* **Your hive box or a cardboard nuc box**
* **Empty frames, fitted with starter strips and prestrung on one side**
* **String and tacks or nails ready to go to finish stringing the frames. (Rubber bands make a good backup system—we don't like the idea of bees chewing on them, cotton string is better, but they're really handy if you're in a rush and the string is giving you trouble.)**
* **2 lidded buckets or plastic bags ready to go (one for garbage; the other for honeycomb)**
* **Smoker filled with newspaper and twigs, and something to light it with**
* **Sharp knife**
* **Bee brush and dustpan**
* **Spray bottle of sugar water**
* **Premixed bag of sugar water**
* **Assembled spacer for feeding**
* **Whatever implements of destruction you need to open up the hive**
* **A work surface would be a handy thing, like a picnic table, or a board on horses. Cover it with something, because there will be honey everywhere.**
* **A brave friend or two, also in bee suits. You really don't want to do this alone. It's too much work.**

Put on your gear and take a deep breath. Try to relax and stay relaxed and focused. Cutouts are intense. The bees will be angry, and they're good at intimidating invaders. You need to keep calm and clear. Keep your movement slow and deliberate. Remember, your gear will protect you, and the smoke will pacify them. But be extra careful with your gear in this situation. Make sure everything is zipped up tight. Tuck your pants into your socks and your sleeves into your gloves.

The very first thing you should do is light the smoker and send a few puffs into the hive by poking the nose of the smoker into any available opening.

Smoke tells them there's an emergency at hand, and in response, they run to eat honey. When they're stuffed with honey, they're less aggressive. So give them a few puffs, then wait about 10 minutes for them to calm down. Smoking is vital to this process. Throughout the cutout, give them more puffs if their aggression level rises. Don't overdo it, though. You don't want to suffocate them. They just have to smell the smoke.

If the colony is in a wall, carefully remove the siding, using a knife to cut the comb away from the siding if it's attached. You don't want to tear apart their comb. The hive is warm—you'll be able to find its outlines from the outside by touch. If the hive is in something portable, open it up as best you can, trying not to harm the comb. The idea in both cases is to expose the comb so you can remove it.

When you can see the comb, take out your long knife. You have to be ruthless here. You're going to cut up their beautiful home, and some bees are going to die because they won't move for the knife. Remember, this is better than extermination, which is the fate of most feral beehives. The hive is an entity in itself, a living mind. The individuals are not as important as the welfare of the hive as a whole, and you are ensuring its survival as best you can.

Every comb arrangement is different in the wild, but it is formed in bulbous individual sheets. Try to cut out those sheets at their attachment points, keeping them as whole as possible. They will be crawling with bees. You are looking for brood comb, the cells where the larvae are being raised. If you hold the comb up to the light, you can see little ricelike larvae tucked into the cells. This is the heart of the hive. You must get this comb into the new hive. Also, the queen is likely to be in this area, laying eggs in empty cells. She's noticeably larger than the other bees, but you may not spot her in the chaos. Cross your fingers and pray to the bee gods that you don't kill her accidentally. If you do, they'll make a new queen, but they'll be aggressive and unsettled until a new queen has hatched and taken the throne.

The best way to work is to have one person dissecting and another one or two stringing the comb into frames. Shake the bees off the comb and lay it on your work surface. You need to fit it into the strung frames. If it's too big, cut it to size. Lay the frame string-side down, and add the comb in pieces to roughly fill the frame. Then enclose the open side with another quick zigzag of string.

Save any small or spare chunks of honeycomb by tossing it in one of the buckets or bags. You'll use it later to feed the bees. Shut the bag or bucket to keep the bees out. Use the other bag for garbage—you might find some dirty old comb in the process—and general cleanup.

As you fill each frame, transfer it to the hive box or nuc box. Fill frames until there's no comb left in the original hive.

Spritz any bees hanging around on the table or the original hive site with sugar water. Then you can sweep them into a dust pan with the bee brush and dump them over the frames in the new hive. They'll crawl in. The ones in the air will be attracted to the scent of the queen. They'll also be drawn toward the honey and the brood.

When you're done, put the lid on the nuc box or hive. If you're planning to transport the box, wait a few hours if you can, until sunset preferably, to give the workers who are out in the field a chance to return to the hive. Meanwhile, plug up entrances to the old hive so that a new colony does not take up residence in the same spot. When you're ready to go, tape up the nuc box or hive box so that all the exits are sealed and the lid is on tight for safe transport.

Once home, put the hive box on its stand or the nuc box on top of the permanent hive box until you have a chance to transfer the frames. Unseal the entrances so the bees can come out in the morning and take a look around.

The next day, or soon after, suit up again at midday and carefully transfer the frames from the nuc box (if you used one) into the permanent hive. Remove some of the empty frames from the hive box so you have lots of room to lower the bee-covered Franken-frames into the hive gently. Fill the lower box first. If you have more than 10 filled frames, put a few in the upper box. Otherwise leave the upper box full of empty frames for the bees to build on in the future. Put the second box on top of the first box. If any spare bees are in the nuc box, upend the box over the permanent hive. The bees should fall down between the frames. Any that are flying will figure things out.

FEED THE HIVE

It's a good idea to feed the bees to keep them happy and healthy until they can reestablish their hive. To do this, you'll use a spacer frame to create a feeding area on top of the hive. See directions for how to build one on page 283. Put on your gear, and as usual, it's best to do this during daylight hours, when the workers are out. Have everything ready so you can move quickly. Remove the lid of the hive. Take the spacer frame you assembled and put it on top of the hive, on the topmost hive box. This will provide a little head space for feeding. Lay any chunks of honeycomb that you reserved from the cutout there, right on top of the frames. Also give the bees the prepared bag of sugar water. Spread the bag out flat. Take a razor blade or sharp knife and cut a 2-inch slit in the center, just enough that the sugar water puddles out a little onto the surface of the bag, not so much that the sugar water gushes into the hive. This cut will become a feeding trough for the bees. Put the lid on top of the spacer and leave the bees alone.

After 3 or 4 days, put on your gear again and lift the lid to check on the bag. If the bag is empty, swap it out for another. Feed the bees this way for a couple weeks. If flowers are plentiful, they'll soon have enough supplies of their own. If there's not much in bloom, you might have to feed a bit longer. They'll lose interest in the sugar water when they don't need it anymore.

TIPS ON KEEPING BEES

Mostly you're just there to watch. The bees will take care of themselves. Observe your hive as much as you can, to get to know the bees' behavior. Happy working bees don't mind if you walk up close to the hive, so we often spend time with no gear on, right in front of the hive, watching their comings and goings. By observing, you'll learn to identify normal bee behavior. You can see workers returning from the field with pollen panniers packed on their back legs. This is a good sign that they're tending brood. You'll see how the hive hums with activity on a sunny day and how they hunker down when it rains. Some of the behaviors you see you won't understand. That's okay, just keep watching. Remember, you have to let bees be bees. If they're having any internal problems, you have to trust them to sort it out.

The one thing you should do is suit up every month or so, smoke the hive, and peek inside to make sure they have enough room. If they've filled about seven out of ten frames in the topmost box, it's time to stack another box full of empty frames on top of the hive. If they get crowded, they might swarm. That is, half of them, or all of them, might leave your hive to look for more spacious digs. Bees from a crowded hive also tend to become aggressive, so it's in everyone's best interests to make sure they have plenty of room.

Finally, for support and ongoing education, seek out other beekeepers in your area—preferably backward-style or natural beekeepers—through beekeeping clubs or online groups. Visit them and lend a hand when they work with their hives. For further reading, we suggest *The Complete Idiot's Guide to Beekeeping*, which was written by two backward-style beekeepers. See our resource listing at the end of this book for more beekeeping books and links.

APARTMENT DWELLERS MAKE GREAT BEEKEEPERS!

You don't need a yard to keep bees. You can keep them on a flat roof or a balcony. You can also keep hives in remote locations—in community gardens or in a little corner of someone's yard. Bribe your hosts with honey.

69 ›

Build a Honey Extractor and Collect Some Honey

Traditional honey extractors are expensive devices designed to spin honeycomb at high speed. The centrifugal action sucks the honey from the comb, leaving the wax cells intact. The empty comb is then returned to the hive, where the bees will refill it. Since they don't have to rebuild the comb, they put more energy into honey making, thus upping the hive's productivity. As backward beekeepers, our primary concern is the bees, not the honey. We don't provide them with prebuilt comb, so they don't make comb that would do well in a centrifuge. When we collect honey, we use a simple crush-and-strain method.

All this requires is a few pieces of easy-to-assemble, inexpensive filtering equipment and the assistance of gravity. The comb is lost to the bees, so they have to rebuild, but building is what they do best. We get to keep the honey and the wax.

YOU'LL NEED

- 2 (5-gallon) food-grade buckets with lids
- Sharp knife, like a utility knife with a new blade
- 5-gallon (60-pound) plastic pail with a honey gate installed at the bottom, and a lid (available at beekeeping supply companies)
- 5-gallon nylon paint strainer (available at painters' supply stores)
- Drill with ½-inch bit
- Something to crush the comb, like a sharp paint scraper mounted on a pole or a very clean spade
- Ordinary beekeeping equipment for collecting the honey: bee suit, gloves, smoker, bee brush

PUTTING IT TOGETHER

ASSEMBLE THE BUCKETS

Set aside one 5-gallon bucket for collecting honey. You won't need it right now.

Using a knife with a sharp blade, cut the center out of the lid[A] belonging to the bucket with the honey gate.[B] Leave about 1 inch around the rim.

Drill two rings of ½-inch holes in the bottom of the regular bucket: a small ring dead center and a second ring close around it.[C] Arrange the holes so

C

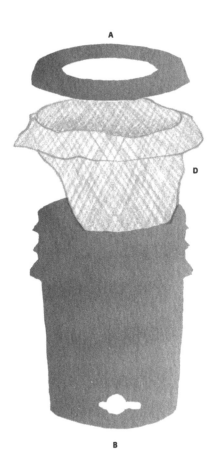

A

D

B

that they lie within the circumference of the hole you cut in the lid of the honey-gate bucket. This bucket will sit on that lid. The honey will pass through these holes into the lower bucket, so the holes must be positioned within the circumference of the hole in the cutout lid.

Tuck the paint strainer [D] into the bucket fitted with the honey gate. The paint strainer is bag shaped. Fold the edges of the bag over the rim of the bucket and snap the cutout lid onto the bucket to hold the strainer in place. Balance the bucket with the holes in the bottom on top of this lid. That's it. That's your fancy setup.

COLLECT THE HONEY

The honey is cut out of the frames at the site of the hive. Have the second clean 5-gallon bucket ready to collect the comb. Smoke the entrances and wait 5 to 10 minutes for the bees to pacify, then lift off the top of the hive. If they still seem a little aggressive, give them another puff of smoke. Lift the frames from the hive, one by one, looking for those that are full of honey. When you find a likely candidate, give it a sharp shake to knock off the clinging bees. Using the bee brush, sweep away any stubborn bees. Standing over the bucket, cut the honeycomb out of the frame with a sharp knife, leaving a ¾-inch strip of comb at the top of the frame to serve as foundation for rebuilding. Let the honeycomb fall into the bucket. Put the lid on the bucket to keep bees out, replace the empty frame in the hive, and repeat. Always be sure to leave enough honey for the hive.

When do you harvest honey? How much honey should you leave? Generally speaking, there won't be enough to harvest until a year after you've started a new hive. Both a captured swarm and a cutout swarm have a lot of rebuilding to do. The presence of excess honey means they have time and energy to concentrate on stockpiling food. We don't begin to consider harvesting honey until the hive has expanded to fill 5 boxes. Knowing how much to take and when to take it is part of the art of beekeeping. The answers vary, depending on the size and health of the hive, the season, and the availability of resources for the bees. Some hives can yield a hundred pounds of honey at a shot, others can't afford to spare any at all. Until you get the knack of it, you'll want the advice of a beekeeping mentor who can evaluate your specific set of conditions. If in doubt, don't harvest. It's better to err on the side of caution.

CRUSH THE HONEY

Inside the house, away from the bees, open the collection bucket. Crush the comb using a long, sharp implement of some sort, like a paint scraper mounted on a pole or a clean spade. A sturdy metal spatula might do for smaller quantities of honey. With sharp downward motions, cut through the comb until there's no more resistance to the blade. The crushed comb and honey will be a semiliquid mass.

STRAIN THE HONEY

Tip the collection bucket full of honey and mashed comb into the top bucket of your strainer. The holes in this bucket will catch the larger chunks of wax, then the honey will drip down into the lower bucket, where the paint strainer will catch smaller pieces and other impurities. This will take a good while, so put a lid on the top bucket to keep out flies and leave it overnight.

ENJOY THE SPOILS

The next day, put a sanitized jar beneath the honey gate and open the gate. Sample your very own raw, unfiltered, local honey collected from wild bees. It tastes like sweet joy.

SMALL-SCALE HARVESTING

The double-bucket system is designed to accommodate large quantities of honey. If you have only a comb or two, you can use the same basic principles to improvise an extractor. Line a colander with cheesecloth. Balance the colander over a large bowl. Put the honeycomb in the colander and crush it into pulp with a spatula. Cover the colander with a kitchen towel and let the honey drain into the bowl overnight. The next day, bottle the honey or strain it through fresh cheesecloth a second time, if necessary.

70 ›

PREPARATION: 2 hours

Make a Native Pollinator Habitat

In this time of honeybee decline, native pollinators—like bumblebees, orchard mason bees, and leafcutter bees— become all the more important. However, they are under threat, too, because their habitat is vanishing.

Native pollinators need wild places to build their homes: dead branches, empty mouse nests, undisturbed patches of soil. In the wild, they live in the unattended margins of nature, where forest meets field, where field meets ditch. Our suburbs stretch out to eat open fields, replacing these marginal spaces with tidy lawns interspersed with acres of concrete and asphalt. Hanging a native bee house in your backyard is a good deed—and it's fascinating, too. There are too many different types of native pollinators to mention, but most are solitary bees, and all are very gentle.

To start, make your yard an oasis for pollinators and all of the other little creatures that need a safe place to make their homes, like butterflies, ladybugs, lacewings and spiders, lizards, snakes, toads, and songbirds. The more complex your yard's ecosystem, the healthier it will be. The best way to protect your veg-etable beds and fruit trees is by letting other plants and creatures thrive in your yard. A diverse garden finds its own balance between pests and predators.

We believe that every garden should have a corner left entirely to nature, a zone off-limits to humans. This corner should never be tidied or improved. Leaves are not collected. Wildflowers and weeds are allowed to bloom and seed there unimpeded. The most you might do is lay down an armload of sticks there as an offering to the lizards and toads. This ground is an incubator for the wild spirit of the garden.

Beyond that, you can support native pollinators by doing a few things. First and foremost, you must banish all pesticides and herbicides from the garden. Second, plant lots of flowering native plants, short-lived wildflowers, fruit trees, and flowering herbs. Plant enough of these so that there's always something blooming in your yard throughout the growing season. Then add water, in the form of birdbath or a pond. Our birdbath draws everything from honeybees to fierce hawks. Do these simple things and your yard will hum with life. Ladybugs and lacewings will patrol your crops, while dragonflies and butterflies color the air. Obliging little birds show up to eat up your aphids and grasshoppers. And in the meantime, hardly noticeable in the background, modest little native pollina-tors will establish themselves in your yard—if they can find a spot.

Thirty percent of native pollinators live in dead wood or the hollows of plant stalks. The rest live underground—including bumblebees. Bumblebees prefer to live in old mouse nests. Who knew? Some garden stores sell bumblebee houses. While this is a charming idea, the truth is, bumblebees rarely adopt these artificial homes. Support ground-dwelling pollinators by simply leaving bare patches of ground for them to dig into—some like soil, some like clay, others like sand.

The pollinators that live in stalks and wood are easier to help. The first thing you can do, as mentioned already, is to just leave dead plant stalks in the ground to overwinter, and let a few dead branches or logs accumulate on your property. Beetles bore holes into the wood, and the pollinators adopt those holes as nests.

Or you can build a house full of stalks to tempt native pollinators to move in.

Pollinator Condo

The bees served by this project are solitary bees that build their nests in tubes—in plant stems or holes in wood. A solitary female lays several eggs in each tube, starting at the back and working forward. Each egg is sealed in its own compartment along with a supply of pollen for the hatchling. In profile view, these nests look like train cars. When the bee fills the entire tube, she seals the front with a plug of mud or plant matter. The next generation hatches in the following spring and begins building its own nests.

It's hard to predict which types of pollinators might pass through your yard. Different types of native bees have different preferences in the size of the nest they prefer and the materials from which it's made. So you're going to collect a variety of potential nesting materials, put them in a bee house, and see who moves in. The first step is to build the house.

YOU'LL NEED

* 1x10 lumber, 20 inches total
* 1x8 lumber, 21 inches total
* Galvanized nails or wood screws, about 1 ½ inches long
* Exterior (waterproof) wood glue
* Mounting hardware of your choice

PUTTING IT TOGETHER

PRECUT THE LUMBER

Cut the 1x10 lumber into two pieces: one 10 inches long[A] and the other 9 ¼ inches.[B] These two pieces will form the roof.

Cut the 1x8 lumber into three pieces: 2 pieces that are 7 ¼ inches and one 6 ½ inches. These will form the sides[C,D] and the back.[E]

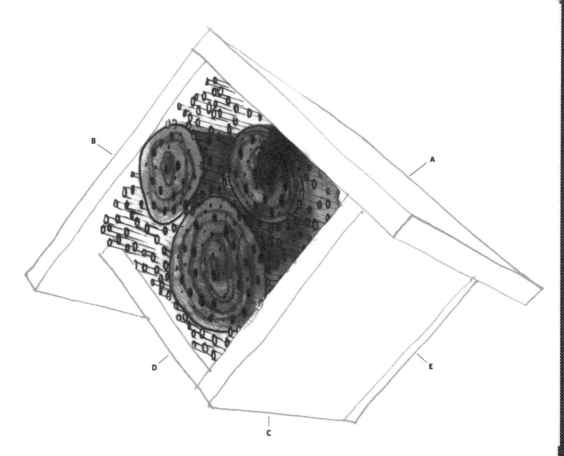

"GLUE AND SCREW" THE PIECES TOGETHER

Start by assembling the roof. Apply a bead of wood glue to both surfaces of the roof pieces, then attach the two pieces together with two nails or screws, one on each side. If you predrill guide holes, it will be easier to drive in the screws. Wipe up any excess glue with a damp cloth.

Next, in exactly the same way, join one 7 ¼-inch piece [C] with the 6 ½-inch piece [D] to form the body of the house. Then attach the back, the other 7 ¼-inch piece. [E]

Attach the assembled body of the house to the roof, aligning the back sides of both roof and house so that the roof projects 2 inches over the front of the house.

FINISH THE PIECE

You could hang the bee house as is. If you built it out of redwood or cedar, it will last a long time untreated. If it's made of pine, it may start breaking down after a few years. If you want it to last longer, coat the exterior with latex house paint or a water-based polyurethane finish. Leave the interior unfinished because the bees might be sensitive to the chemicals in finishes.

NOTES ON WOOD

You can use any type of wood you wish, except pressure-treated lumber, which is full of chemicals that will harm the insects. Cedar and redwood are more expensive than pine but last longer outdoors untreated. Newbie woodworkers should note that the nominal dimensions of 1x8 lumber are actually ¾ x 7 ¼ inches, and 1x10 lumber actually measures ¾ x 9 ¼ inches. This project is designed so that you only have to cut the lumber to the proper length. The widths are standard.

MOUNT IT

The house must be mounted against a wall or secured to a post. It's not meant to dangle from a tree like a birdhouse. So you'll need to decide where you're going to mount it and choose the correct mounting hardware for that location. The most direct method would be to screw the box directly to a wooden fence or wall. If you're going to do that, predrill 2 to 4 holes in the back of the box to make this easier. If you don't want to drill lots of holes in your walls, attach a mounting bracket to the back of the box, which would allow you to hang it from one nail. Hardware stores sell mounting hardware designed for different situations.

GATHER NESTING MATERIALS

Take a pair of shears and forage for plant stalks with soft piths (cores). Some solitary bees like to chew their way into old plant stalks. Good candidates are wild rose, raspberry canes, mullein stalks, and thistle stalks. Poke around and see what you can find. The more variety in size and type, the better.

Also look for plants with hollow stalks, like reeds and bamboo, dry or fresh, in various widths. There's a common type of patio-screening material made up of dried reeds. If you have some of this around, slice off a few reeds from one end.

For wood-dwelling bees, you'll want a thick branch or log section of dry hardwood or fruitwood, cut 6½ inches long, width variable. You'll pack one or more branches in the house along with the stalks or reeds. (See the illustration on page 305.) How many branch pieces you use depends on their width—how many will fit in the house—and your preference. The house could be filled mostly with wood chunks, entirely with plant stalks, or with a mix.

Note: Instead of branches, you could use scraps of hardwood lumber.

PREPARE THE MATERIALS

The house looks neatest if all the nesting material is cut to the same length, but the native bees don't care. So let aesthetics be your guide. Using pruning shears, cut all plant stalks, canes, and reeds to approximately 6½ inches.

Cut bamboo canes just beneath the nodes (where there's a ridge on the outside). The nodes indicate the presence of an interior wall. Let one of those nodes be a back wall for your tube. Bees like back walls, which make them feel secure. Make sure you arrange the bamboo so the walls are at the "back" of the canes and the front portion of the cane is open.

Drill holes in the branches you collected to tempt wood-dwelling bees. One of the most widespread native pollinators in North America is the orchard mason bee. It prefers nests that are ¼ inches wide and 6 inches deep. Using a ¼-inch drill bit, drill 6-inch tunnels into the hardwood you collected. Space the holes about ¾ inches apart. It doesn't matter if the holes are drilled with or against the grain of the wood, as long as the holes are 6 inches deep. But make sure to leave a back wall in the wood—in other words, don't drill all the way through to the other side. If you wish, you can also make a few holes with finer bits ($^3/_{16}$ inch, $^1/_8$ inch, etc.) to attract smaller-bodied pollinators that might live in your area.

Note: If you don't have a drill, just fill your house with stalks.

MOUNT AND FILL THE HOUSE

First, mount the house in its final location. Choose a spot that gets some morning sun; an east- or southeast-facing position is ideal. It should be mounted at least 5 feet off the ground to discourage animals from disturbing it.

Then fill the house with your assembled materials. Pack them in so everything is nice and snug, arranging them any way that pleases you. All that matters is that everything is pressed flush against the back of the house and none of it protrudes past the protection of the roofline.

MAINTENANCE

You don't have to do much from here on out but watch. If the bees are interested, you'll see them flying around the house, entering and exiting the tubes and holes. If they plug up some of the holes, you'll know your house is successful. If it's not adopted the first year, consider planting more flowering plants the next year and trying again. Native bees don't travel far from their nest in search of pollen. If your yard isn't rich with flowers, they won't stick around.

If you notice birds pecking at the bee nests, curl a piece of chicken wire around the front of the house.

Orchard mason bees start building their nests in the early spring, when the blossoms appear, and use mud in their construction, so if your yard is dry (unlikely as that is in the spring), you could make it a point to maintain a little mud puddle near their house.

When winter comes, leave the house where it is. The eggs in the sealed holes will incubate until the next year. The baby bees will be fine over winter. They actually depend on the cold as part of their life cycle. The one thing that can harm them, though, is unusual winter wetness—unusual for your climate, that is. If you usually have snowy winters but are getting driving rainstorms instead, you could take down the box and move it somewhere cold but sheltered, like a garage or shed or covered porch. Move it carefully and put it where it will not be disturbed—either by people or mice. Return the house to the outdoors as soon as you can, before you see the first signs of spring. The bees won't want to miss the first blooms.

The next spring, the bees might recolonize old nesting materials, but they also might appreciate some fresh stuff. Switch some of it out and see which they prefer.

Resources

BEEKEEPING

Backwards Beekeepers. beehuman.blogspot.com.

Bush, Michael. "Beekeeping Naturally, Bush Bees." bushfarms.com/bees.htm.

Beesource.com. "Charles Martin Simon." beesource.com/point-of-view/charles-martin-simon.

Frauenfelder, Mark. "Keeping Bees," in *Made by Hand: Searching for Meaning in a Throwaway World*. Ottawa: Portfolio Hardcover, 2010.

Stiglitz, Dean, and Laurie Herboldsheimer. *The Complete Idiot's Guide to Beekeeping*. New York: Alpha, 2010.

CHICKENS

Damerow, Gail. *The Chicken Health Handbook*. North Adams, MA: Storey Publishing, 1994.

English, Ashley. *Homemade Living: Keeping Chickens with Ashley English: All You Need to Know to Care for a Happy, Healthy Flock*. New York: Lark Books, 2010.

Gardeners' and Poultry Keepers' Guide and Illustrated Catalogue of W. Cooper, Ltd.: 500 Drawings of Greenhouses, Farm and Garden Buildings, and Rustic Furniture, abridged. Bolinas, CA: Shelter Publications, 2010. First published in 1914 by William Cooper Ltd., London.

Heinrichs, Christine. *How to Raise Poultry*. Minneapolis: Voyageur Press, 2009.

Luttmann, Gail, and Rick Luttmann. *Chickens in Your Backyard: A Beginner's Guide*. Emmaus, PA: Rodale Books, 1976.

DIY LIFESTYLE

Carpenter, Novella. *Farm City: The Education of an Urban Farmer*. New York: Penguin Press, 2009.

Frauenfelder, Mark. *Made by Hand: My Year of Searching for Meaning in a Throwaway World*. New York: Portfolio Hardcover, 2010.

Hayes, Shannon. *Radical Homemakers: Reclaiming Domesticity from a Consumer Culture*. Walnut Creek, CA: Left To Write Press, 2010.

FERMENTATION AND PRESERVATION

Alley, Lynn. *Lost Arts*. Berkeley, CA: Ten Speed Press, 1995.

Aubert, Claude, ed. *Keeping Food Fresh: Old World Techniques and Recipes; The Gardeners and Farmers of Terre Vivante*. White River Junction, VT: Chelsea Green Publishing, 1999.

Buhner, Stephen Harrod. *Sacred and Herbal Healing Beers: The Secrets of Ancient Fermentation*. Boulder, CO: Siris Books, 1998.

Fisher, Dennis, and Joe Fisher. *The Homebrewer's Garden: How to Easily Grow, Prepare, and Use Your Own Hops, Malts, Brewing Herbs*. North Adams, MA: Storey Publishing, 1998.

Katz, Sandor Ellix. *Wild Fermentation: The Flavor, Nutrition, and Craft of Live-Culture Foods*. White River Junction, VT: Chelsea Green Publishing, 2003.

Palmer, John J. *How to Brew: Everything You Need to Know to Brew Beer Right the First Time*, 3rd ed. Boulder, CO: Brewers Publications, 2006.

Schramm, Ken. *The Compleat Meadmaker: Home Production of Honey Wine from Your First Batch to Award-Winning Fruit and Herb Variations*. Boulder, CO: Brewers Publications, 2003.

GARDENING AND COMPOSTING

Ashworth, Suzanne, and Kent Whealy. *Seed to Seed: Seed Saving and Growing Techniques for Vegetable Gardeners*, 2nd ed. Decorah, IA: Seed Savers Exchange, 2002.

Coyne, Kelly, and Erik Knutzen. *The Urban Homestead: Your Guide to Self-Sufficient Living in the Heart of the City*, rev. New York: Process, 2010.

Fukuoka, Masanobu. *The One-Straw Revolution: An Introduction to Natural Farming*. New York: NYRB Classics, 2009.

Jeavons, John. *How to Grow More Vegetables (and Fruits, Nuts, Berries, Grains, and Other Crops)*, 7th ed. Berkeley, CA: Ten Speed Press, 2006.

Jenkins, Joseph C. *The Humanure Handbook: A Guide to Composting Human Manure*, 3rd ed. Grove City, PA: Joseph Jenkins, Inc., 2005.

Lowenfels, Jeff, and Wayne Lewis. *Teaming with Microbes: The Organic Gardener's Guide to the Soil Food Web*, rev. Portland, OR: Timber Press, 2010.

Pfeiffer, Ehrenfried. *Bio-Dynamic Farming and Gardening: Soil Fertility, Renewal and Preservation*. Ithaca: Mercury Press, 1984.

Pleasant, Barbara, and Deborah L. Martin. *The Complete Compost Gardening Guide: Banner Batches, Grow Heaps, Comforter Compost, and Other Amazing Techniques for Saving Time and Money, and Producing the Most Flavorful, Nutritious Vegetables Ever*. North Adams, MA: Storey Publishing, 2008.

The Rodale Book of Composting: Easy Methods for Every Gardener. Emmaus, PA: Rodale Press, 1992.

Rodale, J. I. *Pay Dirt: Farming and Gardening with Composts*. New York: Devin-Adair Company, 1948.

Storl, Wolf-Dieter. *Culture and Horticulture: A Philosophy of Gardening*. Berlin: Steiner Books, 1979.

Toensmeier, Eric. *Perennial Vegetables: From Artichokes to Zuiki Taro, A Gardener's Guide to Over 100 Delicious and Easy-to-Grow Edibles*. White River Junction, VT: Chelsea Green Publishing, 2007.

HERBALISM

Bruton-Seal, Julie, and Matthew Seal. *Backyard Medicine: Harvest and Make Your Own Herbal Remedies*. New York: Skyhorse Publishing, 2009.

Buhner, Stephen Harrod. *The Lost Language of Plants: The Ecological Importance of Plant Medicines for Life on Earth*. White River Junction, VT: Chelsea Green Publishing, 2002.

Falconi, Dina. *Earthly Bodies and Heavenly Hair: Natural and Healthy Personal Care for Every Body*. Woodstock, NY: Ceres Press, 1998.

Gladstar, Rosemary. *Rosemary Gladstar's Herbal Recipes for Vibrant Health: 175 Teas, Tonics, Oils, Salves, Tinctures, and Other Natural Remedies for the Entire Family*. North Adams, MA: Storey Publishing, 2008.

Henriette's Herbal Homepage. henriettesherbal.com.

Moore, Michael. *Herbal Materia Medica 5.0*. swsbm.com/ManualsMM/Mat Med5.txt, 1995.

Weed, Susun. Herbal Medicine and Spirit Healing the Wise Woman Way. susunweed.com.

HOUSECLEANING

Hollender, Jeffrey, Geoff Davis, Meika Hollender, and Reed Doyle. *Naturally Clean: The Seventh Generation Guide to Safe and Healthy, Non-Toxic Cleaning.* Gabriola Island, BC: New Society Publishers, 2006.

Sandbeck, Ellen. *Organic Housekeeping: In Which the Nontoxic Avenger Shows You How to Improve Your Health and That of Your Family, While You Save Time, Money, and, Perhaps, Your Sanity.* New York: Scribner, 2006.

Siegel-Maier, Karyn. *The Naturally Clean Home.* North Adams, MA: Storey Publishing, 2008.

SOAPMAKING

Cavitch, Susan Miller. *Soapmaker's Companion: A Comprehensive Guide with Recipes, Techniques and Know-How.* North Adams, MA: Storey Publishing, 1997.

Watson, Anne L. *Smart Soapmaking: The Simple Guide to Making Traditional Handmade Soap Quickly, Safely, and Reliably, or How to Make Luxurious Handcrafted Soaps for Family, Friends, and Yourself.* Olympia, WA: Shepard Publications, 2007.

Acknowledgments

We'd like to thank Gena Smith, Colin Dickerman, and all the good people at Rodale for making this book possible. *Making It* was designed by Roman Jaster and illustrated by Teira Johnson. We're extraordinarily grateful to both of them for their insight, dedication, and passion for the subject. Go Team! And if our agent, Byrd Leavell, ever comes west, we owe him at least a couple of home brews for his advice and support.

We'd also like to thank the following people who've contributed to this book by sharing knowledge, lending a hand, or just being generally wonderful and inspirational: Kirk Anderson, Thomas Lee Bakofsky, Russell Bates, Colin Bogart, Caroline Clerc, Art Detrich, Bruce Fields, Mark Frauenfelder, Ben Guzman, Lora Hall, Shannon Hayes, Heidi Hough, David Kahn, Nancy Klehm, Tara Kolla, Steve Linsley, Jean-Paul Monché, Ray Narkevicius, Craig Ruggless, Jennifer Seeley, Amy Seidenwurm, and of course, our ever-supportive families. We love you, guys!

Index

Underscored page references indicate boxed text. **Boldface** references indicate illustrations.

A

Acetobacter, in vinegar making, 199, 202, 202
Aches, muscle, 33
Acidophilus capsules, for yeast infections, 35
African bees, 272
Aguas Frescas, 37–38
Alcoholic beverages
    beer, 207–15, **208**
    mead, 203–6, **205**
All-grain brewing, in beer making, 207
Almost Castile Soap, 154
Almost Universal Spray, 70
Aloe vera, for treating
    burns, 31
    cuts and scrapes, 32
Animal fat, in soap making, 157, 159–61, 160
Anxiety, 35

B

Back stitch, for basic mending, 85, **85**
Baking soda
    in Baking Soda Cleansing Spray, 132
    in Baking Soda Shampoo, 17–18
    for facial, 25
    in homemade cleaning products, 69, 71, 72, 73, 74
    in homemade laundry detergent, 76, 77
    in Homemade Tooth Powder, 14
    for indigestion, 35
    in A Minimalist Mouthwash, 15
    as shaving preparation, 26
    for skin irritations, 33
Baking Soda Cleansing Spray, as deodorant, 132
Baking Soda Shampoo, 17–18
Beans
    dried
        vs. canned, 42
        how to cook, 48–49
    Quick Soup, 53–54
    seed saving and, 191
Beehives. *See also* Beekeeping, backward; Honeybees
    assembling, 274
    benefits of, 270
    from cutout capture
        building spacer frame, 283
        feeding, 286
        stringing frames, 282–83, **282**
    man-made
        frames for, 272, 273, 274
        positioning, 274–75, **274**
        transferring bees to, 279
Beekeeper protective gear, 277, 278
Beekeeping, backward
    assembling equipment for, 273–75
    capture methods for, 275
        cutout, 1, 275, 281–87
        swarm capture, 277–80
    conventional beekeeping vs., 271
    honey extractor and honey collection methods and, 288–90
    legality of, 274
    locations for, 287
    native pollinator habitat and, 291–95
    technique of, 271–73
    tips for, 287
Beer making, 207–15, **208**
    building mash tun for, 248, **249**, 250, **251**, 252, **252**
    building wort chiller for, 253–54, **254**
Bees. *See* Beehives; Beekeeping, backward; Honeybees
Bee smoker, for use with cutout, 283, 284–85
Bee stings, 30
Berry stains, 81
Beverages
    beer, 207–15, **208**
    herb and fruit infusions, 36–38
    mead, 203–6, **205**
    vinegar-based, 65–67
Bites, insect, 113
Blackberry leaf tea, for diarrhea, 32
Bleaches
    chlorine, 78
    oxygen, 80
Bleeding, 30
Blender, for easy-method soap making, 148, 149
Blood stains, 81
Bluing, laundry, for whitening, 80
Body Polish, 29
Body washing, 28
Borax
    in homemade cleaning products, 69, 69, 70, 71, 72, 74
    in homemade laundry products, 69, 69, 76, 77, 79
Bottling
    beer, 214
    mead, 206

Botulism, 117
Bread, homemade
    reasons for making, 42
    sourdough starter for, 59, 60
    Vollkornbrot, 58–60
Breath fresheners, 15, 15
Brining a chicken, 173
Brood comb, in beekeeping, 275, 285
Bucket, for honey extractor, 288–89, **289**
Bug bites, 30
Bulk bin seeds, for microgreens, 102, 103
Bulk foods, for home cooking, 42
    storing, 43, 43
Burns, 31
Button, sewing, 85–86, **86**

C

Cabbage
    Kimchi, 94–95
    Kimchi Pancakes, 95
    Kraut Quesadillas, 93
    Pink Kraut "Salad," 93
    Sauerkraut, 91–93
Cabbage Patch pH Indicator, 163–64
Carbonation
    beer, 207, 215
    mead, 206, 206
Castile soap
    Almost Castile Soap, 154
    Genuine Castile Soap, 150–53
    in homemade cleaning products, 69, 70,
        72, 73
    liquid, in foam pumps, 156
    for washing delicate fabrics, 78
Catnip
    Catnip Honey, 110
    for sleeplessness or anxiety, 35
Catnip Honey, 110
Chamomile
    Chamomile Honey, 110
    for sleeplessness or anxiety, 35
Chamomile Honey, 110
Chew sticks, for tooth cleaning, 12, 13
Chicken(s). *See also* Chicken coop, building
    brining, 173
    raising, 270
        benefits of, 261
        general tips for, 267–69
        responsibility of, 261
    slaughtering, 165–73, **166**, **171**
    Whole Chicken Stock, 46–47
Chicken coop, building, 261–63, **264–65**, 266–67
Chicken feed, 267
Chickweed
    foraging for, 111, **111**
    for skin irritations, 33

Cleaning products, household
    advantages of, 68, 69
    Almost Universal Spray, 70
    Deodorizer, 74
    Dusting Aids, 73
    Floor Cleaners, 72
    Furniture Polish, 73
    Hard Water Scale Remover, 74
    ingredients and supplies for, 69
    Mildew Removers, 74
    Scouring Powders, 71
    Soap Scum and Bathtub Ring Cleansers, 74
    Soft Scrub, 72
    Spray for Greasy Surfaces, 70
    Stove and Oven Cleaners, 73
    Super-Natural Disinfectant, 71
    Toilet Bowl Cleaners, 72
    Vinegar of the Four Thieves, 71
    Wood Cleaners, 73
Cleaning rags, 69, 70, 73
Cloth menstrual pads, 137, **138**, 139–45, **142**, **144**
Cocoa powder, as dry shampoo, 16
Cocoa Puff Skin Butter, 125–26
Coconut Laundry Soap, 155–56
Coconut oil, in hair conditioner, 23
Coffee stains, 81
Colds, 31, 109
Colony collapse disorder, 271
Comfrey
    as fertilizer, 188
    for muscle aches and strains, 33
Compost or composting
    benefits of, 2, 182, 226
    cautions about, 229
    considerations in making, 228
    container for, 229
        fast compost, 234
        from shipping pallets, 230–31, **231**
        slow compost, 232
    ingredients for, 227, 232–33, 234–35
    methods of
        fast, 226, 234–35
        slow, 226, 232–33
    sifting, 233, 235
    worm bins and, 233, 242–47, **245**
Compost worms, for worm bins, 243
Condiments, homemade
    Harisssa, 63–64
    Mayonnaise, 61–62
    Mustard, 62–63
Conditioner, hair, 23
Congestion
    nasal, 33
    stuffy head, 34
Cooking from scratch. *See also* Salting, foods
            made from
    benefits of, 42
    dried beans, 48–49

Cooking from scratch. (*Cont.*)
    preparation for, 43
    recipes for
        Chicken Stock, 46–47
        Dog's Pot, The, 55–57
        Harissa, 63–64
        Italian Fried Rice, 52–53
        Mayonnaise, 61–62
        Mustard, 62–63
        Oxymel, 65–66
        Quick Soup, 53–54
        Sekanjabin, 66–67
        Switchel, 67
        Vegetable Stock, 44–45
        Vollkornbrot, 58–60
    transitioning to, 42
    whole grains, 50–51
CooKit solar cooker. *See* Solar cooker
Cornstarch, as dry shampoo, 16
Coughs, 31–32, 109, 110, 113
Cross-pollination
    of fruit trees, 193
    seed saving and, 189, 190, 191
Curiously Homemade Peppermints, 15, 35,
    134–36
Cutout, for bee acquisition, 1, 275
    difficulty of, 281
    preparation for, 282–84, **282**
    supplies for, 281–82
Cuts, 32

D

Decoctions, herbal, 116
Deep bedding, in chicken run, 268
Dehydration, 32
Dental care, 11–15
Deodorants
    Baking Soda Cleansing Spray, 132
    Herbal Stick Deodorant, 131
Deodorizer, 74
Diarrhea, 32
Direct sowing of seeds, 180
Disinfectant, Super-Natural, 71
Dog's Pot, The, 55–57
Double-digging soil, for vegetable garden,
    182–83, 183, **183**, 184, 193
Drain opener, in soap making, 149
Dr. Bronner's Sal Suds, for laundry,
    75–76
Drip-irrigation system, for vegetable garden,
    218–22, **219**, **220–21**
Dry toilet
    building, **236**, 237–39
    composting humanure from, 239–41
    ready-made, 238
Dusting Aids, 73

E

Eggplant seeds, saving, 190
Emitter tubing, quarter-inch, in drip-irriga-
    tion system, 219, 220, 221, **221**, 221
Epsom salts, for muscle aches and strains, 33
Espalier, how to, 192–97, **195**, **196**
Essential oils
    for headaches, 33
    for scenting laundry, 81

F

Fabric softener, vinegar as, 80
Face washing, 27–28
Facial, quick, 25
Failures, in make-it-yourself projects, 5
Fast compost, 226, 234–35
Fat, animal, in soap making, 157, 159–61, 160
Fats, for dogs, 56–57
Fels-Naptha, for cleaning laundry, 75, 76
Female hose beginning, in drip-irrigation
    system, **219**, 220
Fennel seeds, as breath freshener, 15
Feral bees, 272, 272, 273, 275, 281. *See also*
    Beekeeping, backward; Honeybees
Fermentation processes
    beer making, 207–15
    mead making, 203–6
    vinegar making, 199–202
Fertilizer. *See also* Manure
    from stinging nettles, 187–88
Filter, in drip-irrigation system, **219**, 220
Flats, for seed starting, 176
Flaxseed, in hair-styling gel, 24
Flaxseed tea, for sore throat, 34
Floor Cleaners, 72
Flour paste, making, 256
Flour sack towels, 78
Flu, 110
Fluorescent shop lights, as grow lights,
    185–86
Food production systems, problems with, 165
French intensive layout, for arranging plant-
    ing beds, **178**, 180
Fruit infusions, 37–38
Fruit trees
    how to espalier, 192–97, **195**, **196**
    pollination of, 193
    preparing soil for, 193
Furniture Polish, 73

G

Garden-Grown Shampoo, 18–19
Garden projects

espalier, how to, 192–97, **195**, **196**

indoor (*see* Indoor gardening)

vegetable garden (*see* Vegetable garden)

Garlic

    Garlic Honey, 109

    Harissa, 63–64

    for treating

        colds, 31

        yeast infections, 35

Garlic Honey, 109

Genuine Castile Soap, 150–53

Ginger

    Ginger Honey, 109

    for upset stomach, 35

Ginger Honey, 109

Grains. *See also* Whole grains

Grass stains, 83

Gravity, in beer making, 209

Gravlax, 96

Gray water, laundry detergent for, 81

Grease, burnt-on, 71

Grease stains, 83

Greasy Surfaces, Spray for, 70

Green Elixir, 36–37

Greens

    Italian Fried Rice, 52–53

Grist, in beer making, 208

Grow lights, for seed starting, 185–86

Gutting a chicken, after slaughter, 172

H

Hair care

    deep conditioning, 23

    herbs for, 20

    natural shampoos for, 16–20

    rinses for, 21–22

    styling gel, 24

Half-inch mainline tubing, in drip-irrigation system, 218, **219**, 220, 221, 221

Hand Scrub, 29

Hardening off, of seedlings, 179

Hard Water Scale Remover, 74

Harissa, 63–64

Headache Balm, 123

Headaches, 33, 119, 123

Henhouse, for raising chickens, 26, 261, 262, 266–67, 268–69

Herbal infusions, 36–37

Herbal medicine. *See also specific herbs and health conditions*

    decoctions in, 116

    dried vs. fresh herbs for, 115

    drying, infusing, and tincturing herbs for, 115–19

    drying herbs for, 115, 115

    foraging feral greens for, 111–14

medicinal honey, 109–10

    oil infusions in, 115, 116–18, 117

    tinctures in, 115, 118–19

    water infusions in, 115, 116

Herbal Stick Deodorant, 131

Herbs. *See also specific herbs*

    disinfectant, 71

    hair-care, 20, 21–22

    in Herbal Stick Deodorant, 131

    infusions of, 36–37

    in interdependent systems, 2

    medicinal (*see* Herbal medicine)

Home brewing, of beer, 207–15, **208**

Home economics, old-fashioned, 2

Homegrown household

    interdependence in, 2–3

    planning projects for, 3

Homemade Laundry Powder, 76–77

Homemade Liquid Soap, 156

Homemade Shampoo Bars, 17

Homemade Tooth Powder, 14

Honey

    collecting, from honey extractor, 289–90, 290

    in interdependent systems, 3

    in mead making, 203, 204

    medicinal, 109–10

    in Oxymel beverage, 65–66

    for treating

        burns, 31

        coughs, 31

        cuts and scrapes, 32

        pimples, 34

        sore throat, 34

Honeybees. *See also* Beehives; Beekeeping, backward

    African, 272

    benefits of keeping, 270

    endangerment of, 270

    feral, in backward beekeeping, 272, 272, 273, 275, 281

    in interdependent systems, 2–3

    mosquitoes and, 133

    native pollinator habitat for, 291–95

Honeycomb

    in backward beekeeping, 272, 279

    cutting, for cutout, 285

Honey extractors

    building, for backward beekeeping, 288–90, **289**

    traditional, 288

Hops

    in beer making, 207, 208, 209, 210, 212, 213

    growing, 215, **215**

    for sleeplessness or anxiety, 35

Hornet stings, 30

Hose bib vacuum breaker, in drip-irrigation system, 219, **219**

Hose Y connector, in drip-irrigation system, **219**, 220
Houseplant, edible, 104–7
Humanure
    composting, 239–41
    pathogens in, 239, <u>241</u>
Hydrogen peroxide, as laundry whitener, 80

I

Indoor gardening
    best crops for, 100
    difficulty of, 100
    projects
        Microgreens, 101–3, **102**
        Sweet Potato Farm, 104–7, **106**
Infections, yeast, 35
Infusions
    in herbal medicine, 115, 116–18
    herb and fruit, 36–38
Insect bites, 113
Insect contamination, of bulk foods, 43
Insect repellents, 133
Interdependence, in homegrown household, 2–3
Intuition, with make-it-yourself projects, 5
Itching, 33, 35, 113

K

Killing cone, for slaughtering a chicken, 167
Kimchi, 94–95
    Kimchi Pancakes, 95

L

Lacto-fermented foods
    benefits of, 90
    Gravlax, 96
    Kimchi, 94–95
    Nukazuke, 97–99
    Sauerkraut, 91–93
Lalvin 71B-1122, in mead making, 204, 205
Lamps, olive oil, 8–10, **8**, **10**
Lard, in soap making, 157, 159, 160–61
Laundry. *See also* Laundry products
    perfumes for, 80–81
    softener for, 80
    special-fabrics care, 78
    stain treatments, 81, 83
    whiteners for, 78–80
Laundry Powder, Homemade, 76–77
Laundry products. *See also* Laundry
    bluing, for whitening, 80
    commercial, ingredients in, 75

eco-, gray water and, <u>81</u>
    homemade cleaners
        benefits of, 75
        Coconut Laundry Soap, 155–56
        Homemade Laundry Powder, 76–77
        ingredients in, 69, 75–76
        variables affecting, 75
Laundry Soap, Coconut, 155–56
Leave-In Herbal Rinses, for hair, 21–22
Lemon, for cleaning sink, 71
Lettuce seeds, saving, 191
Licorice root, for coughs, 32
Linden flower, for sleeplessness or anxiety, 35
Lip Balm, No-Nonsense, 124–25
Lip balm tubes, <u>124</u>
Liquid Soap, Homemade, <u>156</u>
Lox, 96
Lye, in soap making, 148–49, 157–59
    cautions about, <u>151</u>, <u>162</u>
    in Genuine Castile Soap, 151

M

Mainline tubing, half-inch, in drip-irrigation system, 218, **219**, 220, 221, <u>221</u>
Make-it-yourself projects
    origins of, for authors, 1–2
    principles of, 5
Makin' It California Pale Ale, 209–14
Mallow, foraging for, 112, **112**
Malt, in beer making, **208**, 209, 210
Malt extract, in beer making, 207
Malting, in beer making, 207
Manure
    chicken, 261
    for compost pile, 228
    humanure, composting, 239–41
Mash, in beer making, <u>208</u>, 211
Mash tun, for beer making, <u>208</u>
    building, 248, **249**, 250, **251**, 252, **252**
Mayonnaise, 61–62
Mead, making, 203–6, **205**
    building wort chiller for, 253–54, **254**
Medical treatments, 30–35
Mending, basic, 84–87, **84**, **85**, **86**, **87**
Menstrual cups, <u>145</u>
Menstrual pads, cloth, 137, **138**, 139–45, **142**, **144**
Microgreens, 101–3, **102**
    seed sources for, <u>102</u>
    seed types for, <u>103</u>
Mildew Removers, 74
Milk stains, 81
Minimalist Mouthwash, A, 15
Mint, as breath freshener, <u>15</u>
Mirrors, cleaning, 70

Moisturizing creams, 127, 129–30
   Olive Oil Whip, 129
   Silky Cream, 127–28
Molasses
   Switchel, 67
Mosquito Repellent, Yarrow, 133
Mother, vinegar, 199–202, **200**, <u>201</u>
Mouthwash, A Minimalist, 15
Mullein
   common, foraging for, 112–13, **112**
   for coughs, 31
Muscle aches and strains, 33
Muscle pain, <u>119</u>
Mustard, 62–63
"Must," in mead making, 204

N

Nasal congestion, 33
Nasonov scent, in swarm lure, <u>280</u>
Native pollinator habitat, 291–95
Nature, trusting, for make-it-yourself projects, 5
Needles, for basic mending, 84
Nesting box, in chicken coop, 262, **264**, **265**
No-Nonsense Lip Balm, 124–25
Nosebleeds, 30
Nuc box
   for cutout capture of bees, 286
   for swarm capture of bees, 277, <u>278</u>, 279, <u>280</u>
Nukazuke, 97–99

O

Oasis laundry detergent, for gray water, <u>81</u>
Oatmeal bath, for skin irritations, 33
Oil(s)
   in Almost Castile Soap, 154
   in Body Polish/Hand Scrub, 29
   in Coconut Laundry Soap, 155–56
   for face and body washing, 27–28
   in Genuine Castile Soap, 150, 151
   in Peppermint-Rosemary Shampoo Bar,
      154–55
Oil infusions, herbal, 115, 116–18
   caution with, <u>117</u>
Oil lamps, olive, 8–10, **8**, **10**
Oil-soaked rags, caution about, <u>269</u>
Olive oil
   in Almost Castile Soap, 154
   for face and body washing, 27–28
   in Genuine Castile Soap, 150, 151
   in hair conditioner, 23
   for olive oil lamps, 8–10, **8**, **10**
   in Olive Oil Whip moisturizer, 129
   in Peppermint-Rosemary Shampoo Bar,
      154–55
   for shaving, 26

Olive oil lamps, 8–10, **8**, **10**
Olive Oil Whip moisturizer, 129
One-bowl meals, 52–54
Outdoor run, in chicken coop, 261, 263, **264–65**
Oven Cleaners, Stove and, 73
Oxalis, foraging for, 114, **114**
Oxymel, 65–66

P

Pads, cloth menstrual, 137, **138**, 139–45, **142**, **144**
Pain, 34, <u>119</u>
Pale Ale, Makin' It California, 209–14
Pallets, wooden, for compost bin, 230–31, **231**
Pancakes
   Kimchi Pancakes, 95
Pantry
   making shelves for, <u>43</u>
   stocking, 42, 43
Parsley, Italian, as breath freshener, <u>15</u>
Patch, for mending fabric, 87, **87**
Pathogens, in humanure, 239, <u>241</u>
Peas, seed saving and, 191
Peppermint
   Curiously Homemade Peppermints, <u>15</u>, 35,
      134–36
   Peppermint Honey, 110
   in Peppermint-Rosemary Shampoo, 154–55
   for upset stomach, 35
Peppermint Honey, 110
Peppermint-Rosemary Shampoo Bar, 154–55
Peppers
   Harissa, 63–64
Pepper seeds, saving, 190
Perfumes, laundry, 80–81
Perspiration stains, 83
pH Indicator, Cabbage Patch, 163–64
Pickles
   Nukazuke, 97–99
Pimples, 34
Plantain, common
   foraging for, 113, **113**
   for treating
      bug bites, 30
      coughs, 32
      skin irritations, 30
Planting guide, how to make, <u>177</u>
Planting techniques
   espalier, 192–94
   garden (*see* Garden projects; Vegetable
      garden)
Plucking a chicken, after slaughter, 170
Polenta, cooked in solar cooker, 259
Pollination
   of fruit trees, 193
   seed saving and, 189, 190, 191
Pollinator condo, 292–95, **293**, <u>293</u>

Pollinator habitat, native, 291–95
Potassium hydroxide, for liquid soap, 156
Pressure regulator, in drip-irrigation system, **219**, 220
Protein, for dogs, 56
Pruning fruit trees, for espalier, 195, **195, 196**, 197
Pullets, buying, 267

Q

Quarter-inch emitter tubing, in drip-irrigation system, 220, 221, **221**, 221
Quesadillas
    Kraut Quesadillas, 93

R

Racking
    beer, 213–14
    mead, 205–6
Rags, for cleaning, 69, 70, 73
Raised beds, double-digging, 184
Raspberry leaf tea, for diarrhea, 32
Red clover flowers, for coughs, 32
Red worms, for worm bins, 243
Rice, cooked in solar cooker, 259
Rice bran
    Nukazuke, 97–99
Rinses, hair, 21–22
Roman Bath, A, 27–28
Roosting pole, in henhouse, 262
Rose Hip Honey, 110
Rosemary essential oil, in Peppermint-Rosemary Shampoo Bar, 154–55
Row covers, 189, 190
Running stitch, for basic mending, 84–85, **84**
Rust stains, 83
Rye berries
    Vollkornbrot, 58–60

S

Sage, for tooth cleaning, 11
Sage Honey, 109
Salmon
    Gravlax, 96
Salt, in Body Polish/Hand Scrub, 29
Salting, foods made from, 90
    Gravlax, 96
    Kimchi, 94–95
    Nukazuke, 97–99
    Sauerkraut, 91–93
Salves
    Cocoa Puff Skin Butter, 125–26
    Headache Balm, 123

ingredients for, 120
    No-Nonsense Lip Balm, 124–25
    Skin-Healing Salve, 122–23
    tips for making, 120–21, **121**
Sauerkraut, 91–93
    Kraut Quesadillas, 93
    Pink Kraut "Salad," 93
Scouring Powders, 71
Scrapes, 32
Sea sponge tampons, 145
Seedling flats, for starting seeds, 223, **224**, 225
Seedlings, microgreen, 101–3
Seeds. See also Seed saving; Seed starting
    for microgreens
        sources for, 102
        types of, 103
    vegetable, storing, 191
Seed saving, 189–91
Seed starting
    advantages of, 175
    with direct sowing, 180
    grow lights for, 185–86
    steps in
        choosing container, 176
        hardening off, 179
        planting seeds, 176–77, 177
        sprouting seeds, 177–78
        timing planting of seedlings, 178–79
        transplanting, **178**, 179–80
Sekanjabin, 66–67
Sewing. See Mending, basic
Shampoo
    dry, 16
    natural, 16
        Baking Soda Shampoo, 17–18
        Garden-Grown Shampoo, 18–19
        Homemade Shampoo Bars, 17
        Peppermint-Rosemary Shampoo Bar, 154–55
        Soap Nut Shampoo, 19–20
Shampoo Bars
    Homemade, 17
    Peppermint-Rosemary, 154–55
Shaving cuts, bleeding from, 30
Shaving oil, 26
Shipping pallets, for compost bin, 230–31, **231**
Shovel, sharpening, 183
Silk, washing, 78
Silky Cream moisturizer, 127–28
Sink, cleaning, 71
Sinuses, irritated, 34
Skin Butter, Cocoa Puff, 125–26
Skin care
    Body Polish/Hand Scrub, 29
    body washing, 28
    Cocoa Puff Skin Butter, 125–26
    face washing, 27–28
    facial, 25

for irritations, 30, 33, 111, 113
moisturizers (*see* Moisturizing creams)
for shaving, 26
Skin-Healing Salve, 122–23
Skin-Healing Salve, 122–23
Skin irritations, 30, 33, 111, 113
Slaughtering a chicken, 165–73, **166**, **171**
Sleeplessness, 35
Slow compost, 226, 232–33
Smoker, bee, how to use, 283
Soaker hose, for watering garden, 222
Soap. *See also* Soap making
in homemade laundry detergent, 75–76, 77
testing pH of, 163, 164
Soap making
cautions about, 151, 159, 161
easy method, 148–50
Almost Castile Soap, 154
Genuine Castile Soap, 150–53
Peppermint-Rosemary Shampoo Bar,
154–55
equipment for, 149–50
hard method, 157–162
Soap nuts
for gray water, 81
for washing laundry, 78, 82
Soap Nut Shampoo, 19–20
Soap Scum and Bathtub Ring Cleansers, 74
Soapwort, **18–19**
in Garden-Grown Shampoo, 18–19
for washing delicate fabrics, 78
Sodium hydroxide, in soap making, 148–49.
See also specific soap recipes
Soft Scrub, 72
Soil
compost for (*see* Compost or Composting)
preparing
for fruit trees, 193
for vegetable garden bed, 181–84
Soil tests, 181–82, 182
Solar cooker
making, 255–56, **257**
safety with, 258
setting up, 256, 258, **258**
uses for, 259, 259
when to use, 256
Sore throat, 34, 109, 110
Soup. *See also* Stock
Dog's Pot, The, 55–57
Quick Soup, 53–54
Sourdough starter
how to make and maintain, 60
for *Vollkornbrot*, 59
Spacer frame, for cutout bee acquisition, 283, 286
Spelt
Italian Fried Rice, 52–53
Spray bottles, for homemade cleaning
products, 69

Spray for Greasy Surfaces, 70
Stains, laundry, 81, 83
Staples, for cooking, 42
Starter strip, on beehive frames, 272, 274
Stinging nettles
foraging for, 113–14, **113**
making fertilizer from, 187–88
Stings, bee, wasp, and hornet, 30
Stock
Vegetable Stock, 44–45
Whole Chicken Stock, 46–47
Stomach upset, 35, 109
Stove and Oven Cleaners, 73
Strains, muscle, 33
Stuffy head, 34
Styling gel, hair, 24
Sugar water, for bee acquisition, 278–79, 283,
285, 286
Sunburn, 31
Super-Natural Disinfectant, 71
Swarm capture, for bee acquisition, 275,
277–80
Swarm lure, for baiting nuc box, 280
Sweet potatoes, vs. yams, 105
Sweet Potato Farm, 104–7, **106**
Switchel, 67
Synthetic fabrics, washing, 78

T

Tallow, in soap making, 157, 159, 161
Tampons, sea sponge, 145
Tea, black, for sunburn, 31
Tea, willow bark, 34, 34
Tea, worm, as plant tonic, 247
Tea stains, 81
Terry cloth towels, alternative to, 78
Thread, for basic mending, 84
Throat infections, 109. *See also* Sore throat
Thyme, for coughs, 32
Timer, in drip-irrigation system, **219**, 220
Tinctures, herbal, 115, 118–19, 119
Toilet, dry
building, **236**, 237–39
composting humanure from, 239–41
ready-made, 238
Toilet Bowl Cleaners, 72
Tomato sauce stains, 81
Tomato seeds, saving, 190
Toothbrush, alternatives to, 11–13
Tooth cloths, 11
Tooth Powder, Homemade, 14
Towels, flour sack vs. terry, 78
Transplanting seedlings, **178**, 179–80
Trees. *See also* Fruit trees
suitable for toothbrush twigs, 12, 13
Twigs, for tooth cleaning, 12, 13

U

Universal Spray, Almost, 70
Upset stomach, 35, 109

V

Valerian, for sleeplessness or anxiety, 35
Vegetable garden
    compost for (see Compost or Composting)
    drip irrigation for, 218–22, **219**, **220–21**
    fertilizer for, 187–88
    grow lights for, 185–86
    preparing planting bed for, 181–84
    saving seeds from, 189–91
    seedling flats for, 223, **224**, 225
    seed starting for and planting of, 175–80
    soaker hose for watering, 222
    worm castings for, 242, **242**, 247
Vegetables
    Dog's Pot, The, 55–56, 57
    homegrown, superior taste of, 42
    Nukazuke, 97–99
    Quick Soup, 53–54
    Vegetable Stock, 44–45
Vervain, for sleeplessness or anxiety, 35
Vinegar
    in cleaning products, 69, 70, 71, 72, 73, 74
        caution with, 70
    as fabric softener, 80
    in hair rinse, 21
    as insect repellent, 133
    making, 199–202, **200**
    Oxymel, 65–66
    Sekanjabin, 66–67
    for sore throat, 34
    Switchel, 67
    for washing delicate fabrics, 78
Vinegar of the Four Thieves, 71
Vinegar Rinse, for hair, 21
Vitamin C supplement, rose hip honey as, 110
Vollkornbrot, 58–60

W

Washing soda
    caution with, 71, 73, 76, 76
    in homemade cleaning products, 69, 69, 72, 73
    in homemade laundry products, 69, 69, 76, 77, 79
Wasp stings, 30
Water
    as breath freshener, 15
    for chickens, 268

Water infusions, herbal, 115, 116
Water pasteurization, in solar cooker, 259, 259
Weeds, for compost pile, 228
Wheat berries
    Vollkornbrot, 58–60
Whiteners, laundry, 78–80
Whole grains
    cooking, 50–51
    for dogs, 57
    Italian Fried Rice, 52–53
Wild lettuce, for sleeplessness or anxiety, 35
Willow bark, tincturing, 119
Willow bark tea, for pain, 34, 34
Windows, cleaning, 70
Wine stains, 81
Wood ash, for making lye, 157–58
Wood Cleaners, 73
Wooden pallet, for compost bin, 230–31, **231**
Wood sorrel, foraging for, 114, **114**
Wool, washing, 78
Worm bins
    location for, 243
    making, 244–47, **245**
    purpose of, 233, 242
    worms for
        feeding, 245–46, 245
        finding, 243
        types of, 243
Worm castings, 242, **242**
    harvesting, 247
    making worm tea from, 247
Worm tea, 247
Wort, in beer making, 207, 208, 211–13
Wort chiller
    making, 253–54, **254**
    using, 254
Wounds, 109

Y

Yams, vs. sweet potatoes, 105
Yarrow Mosquito Repellent, 133
Yeast
    in beer making, 207, 209, 210, 213
    in mead making, 203, 204
Yeast infections, 35
Yogurt, for itching from yeast infections, 35

Z

Zote, for cleaning laundry, 75, 76